WARSHIP 2001-2002

WARSHIP 2001-2002

Edited by Antony Preston

CONWAY
MARITIME PRESS

Frontispiece

HMS Agincourt. *Launched in 1865, the impressive fivemasted* Agincourt *symbolised the global supremacy of the Royal Navy to the Victorian public. Despite being one of the worst sailers in the fleet,* Agincourt *was the flagship of fifteen admirals, serving as second flagship of the Channel fleet as late as 1889. She was not retired from the service until 1908 and was sent to the breakers on Trafalgar Day, 1961.* (CPL)

© Conway Maritime Press 2001

First published in Great Britain in 2001 by
Conway Maritime Press, a division of Chrysalis Books Plc
9 Blenheim Court, Brewery Road,
London N7 9NY

A member of the Chrysalis Group plc

British Library Cataloguing in Publication Data
A record of this title is available on request from the British Library.

ISBN 0 85177 901 8

Project editor: Martin Robson
Typesetting and layout by Stephen Dent
Printed and bound in Spain

CONTENTS

EDITORIAL

As 2002 is the twenty-fifth anniversary of *Warship*, it is a good time to reflect on the highlights of a quarter of a century and note how the publication has developed. *Warship*, like any other series, changes for a number of reasons, some commercial, but mostly small alterations reflecting the ideas of the changing team of editorial staff, the production department and the designers. Some developments are more successful than others and bad ideas tend to be dropped when no-one is looking.

The origin of *Warship* was in 1976, when Robert Gardiner of the fledgling Conway Maritime Press in Greenwich approached me to ask if I would edit a new quarterly publication dealing with the technical side of naval history. Robert wanted to make better use of the huge Conway Picture Library and the resources of the National Maritime Museum, which was 'just over the road'. Conway Maritime Press had already forged close links with the Museum and wanted to make better use of its human and material resources on the naval side. The Museum was the official repository of the Admiralty's technical records, but also had an excellent picture library and manuscript collection. But there was another agenda; Robert and I were not the only people who deplored the lack of attention paid by mainstream maritime and naval historians to technical matters. *Warship*, we hoped, would 'raise the level of debate' and provide a body of knowledge, which would give historians ready access to properly argued technical comparisons and assessments. We also decided that there was to be no 'statute of limitations' on subject matter or period. *Warship* is primarily concerned with the post-sail era, but we have looked at earlier topics when appropriate and do not try to isolate technology from tactics and strategy.

With my recent experience as a research assistant at the Museum and my writing experience, I accepted with alacrity. The first editions were an interesting example of publishing as it used to be, with no ISBN numbers or year of publication. In fact, so discreet (or ashamed?) were the publishers that I was merely credited as The Editor. When I found that I had too many commitments to continue as editor, I was succeeded by a number of people who put their own individual stamp on the publication, including Robert Gardiner, John Roberts and Andrew Lambert. As the original editor, my pleasure at being asked to come back can be easily imagined, but it was a self-confident adult publication, not the lusty infant that I remembered from twenty years earlier.

The softback quarterly issues were snapped up by the enthusiastic readership, but as soon as Issue No. 4 was printed, a bound version of all four was prepared in a hardback edition, to meet the longer-term needs, particularly of export customers. But the economics of publishing were working against the concept of a quarterly and another reason for moving to an annual publication was to get rid of the need to chop excellent major features into two, three and even four parts.

Warship was lucky to recruit a galaxy of talent for the first issues, with contributions from the late John Campbell, the late David Lyon, Norman Friedman and David K Brown. As it prospered, new and equally distinguished contributors began to feature in its pages. Now we can say with all modesty that we have published virtually all the leading technical historians, not just specialists on the Royal Navy but many others around the world.

The last quarterly editions and Volume XII of the annual appeared in 1979, to be succeeded by the first proper annual the following year. This also seemed as good a time as any to redesign the publication, with a bigger page-size. Since then the quality of paper and reproduction have shown a steady improvement. But complacency is the enemy of good publishing and there is always room for improvement. The vicissitudes of two changes of ownership are too well known to be dwelt on. Although there were lengthy delays, the *Warship* team continued to nurse the Conway Maritime Press flagship publication and eventually the flagship made a safe landfall with the Chrysalis Book Group. The decision to amalgamate the year-numbers, from 1997-1998 was, however driven by simple marketing requirements. As the publication date had moved towards the end of the year, sales representatives pointed out that a title which contained the new year was easier to sell than one with just 'last' year on its dustjacket. Clearly the first twenty-five years are the hardest and we look forward to the next quarter-century.

In this twenty-fifth issue of *Warship* we have tried as usual to strike a balance of topics and eras, adhering to our conviction that lessons and principles have a life of their own, independent of the changing fashions driven by technology and events. Chris Ware has edited the second instalment of the late David Topliss' charting of the evolution of the 1st class cruiser. This is a subject generally neglected by technical historians, but it spans a critical period of naval technology in the second half of the 19th century, as navies tried to tackle the problems of commerce-protection on the trade routes.

Keith McBride has described those undervalued 'intermediate dreadnoughts', the *King Edward VII* class. Although the design was completed by Philip Watts, their balanced good looks clearly identifies them as the last of the William White battleships. Although they missed Jutland (perhaps fortunately), they saw hard front-line service in the early years of the war, and only two were lost.

Dan Harris describes the evolution of the torpedo cruiser in the Royal Swedish Navy, an important step towards the fleet destroyer. As so often with the Scandinavian navies, local conditions called for special solutions, and the fact that none of these ships saw action does not detract from their significance. Sweden, in particular, equipped its navy with state-of-the-art technology to offset the threat from Russia.

Peter Brook describes the Battle of Santiago in July 1898, another in his studies of well known but little understood actions of the late 19th and early 20th centuries. Santiago attracted enormous attention because it was the first modern 'media war', but the actual events leading to the overwhelming American victory over the obsolescent Spanish squadron are largely ignored. Steve McLaughlin follows the same trend, examining the action off Cape Sarych in the early months of the First World War, when a squadron of Russian pre-dreadnoughts engaged the German/Turkish battlecruiser *Goeben*. The Germans were unpleasantly surprised by the long-range gunnery of the old battleship *Evstafi*, and the author takes a close look at Russian gunnery and fire control.

David Brown looks at Royal Navy mine warfare in the First World War, an interesting contrast between the poor quality of British mines in the early part of the war and the introduction of acoustic and magnetic mines in 1917-18. It can be argued that the mine as much as the submarine dictated the style of warfare in the North Sea from 1914 to the Armistice, and was the biggest threat to submarines.

George Moore has contributed another analysis, this time of the Royal Navy's *Blackwood* class (Type 14) frigates, shedding light on the evolution of late- and post-Second World War planning in the Royal Navy. The Type 14 is an excellent example of a successful attempt to create a 2nd rate warship capable of working with its 1st rate counterparts. Like the 'Flower' class corvette, the Type 14 had the best anti-submarine weaponry available, and other capabilities were virtually omitted to keep numbers up and cost down.

Colin Jones looks at pre-1900 Australian navies, when the individual states maintained their own small forces,

mainly for coast defence against the French and the Russians. Although the threat was largely imaginary, it led to the acquisition of some advanced designs, notably torpedo boats, backed by the Royal Navy's locally-based cruiser squadron, partly funded and manned from local resources.

John Jordan provides a detailed description of the last French 'Washington' heavy cruiser, the *Algérie*. Because her career was tragically short she has tended to be largely overlooked in American and British histories, but in many ways she was the best of the *genre*, striking a good balance between armament, speed and protection. Even more important, she achieved that balance without the flagrant cheating resorted to by the Germans, Italians and Japanese.

Pascal Barras looks at the way in which the Royal Navy underpinned British foreign policy in the years after the Russian War of 1854-56. Although rivers of ink have been spilt on preaching about blue-water seapower, there was and continues to be very little understanding of the close interaction between the size and capability of the Navy and the government of the day's strategic options.

Warship cannot survive without producing the sort of material that readers want, so the message is, as always, questions and corrections are welcome, and contributions will always be looked at with interest. We only hope that *Warship* has achieved what it set out to do twenty-five years ago.

Antony Preston

Obituary

Readers of *Warship* will be saddened to learn of the sudden death of David Brown OBE, FHistS ('JD' to all who knew him, to distinguish him from 'DK'). David had been very ill with throat cancer, but had made a complete recovery; he had a sudden relapse and died on 11 August 2001.

J D Brown served in the Fleet Arm as an observer, and when he left the service he was appointed Deputy Head of the Naval Historical Branch, later taking over as Head of Branch. His authoritative books were about all aspects of naval aviation, particularly his beloved Fleet Air Arm, and he told me a few months back that he had a number of projects 'on the drawing board'. His humour and deep understanding of naval aviation will be greatly missed by both friends and students.

FIRST CLASS CRUISERS

Part Two

In the second part of in this trilogy of articles **David Topliss** and **Chris Ware** examine the development of Royal Navy First Class cruisers in the late 1890s from the protected cruisers of the *Diadem* class to the armoured cruisers of the *Cressy* class, through to the controversial *Monmouths*, the apogee of the hail-of-fire ship.

Diadem *class*

Ordered under the 1895/96 and 1896/97 estimates the *Diadems* were a development of the *Blake* class, with some features of the *Edgar* class and the *Powerfuls*. The ships were ordered in two groups of four, and although it is common practice to refer to them as a single class the Director of Naval Construction's department regarded the second group as a separate design. The principal differences between the two groups were confined to the main machinery, which had little, if any, impact on the rest of the design.

Design work on a modified *Blenheim* had started in late November 1893 when Director of Naval Construction (DNC) Sir William White wrote to his principal assistant, James Dunn, to prepare an outline proposal. White again wished to use watertube boilers, but unlike the *Blakes* there was to be only one set of engines on each shaft. The armament of the new ship was to be the same as the *Royal Arthur* in order to retain the high forecastle, which had proved so successful, but all the broadside 6in guns were to be carried in armoured casemates along the lines of the *Powerful*. Dunn was asked to consider carefully the forecastle armament, there could be one 6in gun

HMS Amphitrite *running trials in September 1901 without her uniform armament of 6in guns in a mix of open mounts and two storey casemates. In 1917 she was converted to a minelayer at Portsmouth.* (Antony Preston)

on the centre line, or two side by side, but White feared that in the latter case, the close proximity of the upper deck casemate guns would make it impossible for the gun crews on the forecastle to work the guns in safety. The hull was to be sheathed and coppered and coal stowage was to be 2000 tons. By April the design team were able to present a preliminary legend for consideration. If the *Blake* was to be sheathed and fitted with the armament and protection of the new ship she would have to carry 1015 tons additional weight. The reduction of the normal coal supply by 500 tons would offset the protective deck, the same as in the *Blake*, but like the *Powerful* it was to be a uniform 4in thick over the machinery spaces. The adoption of the under deck ammunition passages pushed up the displacement, there having been no space for these in the *Blakes*. Raising the forecastle one deck level, as well as the use of two-storey casemates and military masts increased the height of the centre of gravity, forcing a growth in beam of 3ft in order to maintain stability. After making allowance for the use of watertube boilers and a single submerged torpedo tube it was inevitable that the new ship would have to be considerably larger. The weight allowed room forward of the machinery spaces, the length of the new design would have to be 55ft longer than the *Blake*, but 70ft shorter than the *Powerful*.

As in the *Powerfuls* it was decided to use Belleville boilers. To begin with it had been hoped that a British water tube boiler would be available but none was developed in time for these ships. However the boilers were a more advanced design than those in *Powerful*, having so-called economizers fitted which pre-heated the water prior to its entering the boiler proper. Compared with the cylindrical boilers of the *Blake* which had given a continuous 8,000ihp the new boilers promised 45 per cent more power on nine tons less weight. Coal bunkerage was to be less than the *Blakes* at the legend, 1000 tons as to 1500, but total bunkerage was 25 per cent higher at 2000 tons.

Compared with the *Powerful* class the ships were to revert to a more normal level of manning, each steaming watch being able to give 70 per cent of natural draught power. But the ships were heavily constrained for accommodation space, with many men having to berth on the upper deck and some method of reducing the crew size was sought. The solution adopted was to reduce the numbers in each steaming watch, so that the available power would only be 50 per cent of the maximum. This would lower the number of stokers required from 217 to 157. However there was a considerable cost to be paid for this. When a ship went to action stations many of the stokers not required for boiler room duties formed a vital part in fighting the ship, manning magazines, passing ammunition and forming damage control teams. The decision to have only enough stokers in each watch to give 50 per cent of the ship's power inevitably meant that there would only be one-third of the stokers available for action duties if the ship was at full power. The first estimates of the number of men required to fight the ship was 505, this was reduced to 473 by reducing the size of the magazine and shell parties. But further economies in manpower were sought. It was found that if electrical

ammunition hoists were fitted to the 6in guns the complement could be reduced by 40. These measures allowed the estimated complement to be reduced from 700 to 650, but this later crept up to 677 by the time the ships entered service. Even so as many as 100 men had to sleep on deck, only moving below when the weather was foul.

Once again the armament proved a bone of contention. The Director of Naval Ordnance (DNO), Capt. Kane, objected to both the 6in guns on the forecastle and to the 9.2in gun aft. The DNO agreed to the raised forecastle and would not consider giving it up, but felt strongly that the ship should carry a heavy gun there. As in the arguments during the design of the *Powerful* he advocated the adoption of an 8in gun. He wrote:

> a ship like the new *Blenheim* should be prepared to attack the 1st class cruisers of other nations, but in doing so she would be seriously handicapped by her armament, as 8 inch guns have been generally adopted by foreign governments for larger cruisers. While I regard the bow fire as lighter than is desirable, I think that the stern fire is heavier than necessary. A 9.2 inch gun is hardly required against cruisers and against battleships the greater speed would be the best defence. I doubt if the possession of one 9.2 inch gun by the 'New *Blenheim*' would make much difference to a battleship if the *Blenheim*'s engines were broken down or if her speed was in some way reduced below that of the battleship.

The DNO repeated his argument that the 8in gun could be handled as a quick-firer (QF). During a visit to the Chilean cruiser *Blanco Encalada* building at Armstrongs yard he had seen the 8in gun fire four rounds in 62 seconds. To get the 8in gun the DNO was willing to give up the upper deck casemates, leaving the guns there in open shields, or to reduce the number of 6in guns to ten, as well as a reduction of the number of 12pdr guns.

Unfortunately White's reply, and the board discussions, on the DNO's minute have not survived, but once again the DNO lost the argument. Rather than the mixture of heavy and medium calibre guns sought by the DNO, the *Diadems* emerged with the uniform 6in gun armament favoured by White and Fisher for the *Powerful*, losing the 9.2in gun aft. Presumably it was felt that in a design more clearly intended for commerce protection that the 6in gun would be adequate. In addition the disadvantage of having only one 9.2in gun would complicate the magazine supply. From April 1895 the legends show the armament as 15-6in guns. There were to be two military masts the forward one having two fighting tops and the after mast one, with 3pdr QF guns in the fighting tops. The military masts were later discarded in order to allow for the provision of a sixteenth 6in gun on the poop. The second group of ships were designed with an armament of 16-6in guns, and the change in armament of the first four was to bring them in line with the later ships.

There was to be one torpedo room with a submerged TT on each beam, forward of number one boiler room. Another TT was to have been placed above water at the stem, protected by an armoured mantelet, but this was deleted when the armament of the first four ships was brought into line with that of the second group. Protection was to be on the same lines as the *Powerful* with a protective deck 4in thick. There was a further refinement in the protection given by the coal bunkers above the protective deck, which were to be divided by a longitudinal bulkhead. White hoped that this would increase the tendency to leave the bunkers close to the ships side full to give the maximum protection in action. The four ships ordered under the 1896-1897 programme were identical in almost all respects to their earlier sisters, only varying in their designed armament and in their machinery. The armament of the first four ships was quickly brought into line so as to make, to all intents, a unified class. White had to consider whether the new ships should have triple screws, or to continue with the normal British practice of using only two. The three-shaft layout was gaining considerable popularity both in the United States and in other European navies. Indeed, the German Navy would use three shafts for all its battleships down to the *Bismarck* of 1939.

The principal advantage of the three-shaft arrangement was claimed to be a reduced chance of loss of power should the machinery spaces be damaged. White dismissed the argument in his typical manner and the three-shaft arrangement played no part in British warship machinery. The ship's engines were slightly altered in layout, while retaining the same specification as the four earlier ships. In the first four vessels the engine cylinders had been arranged in the order high, intermediate, low

and low; the new ships replaced this by low, high, intermediate and low. It was felt that this layout would give a better distribution of stresses along the crankshaft. The boilers were modified to give another 1500ihp and an extra .25kt of speed.

The Armoured Cruisers

Cressy class

When White had abandoned the principle of side armour for first class cruisers in 1888 it was not due to a fundamental dislike of the system. It was driven by the realization that protection against modern guns could only be obtained by ever greater thickness of steel plate, which would impose such penalties in terms of weight as to destroy the fundamental properties required in a cruiser. By 1894 advances in metallurgy had been such as to persuade White that worthwhile protection by side armour was possible at a reasonable cost in weight. This was made feasible by the development of cemented armour in 1891 by the American H A Harvey, and which was improved upon by the German firm of Krupp in 1894. White wrote:

> Since 1894 we have had the Harvey system, and the successive improvements thereupon. The progress made may

HMS Cressy on trials early in 1901, riding high out of the water before her guns were mounted. Cressy marked a return to the ideal of the Orlando's as powerful adjuncts to the battle fleet. (Antony Preston)

be represented by the fact that in 1889-93 a plate 10 1/2 inches thick was needed to resist the attack of 100 pounds' Holtzer projectiles fired from a 6-inch gun with a striking velocity of 2,000 feet per second. Now a 6-inch plate can afford equal or superior protection. The proportionate thickness and weights are as 100 to 57. This remarkable economy of weight in relation to protection necessarily alters all the conditions of design for cruisers.

But the *Cressy* class cannot simply be explained by the adoption of the new armour, rather it was the new armour which allowed a more fundamental change in cruiser design. For the first time since the *Orlandos* a British cruiser was built to operate with the fleet and to take its place in the battle line.

In 1896 White had been to Italy, largely on account of his health, and had seen warships building there. The Italian Navy was in the grip of a financial crisis and the construction of battleships was almost suspended. Unable to afford battleships the Italians had resorted to designing cruisers, the *Carlo Alberto* and *Garibaldi* classes, that could if necessary take their place with the battlefleet. He wrote that:

the inspection of these vessels confirmed the opinion I had previously entertained, that the time had arrived when it had become necessary to construct cruisers for fleet work which should be capable of taking part in fleet action as adjuncts to battleships. Hitherto the conception generally accepted has been that modern cruisers correspond to, and take the duties of, frigates formally serving with fleets. As scouts and attendants on battleships their place will no doubt be always fairly described in this manner. But whereas frigates in old days took no part in fleet actions, there seems absolutely no reason, under modern conditions, why first-class cruisers should hold aloof if designed and constructed suitably.

In late April 1897 White wrote to Chief Constructor W E (later Sir William) Smith asking him to prepare a

HMS *Sutlej a sister of* Cressy, *shown dressed overall still wearing the Victorian livery to be replaced in 1903 by grey overall, probably at the Coronation Naval Review on 16 August 1902.* (Antony Preston)

design for a cruiser of not more than 11,000 tons displacement with sheathing, and a speed of 21.5kts. Armament was to be two 9.2in guns in barbettes and 12-6in guns in casemates. Coal at legend displacement was to give the same endurance as the *Majestic* class battleships, a clear indication that the ships were to operate with the battlefleet, while total bunkerage was to be 2000 tons. Side armour was to be equal to the new battleships of the *Canopus* class: 6in best quality armour extending to 5ft below the waterline at the legend displacement. The protective deck was to be thinner than in previous classes and less curved, amidships the deck was to be kept as low as possible to allow for the lowering of the upper and main decks to a height less than in the *Diadem* class. The upper edges of the belt were to be joined by a deck 1in thick. White's requirements proved hopelessly optimistic, and when the design was presented to the Board displacement had grown to 11,300 tons, and even this was only achieved by dropping the requirement for sheathing the hull and reducing the bunkerage to 1600 tons.

White had outlined his ideas at a Board meeting in early May and the design was presented to the Board in a memorandum dated 10 June 1897 for detailed discussion. The principals of the design were stated as:

Special adaption for service with the Channel and Mediterranean Fleets, and the performance of all duties hitherto devolving on 1st class cruisers attached to fleets.

The capacity for close action as adjuncts to battleships.

Suitability for employment on detached service, if required to be used for the protection of shipping commerce and communication.

Armament, protection, speed and coal endurance to be such that the new cruisers should be formidable rivals to the best cruisers built or building for foreign navies.

The need for the ships to operate in company with the fleet limited their length, and White asked his designers to cut away the underwater parts of the ship fore and aft as much as possible to increase manoeuvrability. Having originally asked for the hull to be sheathed, White argued that this was a feature that could be dispensed with, saving £40,000 and 550 tons. This would, it was admitted, mean that the ships would be less capable of keeping the sea for long periods, but experience with both the *Blakes* and the *Edgars* had shown that this was not as great a problem as had been feared, even on distant stations. Also, improved docking facilities abroad had reduced the need for sheathing. The Board, however, remained in favour of sheathing despite the increased cost and weight, and a reduction in speed. It was therefore decided that the ships should be sheathed even though this would increase the displacement to 11,850 tons.

The buoyancy, stability and trim were to be protected by an armoured citadel, 240ft long by 12ft deep. This was to be 6in thick on the sides, closed at each end by transverse bulkheads 5in thick. The protective deck was 1.5in and the main deck 1in thick within the citadel, coal bunkers were to be placed between the protective decks. The waterline forward of the 6in belt was protected by

2in nickel steel plate, the same depth as the belt, extending up to the bow. The nickel steel plate was, like the armour belt, an innovation and the orders for it were deliberately spread among all the armour manufacturers, rather than to the lowest tender, so that they could gain experience in its production. Outside the citadel the protective deck was 1.5in thick forward and 2.5in aft, increasing to 3in over the steering gear.

For both the *Powerful* and *Diadem* classes White had favoured a uniform 6in armament. This came from his view that these ships' primary purpose was to hunt down enemy commerce destroyers, such as the *Rurik* and the *Brooklyn*. The *Cressys* were to be armed differently to reflect their role with the fleet. Their 6in battery was intended to multiply the effect of the battleships 6in guns, but to augment the effect the ships were to be given a medium-calibre gun that could wreck the secondary turrets of the enemy's ships. Therefore there was to be a 9.2in gun fore and aft to make the *Cressys* more fit to take their place in the battleline. Both the 6in and the 9.2in guns and mountings were to be of a new, more powerful pattern. The development of the new guns caused problems for the design team in that they found themselves trying to calculate the weight and form of the ship without definite information.

White wrote to the Controller that the new 9.2in guns could add 120 tons and the 6in guns about 30 tons more than had been allowed for. To compensate for this the displacement was increased to 12,000 tons, but this was to be done without altering the dimensions of the hull, or increasing the draught, and a new hull form was designed to give the necessary displacement. The 9.2in mounting was to have power-loading and training and carry 32 rounds on the mounting.

As in the previous classes the scale of complement once again became a source of controversy. White had always accepted the need for power assistance for 9.2in guns, and had agreed to the fitting of power hoists for the 6in guns of the *Diadem* class, but this was not a precedent he wished to follow for the new ships. His opposition came not so much from a concern that mechanical loading was vulnerable to breakdown in action, but rather that it would increase the auxiliary machinery and therefore the coal consumption.

The Controller was opposed to any reduction in the scale of complement. He felt it was very important that the engineering department should be well manned to maintain high steaming speeds, but even more that to reduce the size of the fighting complement would be to negate the very *rationale* of the new ships. The new QF guns, combined with new smokeless powders meant that it was possible to maintain a very much higher rate of fire from the 6in battery. Since a major purpose of the ships was to add to the hail-of-fire from the fleet's 6in guns, it would be self-defeating to limit the fire by skimping on the ammunition parties:

> With equal accuracy, greater rapidity of fire gives an advantage in geometrical proportion because every hit tends more or less to check the enemy's rate of fire, either by actual damage or morale effect. We ought not to grudge a single man who can be shown to have an appreciable effect in increasing the rapidity of fire.

It was also argued that the 32 rounds carried on the 9.2in mounting reduced the number of men needed in the shell rooms by 16. This, said the Controller, was the same as saying that the ship should haul down its flag the moment 32 rounds had been fired; the size of the crews should be at least enough to keep up the rate of fire, and this could not be determined until the design of the mountings were complete. The improvements in the design were intended solely to increase the rate of fire, not to reduce the size of the crew

The Controller did, however, make the telling admission that no one really knew how many men were needed to maintain the ammunition supply to the 6in batteries. During trials charges were not passed up the hoists for fear that they might have been damaged. He suggested that a number of dummy charges should be made in order to test what the rate of supply would be on different ships!

Machinery was to be on the same basis as the *Diadem* class, although cruising radius was to be reduced due to the lower amount of bunkerage available. This was partly a result of attempts to keep the size of the ship with reasonable limits, but also because the naval members of the Board thought that the coal supply and endurance should match modem battleships.

Drake *class*

In 1896 in a last flourish of the *Jeune Ecole* the French navy laid down a large armoured cruiser, the *Jeanne d' Arc*. With a speed of 22kts and a range of 13,500nm on a displacement of 11,400 tons the *Jeanne d'Arc* appeared to the British as much of a threat as the *Rurik* had seemed

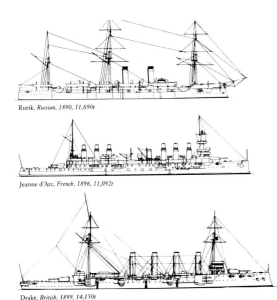

Rurik, Russian, 1890, 11,690t

Jeanne d'Arc, French, 1896, 11,092t

Drake, British, 1899, 14,150t

Contemporary armoured cruisers: (top to bottom) the Russian Rurik *(1895); the French* Jeanne d'Arc *(1902); HMS Drake. (CPL)*

six years earlier. The Senior Naval Lord wrote in February 1898:

> A *Jeanne d 'Arc* which realizes the speed promised by her designers could do incalculable damage in the English and St. George's Channels with comparative impunity, if we possessed nothing fast enough to catch her, and it must be clear that under the conditions which steam power admits of, viz, that a vessel may turn in any direction at will, it will require more than one to run her down.

White had begun to look at the problem of a reply to the French ship in late 1897, when he had asked Froude to look at the power required for 23kts for ships of 11,250 and 9,400 tons displacement. There is no doubt that both White and the Board would have liked a ship of moderate dimensions but, as in the case of the *Powerful*, the requirement for high speed and a powerful armament inevitably resulted in a large vessel.

> It is very much regretted that we should be forced to increase the number of very large and 'man eating' vessels touching the *Powerful* in dimensions but there seems no help for it.

This does not mean that the Navy had not learnt the major lesson of the *Rurik* episode, that it was dangerous to act on the reported performance of an uncompleted ship, and like the Russian ship the *Jeanne d'Arc* did not live up to expectations. But the Board felt forced to act. Normally the Admiralty was confident that it could wait on developments in France, since the size of the British shipbuilding industry, and the faster rate of building meant that any French advance could be swiftly overtaken. However in 1897 there had been an engineer's strike that had lasted seven months, and the Board believed that such events meant that it could no longer rely on any industrial advantage.

White presented his thoughts on the new design to the Board in a minute dated 23 May 1898, and he took the then unusual step of providing a series of alternative designs for discussion. Unlike later practise, when the object was to allow the Board to make an informed choice, White used the alternatives to demonstrate why it was necessary to build such large and expensive ships. This does not mean that White was not prepared to ask quite hard questions as to how the displacement could be kept down, only that, on examination, the price was too high to pay. The Ship's Cover contains a paper, undated but clearly written before May 1898, which looks at how the dimensions of the ship could be reduced; some of these ideas were adopted in the *Drakes* and more in the next class, the *Monmouths*.

The dimensions of the design were dictated by the need for the ships to be able to enter dry docks both at home and abroad, and to be able to pass through the Suez Canal fully armed and equipped. This limited the length to 500ft, even though it would have been better from the point of power-consumption to have made them longer. If the ships had the same speed-length ratio as the

Powerful, then they would have had to be 50ft longer. With the length and draught set, the only parameter open was the beam; the question was how much could the beam be reduced without endangering stability, and the operation of the ship?

Compared to the *Powerful* the main increase in weight was the side armour, less the difference in weight of the protective decks, but the height of the armour raised the centre of gravity. Equally, the depth of the hull was determined by the height of the machinery in the hold, the need to be able to work the coal bunkers on the lower deck, to give the guns in the lower casemates a reasonable freeboard and a sufficient deck height in the casemates. These requirements fixed the freeboard amidships at 14ft. But it was felt possible to save weight high up in the ship by not having a boat deck, the boats being carried on beams, and moving the 12pdr guns down on to the main deck. The poop deck could be dispensed with, and the forecastle lowered one deck, reducing the height of the 9.2in guns. If the height of the casings around the funnels were lowered and the ventilating cowls dispensed with there would be a reduction in top weight. These measures would reduce the centre of gravity and could permit a reduction in the beam. This reduction could be achieved by dispensing with the ammunition passages, and their replacement by magazines near the individual guns they were intended to serve, and if the practice of having a space between the lower bunkers and the ship's side were abandoned it would allow for more of the coal to be carried in the lower bunkers, again lowering the ship's centre of gravity. It was argued that in the case of a major collision or torpedo hit that the triple side would be ruptured anyway, and in a minor collision there would be ample time to close the watertight doors in the bunkers. Torpedo protection would be obtained by careful arrangement of the transverse bulkheads in the boiler rooms.

While the designs put forward by White rejected the most radical of these suggestions, the boat deck was abandoned, as were the high ventilation cowls to the boiler rooms. However, in the case of the latter, the Engineer in Chief (EIC) stressed the need to ensure good ventilation of the boiler rooms, both to ensure good combustion in the boilers and 'to permit a condition of *existence to the men below, which the service afloat may reasonably be expected to accept*'.

As in *Powerful* the main problem was the need for a large machinery installation. Since the overall length of the ship was limited by external factors the large machinery compartments constrained the relative capacity of the magazines. While on average a cruiser's engines and machinery took up about 44 per cent of the ship's length, in both the *Powerful* and the *Drakes* the figure was 50 per cent.

Design No 2 was included by White to show that in a smaller ship for a given speed the ratio of power to displacement was actually higher than in a longer ship. For a ship with 20ft less length and 600 tons less displacement, the power requirements would remain the same, she would carry 700 tons less coal and would only save £15,000 in construction costs. Designs Nos. 3 and 4 were a major departure from White's design practice, showing that the required speed could be achieved if there was a change in Royal Naval engineering. Even had he approved of them White must have known that they would be contested by the Engineer-in-Chief (EIC), and it is likely that the designs were included simply to provoke the EIC to comment formally on the present state of machinery.

Design No 3 showed that 23kts could be obtained if the trial conditions were brought more into line with foreign and British commercial practice. In the Royal Navy the key trial was not the maximum speed over the measured mile, but sustained performance over eight hours with natural draft in the boiler rooms. If this was replaced by moderate forced draft and the trial duration reduced to four hours then the ship could make 23kts, but the natural draft power would be 21,000ihp with a speed of 21.5kts, while maximum continuous speed would only be about 20kts. Since White predicted that *Jeanne d'Arc* would be able to maintain 21kts he did not feel able to recommend the design.

Design No 4 was even more radical, much smaller with an all 6in gun armament and amour reduced to a belt 4in thick, the ship could make 23kts if machinery practice was taken to the extremes. It would require the adoption of small watertube boilers and very fast running engines, neither of which would be acceptable to the EIC. Design No 4 was for both White and the EIC the worst-case design, it was ironic therefore that it was to form the basis of the suc-

ceeding class, the *Monmouths*. Design No 5, which followed a month later, was for a version of design No 4 which replaced the armour belt with a protective deck.

White's favoured design, No 1, was submitted with three alternative armaments. The first effectively reproduced the armament of the *Cressys*, with an extra couple of 12pdr guns. The second and third alternatives were for an all 6in gun armament; in the second the forward guns were mounted behind an armoured breastwork, with ports give large angles of training. The remaining alternative was for 6in guns in twin turrets forward and aft. Once again White had to counter a strong argument from the DNO for an 8in gun armament. The DNO stated that the Elswick 8in gun could be loaded with great rapidity and that the weight of fire delivered would be greater than that from the 9.2in gun. White responded by saying that there was all the difference in the world between high rates of fire on Armstrongs test site with plenty of space and large numbers of men, and in the cramped positions aboard a ship in a seaway. Also while rates of fire were important, it was not the correct way to measure relative gun performance against an armoured ship, which was to look at the ability of the gun to penetrate amour.

Protection was to be based on that of the *Cressy* class, with a 6in belt, reducing to 5in and finally thinning to 2in of nickel steel up to the bows. Unlike the *Cressys* there was no armoured bulkhead forward, but there was

HMS King Alfred, *pictured here with no guns just after completion in December 1903, still in Victorian livery. She was built to counter the new foreign armoured cruisers.* (Antony Preston)

one closing the 6in belt aft. The total thickness of the protective decks were the same as in the preceding class, but with the upper deck being the thicker of the two. Aft of the armour belt protection was given by the lower protective deck extending to the stern.

The rationale behind the scheme of protection was to protect the central area of the vessel against medium calibre shells, such as the 9.2in, when in close action against cruisers and battleships. The 6in cemented armour of the main belt would keep out 6in shells and burst larger shells, allowing the force of the explosion to be absorbed by the coal bunkers behind the belt. The thinner belts forward were intended to limit the damage suffered when the ship was chasing an enemy, and to preserve the freeboard in a seaway. It was felt that there was very little chance of damage aft during a chasing action, and that it was safe to dispense with a vertical belt aft, White explained that even if the compartments above the protective deck were flooded there would be little effect on the speed, stability and manoeuvrability.

The Controller favoured an armoured screen rising above the upper deck, behind which two 6in guns were to be mounted, in order to give protection against raking fire. White argued that any protection from such a screen would be illusory, it would give protection at short ranges if the ships were on a parallel course, but at longer ranges the enemy's shells would simply pass over it and at any other bearing they would go around it.

Work continued on design No 1, and by early June 1898 it was found possible to add four more 6in guns to the armament by making the amidships casemates two storey. The cost of this, and the provision of torpedo nets

was nearly 400 tons more weight, which could be secured by increasing the beam to 71ft and legend displacement to 14,100 tons. The extra guns would impact on magazine space and White proposed to get around this by reducing the maximum rounds per gun carried from the normal 200 rounds to 150, he pointed out that with the exception of the *Diadem* class no cruiser had carried more than 2400 rounds of 6in shell. Presumably both White and the Board remained sensitive about the criticism of the *Powerful's* armament and were prepared to alter the normal practice in an attempt to counter any repetition.

The size of the ship's complement caused some unease, although the DNC was confident that accommodation space would not be a problem. Compared with the *Cressys* the extra four 6in guns would increase the fighting complement by 81 and this could not be avoided. Once again therefore the engineering complement came in for scrutiny and was cut by 15 men.

It was originally intended that there should be only two ships in the class. But in the atmosphere of panic that surrounded the 1898 Supplementary estimates, G J Goschen (later the First Viscount Goschen), the First Lord of the Admiralty, gave way to the wishes of the Controller and other admirals and ordered four, admitting that the proposal for the large cruisers was 'the gravest that has come before me since I became First Lord'.

The Monmouth *and* Suffolk *classes*

While the *Drakes* were intended to deal with the threat posed by one particular ship, the *Jeanne d'Arc*, there was

HMS Leviathan *painted grey overall, with fire control platforms on foremast and mainmast, showing the double casemates with their lack of freeboard in anything other than flat seas.* (Antony Preston)

a growing fear of a new type of cruiser being built in large numbers by other powers. Known as 'Corsair Cruisers' these ships were typified by White as having high speed, moderate protection and light armament. What the Royal Navy's response to this type of ship should be caused some division in the Admiralty. Goschen and a majority of the Naval Lords believed that the correct course was to build a ship very much like those building in France and Russia. The Admiralty's traditional method of dealing with the threat of high-speed opponents, as seen in the design of the *Powerful* and *Drake* classes, was to try to build as balanced a design as possible, regardless of size. The Controller argued that this policy should continue and that more *Drakes* should be laid down. Goschen insisted that the only way to provide ships in sufficient numbers was a smaller ship in which other qualities were sacrificed to speed.

White unusually seems to have taken very little part in the discussion. His biographer wrote:

> For the first time in his life he would seem to have been out of touch with the Board. He neither influenced its decision nor made any stubborn attempt to influence it. Why should the sailors not have the ships they want?

Design work on the new ships was started in July 1898 and the proposed design was presented to the Board at the end of September the same year. The key requirement was to obtain a speed of 23kts, presumably on a displacement of less than 10,000 tons. Yet if any kind of balance was to be maintained in the design both the weight and space allowed for the machinery was to be heavily constrained. Durston the EIC wrote that 24,000ihp could be provided for 1900 tons with Belleville boilers or 1800 tons with small-tube boilers. Such weights were clearly more than could be allowed and White asked what was the best that could be achieved on 1600 tons. If Normand small-tube boilers were used the EIC could provide 21,000ihp on the available displacement, but coal consumption would be 20 per cent higher than with Belleville boilers. If the weight allowance could be raised to 1675 tons then 21,000ihp could be obtained with Bellevilles and in considerably less space. Engine room space, particularly as regards height, was limited and forced the engineers to make a major break with their design practice. Royal Navy preference was to have engines with quite low RPM and a longish stroke; in the *Monmouth* class it was forced to adopt machinery more like that used by firms like Armstrongs in ships built for export, the stroke was reduced and the RPM was the highest ever used in a British triple expansion-engined cruiser. The problem was accentuated when the DNC asked for an extra 1000ihp at the cost of another 45 tons.

Positive that the engineers could deliver the required power, three preliminary designs were prepared. Numbers 1 and 2 were protected by 4in thick belts, while number 3 was for a protected cruiser. The object of the study seems to have been to explore the minimum practicable size for the ship. It also seems likely that the studies did not go beyond the DNC's department, but were only used for internal discussion; as so often White had already made up his mind about the characteristics of the ships. Design number one was presented to the Board in White's minute of 27 September 1898. Protection was to be in the form of a 4in belt of uncemented armour 11ft deep and 225ft long, 6ft would be below the legend waterline. Forward of the main belt the side was to have 2in thick plating up to the bow, while the rear of the belt was to be closed by a 3in bulkhead. The total deck protection was to be 2in thick, 1.5in at main deck level and .75in at the lower deck, with the space in between taken up with coal bunkers. Aft of the armour bulkhead the lower deck was 2in thick to the stern.

There were to be the now usual double-storeyed casemates for 6in guns forward and aft, with a single casemate amidships. The major change was the provision of a twin 6in gun turret at each end. The guns were to be mounted in a common cradle, partly to reduce the weight of the mounting, but primarily so that they could be controlled by one man with one sight. It was felt that the advantages of having the guns in separate cradles was very small. Its only real value lay in the possibility of one gun being put out of action, but it was felt that even if that were to happen to guns in a common cradle it would still be possible to operate the surviving gun. In practise the twin mounting proved a failure almost entirely due to the common cradle, the spread of fire between the two guns was very wide and unpredictable, and there was no way of calibrating the guns together. The DNO recommended that large amounts of ready use ammunition, 80 rounds per gun, should be carried where the guns were some distance from the shell rooms. The all 6in gun main battery placed some strain on the ammunition supply, and it was decided that the magazines should have two handling rooms each to ensure the rate of supply.

White clearly saw that the ships would be criticised both for their armament and protection, in relation to foreign cruisers of similar displacement. However:

> on the dimensions, after fulfilling the essential conditions of Speed (with natural draught in the stokeholds) and coal supply? it is not possible to devote a greater weight to armour and armament than has been assigned thereto….No doubt thicker armour and stronger decks would have been desirable from the point of view of protection, but these changes are not possible on the dimensions. If more powerful armament and better protection are to be obtained, in association with equal speed and coal endurance? then larger and more costly cruisers will be required.

To keep the weight of the hull to a minimum the double bottom only extended up to the bilge. Dispensing with the watertight space at the ship's side increased the coal capacity in a hull tightly constrained for size, and studies of the efficacy of the watertight bulkhead against torpedo or collision damage had been questioned. To help compensate for the loss of the watertight bulkhead the ammunition passages were moved closer to the mid-line of the ship, adjacent to the boiler and engine room spaces, rather than in the middle of the coal bunkers. It was agreed that detailed work would

HMS Cumberland *in Malta in 1913, with funnel bands painted up for identification. The contrast in size with the* Drake *class is very clear.* (Antony Preston)

proceed on design No 1 and the final legend received the Board stamp in February 1899. The beam had grown by 6in and displacement had risen to 9800 tons. The first two ships were ordered under the supplementary estimate to the 1898/99 programme. Originally four ships were to be ordered but the First Lord gave in to pressure from the Admirals and two more *Drakes* and only two *Monmouths* were included in the programme. Two more ships followed in the 1899-1900 Estimates and the remainder in the 1900-01 Programme. The DNC's department regarded the ships ordered under the 1900-01 programme to be a separate class, the *Suffolks*, but as in the case of the *Diadem* class any difference was restricted to the machinery sections.

The original design had provided for Belleville boilers and the first four were fitted as planned, but in the early 1900s the Navy was in the middle of the so called 'Battle of the Boilers' and there were many influential critics of the Belleville boiler. This led to two of the ships of the 1900-01 Programme being fitted with Niclausse boilers, and one with Babcock & Wilcox in order to compare them in practise.

The next class was to show a reversion to the idea of the armoured cruisers as an adjunct to the main battle fleet. Their development would mirror that of the battleships with an increased emphasis on heavier secondary armaments to the point where primary and secondary were virtually indistinguishable, certainly in term of fire control. They would also suffer from the perennial problem of complement, particularly for the engine room, which had been a lief motif throughout the development of the First Class cruisers.

The three last classes of armoured cruisers, the *Devonshires, Duke of Edinburgh's* and *Warriors* will be discussed in the final section of this series; along with wartime experiences and evaluation.

Source notes:

Because of the way that this article came into being it has not been practical to use conventional footnotes, however listed below are the principal sources identified as being used by David Topliss, any amendments will be given at the conclusion of the final article. Quotations in the text of this article are from the Ships Covers or the biography of Sir William White.

Ship's Covers at the National Maritime Museum ADM/138:
  Orlando
  Blake
  Edgar
  Powerful
  Diadem
  Cressy
  Monmouth

Notebooks of naval architect Sir George Thurston, National Maritime Museum, uncatalogued, Ref Mss/72/017.
F Manning, *The Life of Sir William White, KCB*, (London: John Murray, 1923)
[Ed. See also D K Brown 'Sir William White, KCB, FRS, LLD, DSc' in *Warship 2000-2001*, pp.125-131]

THE ROYAL NAVY AND THE ROLE OF SEAPOWER IN GLOBAL POLITICS, 1856-1871

The years 1856-1871 witnessed major upheaval in warship design, in which rapid technological advance made the Royal Navy of the 1870s almost unrecognisable from that of the 1850s. Here **Pascal Barras** argues that the results were largely favourable to the Royal Navy, which in 1871 remained a premier force in global power politics.

'The fear of war…acts in preventing war'.[1]

The fifteen years that followed the Russian (Crimean) War were a period of rapid technological advance in warship design, which made the major fleets of 1871 almost unrecognisable from those which had operated in the Baltic and Black Seas in 1854-1856. The drastic changes in propulsion, armour and armament threatened to erase Britain's long-standing naval dominance, upon which the strength of her global Empire and the sanctity of the home islands was founded. At the same time as naval warfare was being revolutionised, the map of Europe was extensively redrawn through a series of brief, limited wars based on nationalist principles. The end result of all this change was, however, very favourable to Britain. She emerged in 1871 more secure in Europe and stronger globally than at any point since 1815. The containment of France, the ultimate goal of the Congress of Vienna, was finally achieved with the establishment of Prussia as a strong counterbalance in central Europe. The fall of Louis Napoléon, and the weakness of the American navy, meant that there was no immediate great power threat to the Empire. Even the formal removal in 1871 of the restrictions placed on Russia by the 1856 Treaty of Paris presented no significant danger to British security, as Russian power at this point was critically under-developed and posed no imminent danger which could not be effectively countered.

While the fact that Britain did not have to go to war to improve her position was the result of a certain degree of good fortune, credit also must be given to the soundness of her naval policy and diplomacy. She picked up the gauntlet of technological change thrown down by France in the late 1850s and early 1860s by fortifying her dockyards and building a superior ironclad fleet, thus enabling her to maintain her free hand and independence in European politics.[2] Adapting the Royal Navy's traditional strategy of blockade and coastal operations to the new technological circumstances, she refined the offensive doctrine in which gunboats, 'coast defence' ships and seagoing ironclads could provide power-projection to any European coastline. This naval preparation provided a deterrent threat, which enabled British statesmen to patiently observe events on the continent while reserving the intention and capability of intervening on occasions in which British interests were challenged. In this period, as was true since 1688, the Royal Navy provided Britain with the ultimate insurance policy. Command of the sea gave Britain the ability to project power to any coastline in the world, while ensuring a high degree of invulnerability from incurring similar injury herself.

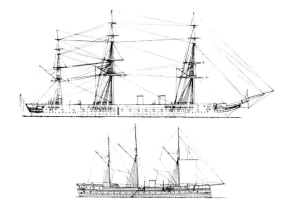

HMS Warrior (*top*) and Gloire (*below*) the world's first seagoing ironclads showing the enormous difference in size although both were rated as frigates. (CPL)

Naval bases used by the Royal Navy in the nineteenth century. (Antony Preston)

The Politics and Strategy of Seapower

Despite the divergent personalities and beliefs represented in British statesmen between 1856 and 1871, naval policy remained largely constant. The concept of the Royal Navy as a deterrent force remained the foundation of government policy from Lord Palmerston through to Benjamin Disraeli and W E Gladstone. Where these men differed in opinion was simply in whether deterrence was to be provided from forward bases scattered around the world, or whether it should be centrally concentrated as a defensive force around the home islands. Through this stability in naval policy, Boards of Admiralty were able to implement a consistent long-term strategy, which enabled deterrence to be effective. Exploiting the capabilities which new technology brought to naval warfare, the offensive coastal-assault doctrine employed by the Admiralty provided a strong base for British security. While this was a case of policy-driven strategy, a symbiotic quality nonetheless existed in that both policy and strategy needed each other to be stable in order that they could individually be of maximum value in protecting British interests.

In this period, Britain's policy of deterrence through naval strength was based on battlefleet supremacy in home waters and a working command of the world's oceans.[3] This not only provided security for the home islands and ensured that no serious threat could be mounted against her global empire, but also enabled Britain to have a voice in European politics. At the end of the Russian War, British naval dominance was clearly established, with only France offering any competition. Further, the war against Russia had demonstrated the efficacy of the Royal Navy's coast-assault doctrine and provided European statesmen with a demonstration of British offensive capabilities. It is against this background that the French ironclad threat must viewed, as British reactions were conditioned by the need not simply to protect against invasion but to retain the ability to project power.

The aim of coast-assault was remarkably simple; deflecting the enemy's mind from offensive operations against Britain by keeping attention focused on the defence of his own shores.[4] A model of the strategy in action was provided in the attack on Kinburn on 14-15 October 1855, in which gunboats landed troops behind the fortress to prevent a Russian retreat and then joined a flotilla of mortar boats, floating batteries and line-of-battle ships to bombard the fortress itself.[5] The advent of new technology in naval warfare had, in itself, little effect on the mechanics of such operations. Even before the French had launched *Gloire*, the Board of Admiralty had given some thought to the potential implications of improved military technology. It fully expected that a change would have to be made in the structure of fleets ordered to attack land positions, given the possibility of facing return fire of molten iron which could immediately set fire to wooden ships. Initially, it was believed that this could be countered by employing smaller ships which would be protected simply by the limited target that they presented, but the possible future use of iron was also contemplated. The Admiralty remained convinced that coastal operations would not only be viable in future conflicts, but that they would remain crucial to British war-fighting capability.[6]

The true danger posed by France's adoption of ironclad seagoing ships was that it threatened to wrest command of European waters away from Britain, making coastal assault impossible and allowing France to employ a similar strategy to gain British acquiescence for European territorial revision.[7] This challenge was negated in two parts. Naval arsenals and dockyards in Britain were strengthened to prevent France from using la Royale in diplomatic initiatives, and a cautious programme of ironclad construction was implemented in order to maintain command of the seas. The two key factors guiding early British ironclad construction were the massive expense required for the building of even one ship and the uncertainty of the new technology. A three-deck line-of-battle ship could be constructed for about £150,000, less than half of the cost of Warrior.[8] As the application of iron armour to ships was still untested, Britain was also wary of spending money needlessly. Had Gloire proved to be a total failure, the French challenge would have been dead in the water. As late as September 1860 the Board of Admiralty was pondering the use of Warrior as a transport if she did not meet expectations in trials.[9] Britain's response was thus tempered and measured, linking its construction policy with reports of the success of the new technology, relying mostly on superior all-iron designs and using wooden conversions only as a stop-gap measure.[10] By the end of 1861, the short-term nature of the French ironclad programme was apparent. The hastily built, and mostly wooden hulled French ironclads were no match for British construction in terms of quality, and her industry lacked the resources to support an extended effort to out-build Britain. Palmerston's government had demonstrated its resolve to maintain British freedom of action, despite the enormous costs involved in laying down fifteen ironclads.

Having laid a solid foundation which would secure future command of the sea, the Admiralty expanded its focus, exploiting the new technology to develop specialised coastal operations craft. The original impetus for the ordering of the Prince Albert and Royal Sovereign came about because Parliament had turned against Palmerston's plans for improving the defences of the Spithead fortification.[11] The Admiralty consequently proposed adopting the recommendation contained in the Report of the Royal Commission on National Defences (1860), which advocated the construction of heavily-armed shallow-draught vessels to protect British dockyards. The decision to utilise turret-mounted guns in these vessels in place of the conventional broadside was based as much on the technical viability of the new system as it was on the fact that its designer, Cowper Coles, had convinced Gladstone that his plans represented a low-cost alternative to traditional means of defence. The other trait that these ships owed to economy-minded liberals was the descriptive term 'coast defence' vessels, with which they were labelled. As the public at large would not support an open admission of a British offensive naval strategy, the Admiralty only acknowledged part of the role these ships would play, keeping secret the fact that they were intended to act offensively against an enemy's coast as much as defending Britain's own.[12] This label stuck not only to these vessels, but also to subsequent craft designed among similar principles, obfuscating their intended purpose to all but those against whom they would be used.

HMS Warrior, with the lengthened bowsprit (post-1867). Note the narrow gunports (possible with pivot guns). (CPL)

The iron-hulled coast defence turret ship HMS Prince Albert (1866) pointed the way to later developments. (CPL)

The theme of economy became increasingly important during this period. Britain's initial response to the iron-clad programme resulted in the Prime Minister, Palmerston, clashing with his Chancellor of the Exchequer, Gladstone, with Palmerston holding sway on most occasions. The cause of disagreement between the two men was their belief in how the Royal Navy should be used to protect British interests. Palmerston's policy of deterrence reflected the beliefs of the pre-industrial age, in which large forces had to be stationed around the world to maintain a watch over British interests. Gladstone, on the other hand, recognised that improvements in technology such as steam propulsion and the telegraph made such expensive measures unnecessary, as

the main naval force could be concentrated in home waters and dispatched to foreign locales when trouble arose.[13] For Gladstone, economy in defence spending was also important as it was the platform on which he based his future political career. That he was unable to gain the upper hand over Palmerston was the result not only of the latter's astute understanding of the machinations of deterrence and international politics, but also the balance of forces in Parliament upon which his policies relied. The ability to draw support from across a broad spectrum of opinion, both from within and outside his party, meant that the disaffected always remained in the minority. This was particularly true of defence issues, where he was able to curry favour with Tories and those

HMS Black Prince, *the second 'Black Snake of the Channel', with funnels lowered.* (CPL)

Radicals who relished ideas of the British lion being a rough animal in foreign questions.[14]

Consequently, Gladstone had to wait for Palmerston's departure from office before any success could be achieved in reducing defence expenditures. Such was his zeal in October 1865 that the corpse of Palmerston was barely cold before he wrote to Lord Russell, the apparent next Prime Minister, advocating cuts to the naval and military establishment.[15] Gladstone's proposals, however, went far beyond what the First Lord of the Admiralty, the Duke of Somerset, thought prudent to maintain the efficiency of the Navy, and were a contributory factor in Somerset's offer to resign.[16] Ignoring calls from leading Whigs to merge the Cabinet position of the First Lord of the Admiralty with that of the Duchy of Lancaster, Russell rejected the resignation.[17] Gladstone continued to press for economy as the annual estimates were being drawn up, arguing that this would be possible through reforming the administration of the Navy. Russell, however, apparently agreeing with the Whig whip, Henry Brand, felt that large reductions in the Navy would be unpopular, and the naval estimates actually increased by £0.4 million in 1866.[18] Gladstone was again forced to wait to implement his programme of reductions.

Part of the Admiralty's concern in 1865-6 was the increasing threat posed to the Empire by foreign warships. Britain's initial ironclad programme reflected the fact that the French challenge was geographically limited to European waters. As British interests on foreign stations could be adequately protected by a force of unarmoured sloops, frigates, and the gunboats built during the Russian War, the stationing of ironclads outside European waters would not only have been a wasteful overkill but would also have dangerously reduced Britain's ability to fight France. Matching a realistic force-structure with the fact that ironclads relied heavily on large dockyards (which did not yet exist outside of Europe) for fitting-out, coaling, and maintenance led the Admiralty to refrain from detaching ironclads overseas until France had done likewise.[19] This dispersal was only achieved with the launch of the French armoured cruiser *Belliqueuse* in September 1865 and the ordering of seven *Alma* class armoured cruisers in the same year. The Admiralty's response to the expanded geographic presence of French ironclads was initially hindered by the design of early British ironclads, which gave priority to fighting qualities at the expense of cruising well under sail. In order to maximise their efficiency on distant stations, they had to be fitted with an auxiliary engine to keep the screw turning at all times at the same speed of the ships' forward progress.[20] This temporary measure was later augmented by the laying down of four *Audacious* class ironclads in 1867 and two *Swiftsure* class ironclads in 1868, all of which were intended for use in distant waters.

Compounding the problem posed by the spread of ironclads outside of European waters was the construction of the large American *Wampanoag* class cruisers designed to attack British commerce. Before these ships were laid down, the Admiralty believed that the US Navy posed no significant threat to Britain. Comprising mostly shallow-draught monitors, it was capable only of defensive coastal operations despite the outlandish claims made by Admiral Porter, USN, towards the close of the American Civil War, that the monitor *Monadnock* could cross the Atlantic, destroy any French or British vessel, lay either nation's towns 'under contribution', and return to America, provided that coal could be acquired for the voyage home.[21] By February 1866, however, the

HMS Prince Consort *was originally a 91-gun 2nd Rate, but, along with* Caledonia *and* Ocean, *was converted during 1861-62 to an ironclad armed with 7in breechloaders and four 100pdr and 12-68pdr smoothbores.* (CPL)

HMS Audacious *at Hong Kong in the 1870s, while serving as flagship of the China Station.* Audacious *and her sisters,* Invincible, Iron Duke *and* Vanguard, *were the first ironclads designed for use on foreign stations.* (CPL)

need the defend against the American cruisers was of considerable importance to the Admiralty, and within two months plans had been drawn up and approved for the unarmoured iron frigate *Inconstant*.[22] By the time she was launched in 1868, however, the American threat had greatly diminished as the *Wampanoag* class were known by the Admiralty to be somewhat less successful, and definitely inferior to the British design.[23]

The first significant modification in government naval policy did not occur until Gladstone climbed to the top rung of British politics in 1868. The Conservative administrations of Lord Derby and Benjamin Disraeli between 1866 and 1868 had not been able to effect any reductions in the Estimates, faced with combative Boards of Admiralty, although some reductions in unarmoured ships on foreign stations had been achieved through ordering six instead of three new ironclads in the 1868-9 Estimates.[24] In contrast to the acrimonious tension on naval questions which hampered the Tory governments,

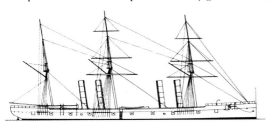

The US Navy's Wampanoag *class wooden screw frigates worried the Admiralty, but proved unsuccessful in service,* Wampanoag *herself was condemned in 1869 a mere five years after her launch.* (CPL)

Gladstone's reductions were implemented with the entire cooperation of his First Lord of the Admiralty, Hugh Childers. The Board of Admiralty was reformed, as was promotion and retirement, and a permanent downsizing of overseas forces was accomplished. The decision to concentrate forces in European waters marked a transformation in British deterrence, in which force-levels on foreign stations were determined by realistic immediate need, and could be augmented rapidly from a centralised reserve in emergencies because of improved communications. One aspect of Childers' reforms, an attempt to institute a consistent building programme, proved a failure almost immediately because it was inconsistent with a policy of deterrence. While Childers believed that adding a fixed number of ships each year would enable Britain to achieve a 'two-power standard' by 1871, such plans relied upon similar construction consistency in other countries.[25] This ignored the lesson provided by Palmerston at the start of the ironclad race that Britain must base her construction policy on that of her rivals in order to maintain command of the seas and thus a credible deterrence. Childers' plan fell apart as a result of increased French naval spending in the build-up to, and during, the Franco-Prussian War, which prompted the other members of the Board of Admiralty to call for Britain to match French efforts.[26] Gladstone's government responded in true Palmerston style with an additional vote of credit of £2,000,000 for the armed forces, £600,000 of which was earmarked for the Navy. The treaty which Gladstone signed with France and Prussia to guarantee the neutrality of Belgium served as an indication of continued British interest in the Low Countries;

the ordering of shallow-draught ironclads and gunboats for coastal assault was a warning that Britain was prepared to use force in the matter.

Recognising the soundness of a deterrent naval policy, even the economy-minded Gladstone proved willing to spend money on the Royal Navy to protect Britain's position in Europe. The manner in which British governments and Boards of Admiralty from 1856 to 1870 adapted construction policy to maintain naval supremacy, first in Europe and later across the globe, served as an indication of their faith in the Navy to operate effectively as the guarantor of Britain's security. The assumption which underlay this reliance was the continued ability of fleets to reflect national power; in short, the continued importance of seapower.

National Power, Seapower, and International Influence

The inherent problem with analysing national power is the simple fact that it is not only relative from one state to another but also to the situation in which it is to be employed. The same is obviously true of its component elements, be they economic, geographical, military or naval; time and place are crucial considerations. Only by answering the question of who gets what, when, where and how can a precise understanding of power, or the factors which comprise it, be achieved. No state, irregardless of how powerful it is, gets what it wants in every situation.[27] Applied to British power in the post-Crimean era, this theoretical premise opens an avenue for questioning what has passed as the accepted understanding of her global position at that time. In particular, statements which link the decline of Britain to the shift of power

from coastal to continental states as railways and telegraphs improved inland communications, should be regarded as merely identifying the growth of another element of power over considerable period of time.[28] Such arguments really say nothing about the decline of seapower as they do not give a context in which the relative merits of each component can be compared and contrasted. Further, statements about the weakness of Britain which are linked to the decline of seapower have tended to view navies as being reduced to strictly defensive assets.[29] Regarding the Royal Navy as employing an offensive strategy, which was intended as a deterrent, gives further impetus to re-examining British power between 1856 and 1871.

Any study of power must be linked to the objectives of the state(s) in question. While Britain had been largely able to flaunt her influence globally before the Russian War, a combination of factors gradually forced a more realistic re-evaluation of foreign policy after 1856 to focus on vital interests, resulting in a stance which has been labelled 'non-interventionism'. The influence of domestic politics, in which liberal ideals of peace and economy were strongly represented, and the increase in industrialisation on the Continent created a situation in which Britain was unable to back up her diplomacy with force unless her interests were being directly challenged. The political and economic costs were simply too high for a government to consider such actions. Consequently, British policy towards Europe in this period was governed primarily by considerations of the balance of power in Europe, the independence of the Low Countries, the maintenance of her naval supremacy and the continuation of a secure line of communication with India. Only a threat to these interests would prompt British action.

Due to the structure of her power, which was geared towards victory through endurance and economic

HMS Wolverine (1864) was one of six Jason class wooden screw corvettes armed with 20-8in SB and a 110pdr Armstrong BL. Their unexceptional performance led to a short service life as speed became increasingly important in cruising vessels. (CPL)

The French Reine Blanche (1868) was one of seven Alma class small wooden central battery ironclad designed for use in distant waters. (CPL)

The French Marengo (1872) was one of three Ocean class woooden central battery ironclads, she is depicted here reduced to barquentine rig. (CPL)

strength, and the fact that she would only act in questions crucial to her national existence, British intervention could be expected to be the beginning of a protracted campaign in which she would eventually seek allies to aid her cause.[30] The beginning of any such action, however, would be an offensive by the Royal Navy. While naval power in itself was unlikely to prove decisive, it had the ability to inflict painful losses when employed on its own, and could alter the strategic balance when used in conjunction with military forces on land. Britain could not only project naval power directly to the geographic regions which were most important to her, but also to any European coastline. No continental state was immune to such disruption from the sea, particularly those who were in a position to challenge her interests: Russia, France and Prussia.

The Russian War demonstrated that even a massive continental state such as Russia could suffer severely in attacks from the sea. Apart from the threat of the disruption of her coastal trade, one of Russia's key weaknesses, as far as the Royal Navy was concerned, was the immense distance and lack of reliable lines of communication between the regions in which seapower could be exercised against her. This was exploited by Britain between 1854 and 1856 through a dual offensive in both the Black Sea and the Baltic theatres. The vulnerability of St Petersburg to naval bombardment and amphibious operations tied up 250,000 first-class troops in the region which could otherwise have been used in the defence of the Crimea.[31] Russian acceptance of her susceptibility to seapower was evidenced by the efforts made after the war with Britain to improve her coastal defences both on land and at sea.[32] She built a respectable number of ironclads in the 1860s, the majority of which were coast-defence vessels incapable of leaving the Baltic, experimented in both contact and electrically-detonated underwater mines, and revised and strengthened the shore defences around Kronstadt, with the aim of bringing them to a constant state of readiness so as to protect against sudden attacks from the sea.[33]

While continental France possessed no area of immense strategic importance open to the sea comparable to the Baltic, Louis Napoléon's colonial ambitions provided a soft underbelly which was vulnerable to seapower. Spurred by a preoccupation with economic prosperity, his chief focus outside of France was Algeria, from which French influence in the Mediterranean was to be spread. The large army of occupation in the colony increased the strategic importance of ensuring communications across the Mediterranean, a role which fell to the French Navy. As well, apart from the expected disruption of coastal trade, the importance of naval power to her lay to a significant extent in the fact that, except during the first years of ironclad construction, la Royale was an instrument of prestige to the Second Empire.[34] Louis Napoléon sought the gains of his uncle, without his uncle's victories, which outside Europe, depended on the French Navy. A naval defeat meant that France would be constrained within her continental borders, a situation unacceptable to a regime which played so heavily on national memories of past glory.[35] As a result of her inability to gain the upper hand in the

Channel at the beginning of the ironclad race, she was consistently forced to factor the Royal Navy into any diplomatic considerations that affected British interests. Consequently, the energy she directed into the protection of her dockyards and naval arsenals took on an added significance.[36] These arrangements culminated during the Franco-Prussian War, when France was forced to prepare for both a defensive war with the Royal Navy as well as for offensive operations against Prussia. Rigault de Genouilly, the French Minister of Marine, ordered a significant number of shallow-draught vessels, including rams and floating batteries, to be kept at Cherbourg during the war so as to defend the arsenal and the Channel littoral.[37] Also at Cherbourg, the coast defences were fully armed, torpedoes were placed in the roads and outside the breakwater to keep an enemy at a distance, and the guns on the breakwaters were replaced with 22cm shell-guns. These preparations, and similar ones carried out at Brest, Toulon and other naval ports were, in the words of the British naval attaché in Paris, 'exaggerated against a power of small naval importance', such as Prussia.[38] Only the threat of a British attack could have prompted such a response.

Of the three leading states in Europe, Prussia's vulnerability to seapower was the least severe as she had no exposed regions of significant strategic importance and had, at the time, no extra-European ambitions. She could, nonetheless, suffer enough economic disruption from an enemy's navy to necessitate her to commit resources to coastal defences in the Baltic and North Seas if faced with an enemy which possessed a superior navy. This became evident during her war with Denmark in 1864, when the Danish fleet inflicted heavy losses on North German commerce. The situation was only improved when Austria gave in to Prussian pleas for assistance and sent ships to the North Sea to lift the Danish blockade.[39] In the following year, a Prussian agent was sent to the British colony of Heligoland and unsuccessfully attempted to incite the inhabitants to ask for annexation to Prussia. The island was of considerable strategic utility, as it not only commanded the entrances to the rivers Elbe, Weser, Jahde and Eyder, but also the entrance to a proposed canal linking the Baltic with the North Sea.[40] The island afforded sheltered anchorage for ships of any size, and was considered by the Royal Navy as invaluable as a station for blockading forces to watch the North German coast.[41] At the same time plans were drawn up in Prussia to erect and fortify a large naval base at Kiel, to speed up the completion of the naval arsenal on the Bay of Jahde and to purchase two ironclad frigates.[42] These were not the actions of a state impervious to seapower. The potential susceptibility of Prussia to naval action was again demonstrated during the Franco-Prussian War, despite the inability of France to take full advantage of it. Only the unsuitability for coastal operations of the French fleet sent to the North Sea, drawing too much water to attack fortified positions and being too unstable to interdict commerce, prevented her from repeating the damage inflicted by Denmark six years previously.[43] Further, the reappearance of the French fleet after the initial blockade had been lifted caused considerable alarm in Hamburg and Berlin, resulting in the reinforcement of Hamburg with

The masted turret ship HMS Monarch (1869) was the first successful sea-going turret ship design, unlike her ill-fated rival HMS Captain. (CPL)

HMS Tenedos, *launched in May 1870 was the last of seven* Eclipse *class small wooden screw corvettes. The class boasted a 2-3kt speed advantage over the* Jason *class. (CPL)*

The Prussian central battery ironclad Kronprinz *(1867) was built on the Thames to a design by Sir Edward Reed.* (CPL)

considerable numbers of troops from Hanover and Berlin to counter any attempted French landing.[44] With the introduction of a torpedo service in the 1872 German naval estimates, Prussia acknowledged its naval suscepti-bilities and shortcomings. 'At the outbreak of the last war and during its continuance, the defence of the seashore has become very apparent', making such defensive prepa-rations necessary 'so that the harbours may be secured against all eventualities'.[45]

The point that European statesmen were aware of the threat to their countries posed by the Royal Navy cannot be over-stated. This was one of the keys to the deterrent effect of British strategy, the other, of course, being the realisation that Britain would actually use force if her interests were challenged.[46] While C J Bartlett makes the valid point that it is hard to measure the effect of deter-rence as it is impossible to ascertain what would have happened in its absence, there can be little other expla-nation for why British interests were challenged so infre-quently between 1856 and 1870, especially as European statesmen were well aware of Britain's resolve not to get involved in continental affairs which had no bearing on her interests.[47] Diplomacy was always to be the preferred course of action for British statesmen, and proved suc-cessful in the relatively minor Luxembourg and Belgian railways crises. These incidents were of a special nature as Britain was aware that French territorial ambitions after Sadowa were simply attempts to compensate for similar Prussian gains, and that, given Prussia's strength in cen-tral Europe, France could not risk antagonising her west-ern neighbour.[48] While Britain did not contemplate naval action during these crises, the degree to which the Royal Navy was respected in Europe was demonstrated by

a Belgian request in April 1870 for two British ironclads to be stationed in the river Scheldt to assist in the defence of Antwerp.[49] A more direct compliment to British seapower was paid by Prince Gortchakoff, the Russian Chancellor and Foreign Minister, during the Gladstone administration's negotiations in 1870 with Prussia and France for the security of Belgium. Querying the diplomatic approach adopted by Britain, Gortchakoff remarked to Sir Andrew Buchanan, the British Ambassador to St. Petersburgh, that 'a few ironclads sent to Antwerp would as effectually secure Belgian neutrali-ty, as an engagement entered into by Treaty'.[50]

On only two occasions during this period was a suffi-cient challenge posed by a potential rival in Europe to warrant an extra-ordinary British naval response: during the build-up to the Franco-Austrian war, and during the Franco-Prussian war. In the first instance, Britain rein-forced the Mediterranean squadron upon hearing rumours of a Franco-Russian alliance to make war on Austria.[51] This was clearly a question of the balance of power, and Britain felt that it might be necessary to go to war in order to guarantee the existence of Austria as a great power and protect the Ottoman Empire.[52] The threat from Russia never materialised, yet the danger of increased French influence in Italy had serious implica-tions for British Mediterranean interests and the route to India. While Palmerston's Italian policy in 1859 was cur-tailed by the early French lead in ironclad construction[53], he was not willing to give France free reign in the region, fearing the French Emperor's eventual designs on Turkey or Morocco.[54] The criteria he stipulated which would lead Britain to war were either a direct French attack on England or a 'great scheme of French aggrandisement'

The Audacious *class central battery ironclad HMS* Iron Duke *achieved notoriety by ramming and sinking her sister* Vanguard *in 1875.* (CPL)

which would jeopardise future British security. Napoléon, however, proved to be more cautious than Palmerston suspected. The Villafranca agreement ensured Austria's continued position as a great power and the immediate danger from France subsided.

A similar fear for the balance of power prompted Britain into action again in 1870. The cruise of the combined Mediterranean and Channel Squadrons in 1870 has come to be remembered primarily for the loss of the *Captain*, yet the movements of the ships is also significant in light of the quarrel between France and Prussia. While the primary purpose of the cruise was intended to be the tests of the qualities of the turret ships *Monarch* and *Captain*, the necessity of making a solid show of strength was decided upon by the British government even before the conflict broke out.[55] On the day after France declared war, Admiral Sir Alexander Milne, the commander of the combined squadron, was informed by the First Lord of the Admiralty that the Cabinet wished the fleets to proceed north, rather than remaining near Gibraltar.[56] Six days later, formal orders were issued to Milne designating Cape Finisterre as the northern, and Cape St Vincent as the southern boundary for fleet exercises, replacing the original southern latitude of Madeira, and requiring him to make arrangements so that the Board of Admiralty could readily communicate with the fleet.[57] On 11 August orders were again changed and Vigo was designated as the headquarters for the fleets, with the necessity of remaining in contact with the Admiralty being re-stated.[58] While initial British concerns were over the safety of Belgium, her preparations for war included the fitting out of ships of the *Audacious* class, which would have allowed her to form a North Sea Squadron if necessary.[59] The fleets were intended to exercise together until 12 September, yet the defeat of

Louis Napoléon made the chances of a serious naval war appear unlikely after 3 September, and the loss of the *Captain* on 7 September further shifted the focus of the Admiralty away from war.[60]

Naval power was not the be-all and end-all of national power between 1856 and 1871 and to suggest such would be foolish. It was, however, still a potent force in international politics that no state could afford to ignore. As Britain's interests in this period were clearly defined and limited to safeguarding her future security, the Royal Navy was able to provide effective and immediate protection against any possible challenge. Apart from its ability to inflict serious injury on any European state, the navy was, in a basic sense, a barometer through which foreign statesmen could gauge the mood in Whitehall. The threat of its employment indicated the potential for a war in which eventually all British resources would be brought to bear. Despite practising a policy of 'non-intervention', Britain proved herself not only willing, but also able to get involved in European affairs under the right circumstances.

The territorial changes in Europe and the revolution in naval warfare that followed the Russian War had the potential to deal a serious blow to Britain's world power. That they did not was a testament to a realistic redefining of British interests by the statesmen of the day to identify the minimum requirements for national security, and to the soundness and consistency of British naval policy. Through the reliance on an offensive strategy based on coastal operations, the Royal Navy was able to project power to any point of the globe accessible from the sea, providing strong deterrence against any challenge to Britain or her Empire. In consequence, Britain emerged in 1871 stronger globally and more secure at home than she had been fifteen years previously, all the while abstaining from involvement in European conflict.

Although there were hiccups in the practice of deterrence, especially in Europe, the efficacy of Britain's approach was demonstrated in the absence of any serious challenges to her interests. The Schleswig-Holstein affair, in particular, seems less of a disaster in British diplomacy when contrasted with the British response to the Franco-Prussian war. In this light, the events of 1864 become a simply diplomatic over-extension by Palmerston, compounded by Russell's impetuous behaviour, in a question that had no real significance to the nation. All European statesmen were aware of the exact nature of British interests and the continued importance of seapower. While this circumstance did lead to a certain lessening of British influence in continental matters which were of little importance to her and increased the chances of embarrassment if she played her hand badly, it also ensured the respect of the Great Powers of Europe, and their avoidance of treading on her toes in matters in which she was more directly concerned.

Acknowledgements

I am grateful to the Society for Nautical Research and the University of Hull for giving me the opportunity to present an earlier draft of this article to the 'New Researchers in Maritime History Conference' in March 1999. I wish also to acknowledge the assistance of the 'Regional Security in a Global Context' Programme at King's College London for the award of a John D and Catherine T MacArthur Scholarship during the research and writing of this paper. Finally, thanks are due to Professor Andrew Lambert for his comments and suggestions at various stages of this project.

Notes

1 Russell to the Attorney General, copy, 2 March 1866, Russell Papers, PRO 30/22/16B.
2 A Lambert, 'Politics, Technology and Policy-Making 1859-1865: Palmerston, Gladstone and the Management of the Ironclad Naval Race', *Northern Mariner/Le marin du nord*, VIII, No. 3 (July 1998), p.2.
3 A Lambert, 'The Royal Navy, 1856-1914: Deterrence and Strategy of World Power' in K Neilson and E J Errington (eds.), *Navies and Global Defense*, (London: Praeger, 1995), p.73.
4 A Milne, 'Response to three questions put by the Queen to the Board of Admiralty in 1858', [no date] May, 1858, Milne Papers, MLN 142/2 (NMM). For more on British coastal-assault doctrine, see P Barras, 'British Offensive Strategy and the Political Myth of Gunboats and "Coastal- Defence" Vessels in the 1860s', in J Ferris (ed.), *New Currents in Naval History* (London: Praeger, forthcoming).
5 For a more thorough discussion of this action, see J P Baxter, *The Introduction of the Ironclad Warship* (Cambridge, Mass: Harvard University Press, 1933), pp. 83-85, and A Lambert, *The Crimean War: British Grand Strategy, 1853-1856* (Manchester: Manchester University Press, 1990), pp.257-261.
6 A Milne, 'Response to three questions put by the Queen to the Board of Admiralty in 1858', [no date] May, 1858. Milne Papers, MLN 142/2 (NMM).
7 Lambert, 'Ironclad Naval Race', p.1.
8 D K Brown, *Warrior to Dreadnought; Warship Development, 1860-1905* (London: Chatham, 1997), p.15.
9 Board minute, 22 September 1860, ADM 1/5749 (all ADM files are from the PRO).
10 Lambert, 'Ironclad Naval Race', p.29.
11 *Ibid.*, p.27.

The French-built Prussian central battery ironclad Friedrich Carl *(1867) was similar to the British-built* Kronprinz. (CPL)

12 J C D Hay, minute, no date, [December, 1866?], Milne Papers, MLN 143/2 (NMM). Sir John Pakington, minute, 4 November 1866, ADM 1/5983.

13 A Lambert, 'The Admiralty, the "Trent" Crisis of 1861 and the Strategy of Imperial Defence', pp.5-6. I wish to thank Professor Lambert for permission to consult and cite his yet unpublished paper.

14 P M Gurowich, 'The Continuation of War by Other Mean: Party and Politics, 1855-1865', *The Historical Journal*, 27, 3 (1984), pp.616-618.

15 Gladstone to Russell, 18 October 1865, Russell Papers, PRO 30/22/15F.

16 Somerset to Russell, (private), 20 October 1865, 21 October 1865, 23 October 1865, Russell Papers, PRO 30/22/15F. Also relevant to Somerset's decision to put his office at Russell's disposal was the concern shared among many members of the incoming administration that the new government was unbalanced in Parliament, with too many departments led by individuals sitting in the House of Lords.

17 Brand to Russell, 23 October 1865; unsigned [George Elliot?], minute, 24 October 1865, Russell Papers, PRO 30/22/15F.

18 B R Mitchell, *British Historical Statistics*, (Cambridge: Cambridge University Press, 1988).

19 Controller's submission, confidential, 11 February 1863, ADM 1/5840.

20 Controller's submission, 19 January 1866, ADM 1/5980.

21 Controller's submission, 20 January 1863, ADM 1/5840; Rear Admiral Porter to the Secretary of the United States Navy, copy, 15 January 1865, ADM 1/5952.

22 F W Grey, minute, 13 February 1866; Controller's submission, 25 April 1866; F W Grey minute, 26 September 1866, ADM 1/5980.

23 Childers to Russell, private, 17 February 1869, Russell Papers, PRO 30/22/16F.

24 J F Beeler, *British Naval Policy in the Gladstone-Disraeli Era, 1866-1880* (Stanford, California: Stanford University Press, 1997), pp.71-79.

25 Childers to Russell, 17 February 1869, Russell Papers, PRO 30/22/16F.

26 Robinson to Dacres, 4 August 1870; Sidney Dacres, memorandum, 8 August 1870. ADM 1/6159.

27 Gordon Martel, 'The Meaning of Power: Rethinking the Decline and Fall of Great Britain' *International History Review*, 13:14 (November, 1991), pp.677-678.

28 Arguments which emphasise the shift in power from coastal to continental states can be found in M Chamberlain, *'Pax Britannica'? British Foreign Policy, 1789-1914* (London and New York: Longman, 1988) and C J Bartlett, 'Statecraft, Power and Influence' in Bartlett, ed. *Britain Pre-eminent* (London: Macmillan, 1969).

29 Lambert, 'Deterrence and Strategy of World Power', p.73.

30 *Ibid.*, p.83.

31 A Lambert, 'Part of a Long Line of Circumvallation to Confine the Future Expansion of Russia; Great Britain and the Baltic, 1809-1890', in G Rystad, K R Böhme and W M Carlgren (eds.), *In Quest of Trade and Security: The Baltic in Power Politics, 1500-1990*, vol. 1 (Stockholm: PROBUS Förlag, 1994), p.310.

32 W C Fuller Jr. *Strategy and Naval Power in Russia, 1600-1914* (New York: The Free Press, 1992), p.287.

33 Crealoch to Buchanan, copy, 2 November 1865, ADM 1/5954. Buchanan to Clarendon, copy, 5 October 1869, ADM 1/6128. Beeler, p.202. D W Mitchell, *A History of Russian and Soviet Seapower* (London: André Deutsch, 1973), p.177. Fuller, p.287.

34 T Ropp, *The Development of a Modern Navy: French Naval Policy 1871-1904* (Annapolis, Maryland: Naval Institute Press, 1987), p.7.

35 J F MacMillan, *Napoleon III* (London and New York: Longman, 1991), pp.60-63.

36 Barras, *op.cit.*

37 M Battesti, *La Marine de Napoléon III, Une politique navale* (Paris: Service historique de la marine, 1996), vol 2., p.1054.

38 Hore to Lyons, copy, 29 July 1870; Hamond to Granville, copy, 7 August 1870 ADM 1/6170.

39 R Gardiner (ed.), *Conway's All the World's Fighting Ships 1860-1905* (London: Conway Maritime Press, 1979), p.266. Russell to Grey, 3 May 1864, quoted in G P Gooch (ed.), *The Later Correspondence of Lord John Russell* vol. 2 (London: Longmans, Green and Co., 1925), p.310.

40 A Green, 'Memorandum on such Points connected with the acquisition and retention of Heligoland', 18 September 1869, ADM 1/6128.

41 G H Richards, 'Heligoland', copy, 23 September 1869, CO 118/45 (PRO).

42 Napier to Russell, copy, 20 April 1865, ADM 1/5953.

43 Extract from *Electuer Libre*, no date, enclosed in Hore to Lyons, copy, 4 October 1870, ADM 1/6171.

44 Loftus to Granville, copy, 12 November 1870, ADM 1/6171.

45 Translation from the 1872 German naval estimates, in Goodenough to Odo Russell, 'The German Torpedo Corps', no date, ADM 1/6198.

46 Lambert, '"Trent" Crisis', p.18.

47 Bartlett, 'Statecraft', p. 184. K Bourne, *The Foreign Policy of Victorian England, 1830-1902* (Oxford: Clarendon Press, 1970), pp.118-119.

48 C I Hamilton, Anglo-French Naval Rivalry, 1840-1870 (Oxford: Clarendon Press, 1993), p.297.

49 Lumley to Clarendon, most confidential, copy, 12 April 1870, ADM 1/6168.

50 Buchanan to Granville, no. 301, 8 August 1870, FO 65/803 (PRO).

51 Baxter, p.137.

52 Russell to Clarendon, 26 December 1858, Gooch, *Correspondence*, p.228.

53 Lambert, 'Ironclad Naval Race', p.14.

54 Palmerston to Russell, 26 October 1859, Gooch, *Correspondence*, p.244.

55 Lushington to Hammond, duplicate copy, 8 February 1870, ADM 1/6168. Childers to Milne, 12 July 1870, Milne Papers, MLN 165/1 (NMM).

56 Childers to Milne, confidential, 20 July 1870, Milne Papers, MLN 1165/1 (NMM).

57 Wolley to Milne, duplicate copy, 8 July 1870; Wolley to Milne, duplicate copy, 26 July 1870, ADM 1/6168.

58 Lushington to Milne, secret, duplicate copy, 11 August 1870, ADM 1/6168.

59 Childers to Milne, 12 August 1870, Milne Papers, MLN 165/1 (NMM).

60 Lushington to Milne, secret, duplicate copy, 11 August 1870, ADM 1/6168. Childers to Milne, 6 September 1870, Milne Papers, MLN 165/1 (NMM).

SPAIN'S FAREWELL TO GREATNESS:

The Battle of Santiago, 3 July 1898

At 09:30 on 3 July 1898 a Spanish squadron of four armoured cruisers and two destroyers under the command of Admiral Pascual Cervera, began to leave the narrow entrance of the harbour of Santiago de Cuba under the waiting guns of Admiral Sampson's North American Squadron. Four hours later every Spanish ship had been sunk or run aground, having inflicted no significant damage on the American ships. **Peter Brook** examines how Spain lost an empire and the United States gained one.

Background

The Spanish colony of Cuba had been in a state of simmering discontent for much of the nineteenth century, with Spain treating the island as a 'milch cow', denying political rights to the islanders and with much maladministration and corruption on the part of the Spanish officials. Guerilla war broke out in 1869 and lasted for ten years and again flared up in 1895: at this time the war was marked by brutal methods introduced by the Captain General, Weyler. His tactics included lines of barbed wire supplemented by blockhouses and, in order to deny the rebels food and shelter, a scorched earth policy was introduced, with the wretched peasants, the *reconcentrados*, being herded into camps where large numbers died of disease and starvation.

The USA had long taken an interest in Cuba; indeed in the 1850s there was serious thought of purchasing the island, which would have added an extra slave state to the Union, but nothing came of this. American citizens were involved in the ten-year war and public unhappiness increased after 1895, the flames being fanned by William Randolph Hearst's 'Yellow Press'. The US Minister in Madrid began negotiations in September 1897 with a new liberal government, whose first act was to dismiss Weyler. Proceedings were slow because the Spanish feared that precipitate granting of independence might endanger the monarchy[1]; the whole situation was transformed by the sinking of the armoured cruiser USS *Maine* in Havana harbour after an explosion on the night of 15 February 1898. *Maine* had been despatched to Cuba as a show of force after anti-American riots. An American Court of Enquiry concluded that the explosion was due to a mine, whereas the Spanish asserted that the cause was spontaneous combustion in a coal bunker adjacent to a powder magazine. At the time a distinguished British engineer supported the spontaneous combustion theory and many years later Admiral Rickover USN produced powerful arguments against the mine hypothesis.[2]

War might still have been averted as Spain acceded to all American demands, but Congress was determined on war and President McKinley did nothing to stop the bellicosity. On 20 April an ultimatum was sent to Spain demanding immediate evacuation of Cuba; Spain made no response and hostilities began on 21 April.[3]

The Two Fleets Compared

Both countries had powerful navies in the mid-1860s but both had allowed them to run down, the USA because of the lack of any external threat, binding the wounds of the Civil War and expansion westwards. Spain because of twenty years of civil wars, insurrections, *pronunciamentos* and unstable governments, finally resolved by the restoration of the monarchy. Both countries began to rebuild their navies in the late 1880s but here the USA had the advantages of being vastly wealthier and having a flourishing industrial base, while Spain either had to buy warships from abroad or use foreign designers and imported materials, usually from Britain or France.

At the beginning of the war the USA had four 1st class and one 2nd class battleship, two armoured and eleven protected cruisers, and a number of low freeboard monitors which proved to be almost useless. Spain had one 2nd class battleship undergoing modernisation, a large armoured cruiser not ready for service after several years building, three armoured cruisers designed by Palmers and built under that firm's supervision at Bilbao of largely imported material, and a very fine Italian built armoured cruiser the *Cristobal Colon*. Unfortunately she was lacking her main armament of two 10in guns, these having been rejected for some reason by the purchasing commission. There were a number of torpedo craft but the only effective ones were six British-built destroyers; like all their contemporaries they proved too fragile for open sea work. The US Navy (USN) had a number of torpedo boats but no destroyers. The Spanish had only

Admiral Cervera. (Author's collection)

three effective protected cruisers; they were small and two were stationed in the Philippines. The USN was incomparably superior to the Spanish, better officered and manned and with clear strategic plans. Almost immediately after war broke out an 80 mile stretch of the north coast of Cuba, centred on Havana, was blockaded and on 1 May Commodore Dewey, commanding the Asiatic Squadron totally destroyed the feeble Spanish fleet in Manila Bay.[4]

Colon, quarterdeck showing missing 10in gun. (Navy and Army Illustrated)

Cervera and the Spanish Atlantic Squadron

A unique insight into the problems facing Admiral Cervera, commanding the main Spanish squadron, is provided in a series of letters from the Admiral to his 'Dear Admiral and friend', Admiral Segismondo Bermejo, Minister of Marine during the first part of the war. Cervera arranged for copies to be kept by a trusted friend and after the war and, with the Queen Regent's permission, they were published in Spain and shortly after, translated and published by the US Office of Naval Intelligence. They provide a damming picture of incompetence and obtuseness on the part of the Spanish authorities.

The correspondence began in November 1897; the constant themes were the lack of supplies, money, cartridge cases for all the QFs, thus preventing target practice, and the lack of *Colon's* heavy guns. Cervera suggested either accepting Ansaldo's defective ones or buying a pair of older ones from Armstrong's. Nothing was done and Cervera, reaching the end of his tether, pointed out the futility of going to war with a superior power for the sake of an island effectively lost to Spain. Bermejo insisted that the two navies were equal and produced a fatuous

Infanta Maria Teresa, *prewar.* (Navy and Army Illustrated)

Vizcaya, *forward turret*. (Navy and Army Illustrated)

plan that Cervera should blockade the southern coast of the USA, using ships months from completion. At the beginning of April Cervera was ordered to the Cap Verde islands off the coast of Africa; the voyage revealed that the torpedo boats were useless because of defective boilers. *Colon* burnt excessive amounts of coal, *Vizcaya* could make no more than 14kts because of a foul bottom and the destroyers had their bow plates pushed in. Cervera convened a council of war which recommended that the squadron sail for the Canaries, but on 22 April Cervera was ordered to make for the West Indies. The four armoured cruisers, three destroyers and three auxiliaries, without proper orders, short of coal, with defective or missing guns and quite inadequate supplies of all sorts but especially ammunition, set off on their hopeless mission on 29 April. After calling in at the French island of Martinique, where the destroyer *Terror* was left behind, Cervera finally reached the port of Santiago on the southern coast of Cuba on 19 May.[5] Conditions were far from ideal, with a narrow, treacherous entrance, poor supplies, no coaling facilities, antiquated shore defences and under siege by Cuban guerillas. Ironically Cervera had been sent orders that he should return to Spain but he received the message too late.[6]

American naval movements

The USN took some time to learn of Cervera's whereabouts and in addition the progress of Commodore

Pluton, *prewar*. (Author's collection)

Furor, *prewar*. (Author's collection)

Indiana, *fore turret*. (*Navy and Army Illustrated*)

Texas, *prewar.* (*Navy and Army Illustrated*)

Brooklyn, *prewar.* (*Navy and Army Illustrated*)

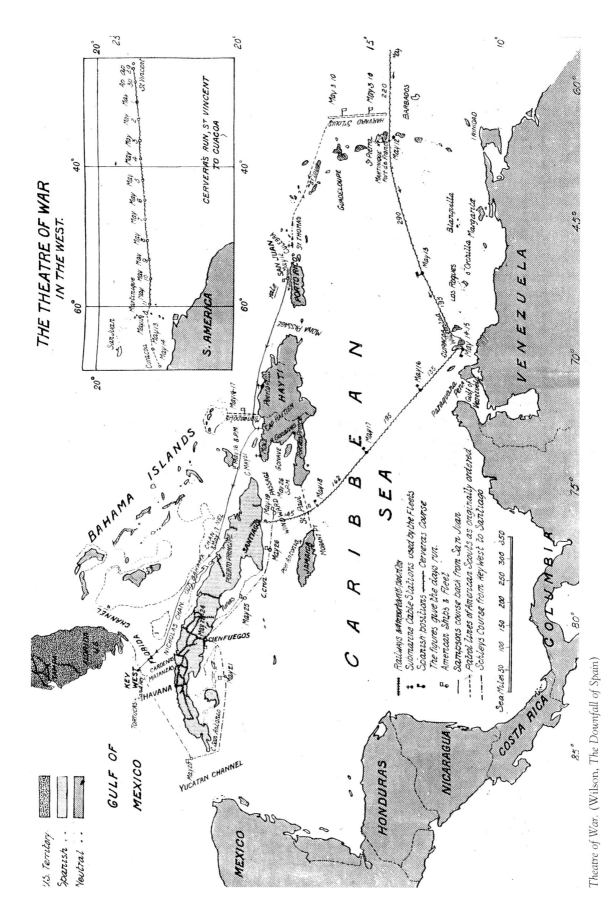

THE THEATRE OF WAR
IN THE WEST.

CERVERA'S RUN, ST VINCENT TO CURACOA

Theatre of War. (Wilson, The Downfall of Spain)

Commodore Schley. (Author's collection)

Admiral Sampson. (Author's collection)

Schley, commanding the Flying Squadron, was vacillating and dilatory but by 1 June Rear Admiral Sampson had taken command with a force of two armoured cruisers, four battleships, two cruisers and a number of auxiliaries. An attempt was made to block the entrance by scuttling a collier, *Merrimac*, but this was unsuccessful. Thereafter the composition of the blockading squadron varied with ships being added and detached for coaling. The US Army then intervened, landing a substantial force to the east of the city and there was a fierce land battle on 1 July both sides suffering heavy casualties but leaving the Americans near the town. On the same day the Captain General of Cuba ordered Cervera to reembark the large numbers of men helping in the city's defence and to sortie in order to prevent the squadron falling into American hands. This order made the squadron's destruction and the early fall of the city inevitable.[7]

The Battle

Cervera decided to break through the American blockading line during daylight hours. His Flag-Captain, Victor Concas, and one other commanding officer wished to break out at night but the Admiral feared that the enemy's searchlights, directed at the harbour entrance throughout the hours of darkness would be too dazzling for safe navigation. So it was not long after 09:30 that the Spanish squadron began to leave the bay, led by Cervera's flagship *Infanta Maria Teresa*, followed at 800yd intervals by *Vizcaya*, *Colon*, *Oquendo*, *Furor* and *Pluton*. The plan was for *Teresa* to engage the nearest enemy ship while the three remaining cruisers headed westwards towards Cienfuegois, the destroyers keeping out of the way waiting for any favourable opportunities, making off at their highest speed if the battle was going against the Spanish. As Cervera cleared the entrance and the dangerous shoal to the west he slowed in order to drop the pilot, each succeeding ship doing the same. The bugles sounded for action, and in Concas' plaintive words they were 'the last echo of those — sounded at the capture of Granada. It was the signal that the history of grandeur was at an end and that Spain was becoming a nation of the fourth class'.[8]

The blockading squadron was two major ships short: *Massachusetts* had been detached to coal at Guantanamo five hours previously, while Sampson in his flagship *New York* had gone a few miles east to confer with the army commander, General Shafter. The remainder were in a rough semi-circle about 6000 yards from the harbour entrance, from east to west, *Gloucester*, *Indiana*, *Oregon*, *Iowa*, *Texas*, *Brooklyn* and *Vixen*. As the Spanish debouched from the entrance, *Teresa* presented a magnificent sight, freshly painted, a great silk scarlet and gold battle flag flying and with a bone in her teeth as she made straight for *Brooklyn*. Cervera, knowing that she was the

Table 1: *THE TWO SQUADRONS*

Spanish Atlantic Squadron

Name	Type	Displacement (tons)	Launched	Trial Speed (kts)	Armament	Armour
Vizcaya	Armoured Cruiser	6890	1890	20.2	2-11in BL 10-5.5in QF 8-TTs	Compound Partial belt, 12-6in Deck, flat, 3-2in Barbettes, 10in Hoods, 2in, CT 12in
Almirante Oquendo	Armoured Cruiser	6890	1891	20.2	2-11in BL 10-5.5in QF 8-TTs	as *Vizcaya*
Infante Maria Teresa (flagship)	Armoured Cruiser	6890	1891	20.2	2-11in BL 10-5.5in QF 8-TTs	as *Vizcaya*
Cristobal Colon	Armoured Cruiser	6732	1896	20.0	10-6in QF 6-4.7in QF 5-TTs	Nickel Steel Belt, 6-2.5in Citadel, 6in, Battery, 6in Deck,1.5-1in, CT, 6in
Furor	Destroyer	380	1896	30.0	2-3in QF, 2-6pdr 2-37mm automatic 2-14in TTs	
Pluton	Destroyer	420	1897	30.0	2-3in QF, 2-6pdr 2-37mm automatic 2-14in TTs	

Source: Admiralty Intelligence Department, No 582, *Modern Naval Operations: Spanish American War, Operations in the Atlantic*, p.114.

Note: The designs of *Teresa*, *Oquendo* and *Vizcaya* were based on British *Orlando* class cruisers and built by Palmers at Bilbao using imported materials. The design was unsatisfactory with a narrow 5.5ft belt and the battery was crowded with shield protection only. Much wood was used in construction upper and lower decks had wood laid directly on beams without steel plates between. *Colon* was one of the *Giuseppe Garibaldi* class laid down for the Italian navy. Belt was 9ft wide.

fastest and thus the potentially most dangerous opponent, decided to engage her closely. As it became clear that the Spanish were heading west the Americans followed suit with the exception of *Brooklyn*. The two ships were converging at about 24kts and at a distance of about 1200 yards her captain ordered the helm to be put hard to port, that is a turn to starboard, an order immediately confirmed by Schley. *Brooklyn* turned three quarters of a circle, eventually heading west, further away from the Spanish and having lost some ground, but still leading the fleet. This was the famous 'loop' which will be discussed later.[9]

Even before the pilot was dropped the Spanish flagship was being hit and sustaining casualties and was quickly put out of action, two 12in or 13in shells hitting near the stern, one destroying a fire main and the other rupturing a steam pipe, making the after part of the ship, including the stern turret, uninhabitable. With the Admiral's cabin being set on fire setting off 6pdr ammunition, the whole stern of the ship was ablaze, with the fire spreading forward. At this juncture Captain Concas was severely wounded and the Admiral assumed command. After a brief consultation with a couple of other officers he ordered the ship to be turned to starboard, running aground in a small bay six and a half miles from the harbour. The ship's hull was not severely damaged as the bay was sandy; Cervera and the other survivors made for shore assisted by boats from *Gloucester* and shortly after there were a series of explosions as the magazines went up.[10]

Oquendo lasted only a little longer, coming under heavy fire from *Iowa* and *Brooklyn* at a range of less than 4000 yards. The breech of one of the 5.5in guns burst, and within a short time only two guns of the port battery were still in action. Both the ammunition hoists broke

US Navy

Name	Type	Displacement (tons)	Launched	Trial Speed (kts)	Armament	Armour
Texas	Battleship 2nd class	6315	1892	17.8	2-12in BL 6-6in BL 2-TTs	Nickel Steel Belt, 12in, Citadel, 12in Deck, 2in CT, 12in
Indiana	Battleship	10288	1893	15.5	4-13in BL 8-8in BL 4-6in 2-TTs	Harvey Nickel Belt, 18-8in, Upper Belt, 4in 13in turrets, 15in 8in turrets, 6in Deck, 2.75-3in, CT.10in
Oregon	Battleship	10288	1893	15.5	4-13in BL 8-8in BL 4-6in 2-TTs	As *Indiana*
Iowa	Battleship	11340	1896	17.0	4-12in BL 8-8in BL 6-4in RF 4-TTs	Harvey Nickel Belt, 14-7in, Upper Belt, 4in 12in turrets, 15in 8in turrets, 5in Deck, 2.75in, CT, 10in
Brooklyn	Armoured Cruiser	9215	1895	21.9	8-8in BL 12-5in RF 4-TTs	Harvey Nickel Belt, 3in, Deck, 6-3in Turrets, 5.5in, Sponsons, 4in CT, 8in
New York (Flagship)	Armoured Cruiser	8200	1891	21.0	6-8in BL 12-4in RF 2-TTs	Nickel Steel Belt, 5in Deck, 6-3in, Turrets, 5.5in.
Gloucester	Armed Yacht	786	1891	17	4-6pdr, 4-3pdr	
Vixen	Armed Yacht	800	1896	16	4-6pdr, 4-1pdr	

Source: Navy Dept Reports 1898, pp.526-531, 578-579.

Note: *Indiana* and *Oregon* were low freeboard vessels. *Iowa* had an extra deck forward. *Brooklyn*, because of her thin narrow belt, was really a large protected cruiser. She had four sets of engines with two mounted in tandem on each shaft, with the forward pair disconnected for cruising and needing 20 minutes to be re-coupled. *New York*, which took no effective part in the battle, had similar arrangements.

and the guns were kept going by manhandling ready-use ammunition. The forward turret fired twice and was then put out of action, an 8in projectile entering the turret between the gun and the gunport, rendering the gun useless and causing heavy casualties. The stern of the ship was now ablaze and as there was a risk of burning debris falling down the open ammunition hoists, orders were given to flood the magazines. Fire broke out in the after torpedo room and at this point *Oquendo* headed for the shore, first firing off her forward torpedoes in case they detonated by the force of beaching. The beach was half a mile beyond the *Teresa*, the bottom was rocky and *Oquendo*'s hull was badly damaged. The crew made for the shore by swimming and using two undamaged boats. Captain Lazaga did not survive, apparently dying of a heart attack. At this stage *Colon* and *Vizcaya* were running westward with the US squadron on the same course but 1500-3000 yards out to sea; *Brooklyn* was leading, followed by *Oregon*, *Texas* and *Iowa*.[11] It was now the turn of *Vizcaya* to come under fire. The 5.5in guns and their ammunition quickly showed their deficiencies. Breeches could not be closed, projectiles jammed and firing pins failed to work; one gun tried seven rounds before one could be fired and another gun, eight. By about 11:50 the

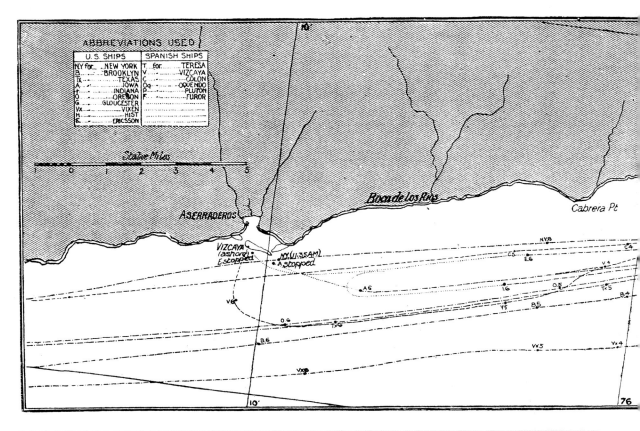

Iowa, *prewar*. (Author's collection)

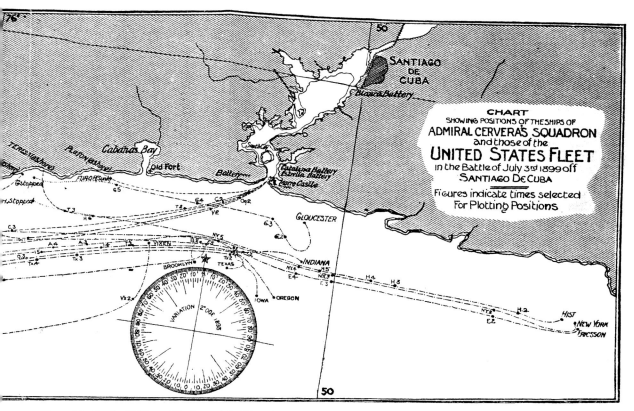

Plan of the Battle. (Wilson, *The Downfall of Spain*)

ship was ablaze, all the guns had been silenced but an attempt was made to ram her chief opponent, *Brooklyn*. This was unsuccessful and with Captain Eulate wounded, the ship's head was turned shoreward. The captain returned on deck and after a brief discussion with the nearest officers confirmed the order. *Vizcaya* ran aground at Asserado, 21 miles from Santiago at 11:05; the crew struggled ashore and not long after a series of explosions racked the ship as the torpedoes fore and aft exploded followed by the two main magazines.[12]

This left only the *Colon* steadily outstripping *Brooklyn*, *Oregon* and *Texas*, with *New York* coming up at her best speed but still some miles away, *Indiana* having been sent back to watch Santiago; *Iowa* was rescuing *Vizcaya*'s crew with Captain Evans returning Eulate's proffered sword. Shortly after 11:00 *Colon* began to lose speed as her best coal was used up. *Oregon* fired a 13in shell, which fell short but the next went over. Commodore Paredes decided to run ashore, although *Colon* was only slightly damaged, to prevent the ship being captured and to avoid a useless sacrifice of life. *Colon* turned into the coast going aground at 13:15 at the Tarquino River, 48 miles from Santiago. To indicate that he had surrendered a lee gun was fired and the colours hauled down. Some American officers believed that the surrender had been made before going ashore and opening and destroying the seacocks. When Captain Chadwick of the *New York* boarded *Colon* at 14:10 he found the Commodore and the Captain having soup in the after cabin. Later the Commodore assured Admiral Sampson that the ship

was watertight but the rising level of water in the hold belied this statement and despite all efforts including *New York* pushing *Colon*'s stern on to the shore, the ship rolled on her starboard beam three-quarters submerged and beyond salvaging.[13]

The two destroyers were put out of action rapidly. *Furor* under the command of Captain Vilaamil was overwhelmed by fire from a number of ships and was soon ablaze with all boilers out of action, no steering and with more than half her crew dead or injured, began to sink with the crew abandoning the ship. Two American boats from *Gloucester* came alongside and took off the few left on board and shortly after the destroyer blew up. More than half the crew including Vilaamil were lost. *Pluton* fared no better. Following in *Furor*'s wake she was hit in the bow by a large projectile at 10:45 and soon after the forward group of boilers blew up after being hit and a fire started in the captain's cabin aft setting off ammunition. The ship was now sinking and her captain, Lt Cdr Vazquez, steered for the shore and ran aground, the crew were picked up by *Gloucester*'s boats. That ship, although armed only with 6pdrs and 3pdrs, played a major part in the sinking of the two destroyers.[14]

The Spanish lost 323 killed and 151 wounded out of 3227 officers and men, with the remainder captured with the exception of about 150 who managed to return to Santiago. American losses were one killed and one wounded both on *Brooklyn*. That ship was hit by about 20 projectiles, sustaining no significant damage, while the remaining ships suffered even less. The Spanish ships

Vizcaya's magazines exploding. (Author's Collection)

were carefully examined shortly after the battle and here an unpleasant surprise was revealed. The hits are recorded here:

Number of hits made by the US Squadron

	12 or 13in	8in	6 or 5in	4in	6pdr	Total
Teresa	2	3	1	4	12	22
Oquendo		4	2	9	53	68
Vizcaya		5	5	4	9	23
Colon			3		3	6
Total	2	12	14	14	77	119

Percentage of hits for each calibre of gun

12 and 13in	2.2%
8in	3.1%
6in and 5in	2.6%
4in	5.1%
6pdr	1.1%

Source: Chadwick, *Spanish American War*, vol 2, p.177.

The USN refused to believe that they had done no better than the Chinese at the battle of the Yalu in 1894 and only half as well as the Japanese at the same battle, claiming that evidence of many hits had been obliterated by fire and explosions. This view was strongly supported by a contemporary British writer, H W Wilson. Writing on Santiago more than twenty years later he suggested that only 'several' hits been lost. The USN quickly accepted that its gunnery was poor and took vigorous measures to correct it.[15]

The Aftermath

The first consequence of the victory was the surrender of Santiago less than a fortnight later. On the day of the battle General Shafter, elderly, obese, sick and depressed at the heavy losses the army had incurred, proposed a retreat but encouraged by the victory, stayed put and Santiago, short of food and ammunition, capitulated. By the end of the month US troops had landed on the nearby island of Puerto Rico which was quickly occupied with little resistance. The Spanish had already been seeking an end to hostilities and a treaty of peace was concluded whereby Spain lost Puerto Rico and all of her Caribbean islands, together with the island of Guam in the Pacific in lieu of an indemnity. The US had only a toehold in the Philippines but they were ceded for the sum of $20,000,000; this part of the treaty proved to be a poisoned chalice as Aguinaldo the Filipino independence fighter turned his guns on the Americans.[16]

The board appointed to inspect the armoured cruisers found that *Vizcaya* and *Oquendo* had suffered so much damage from fire and internal explosions that they could not be salvaged while *Colon* too could not be re-floated. *Teresa* was capable of being made seaworthy locally: this was done and she set off for Norfolk, Virginia, but was abandoned in a gale on 1 November. The Board found that no projectiles had reached the vitals of any of the ships. They recommended that wood for construction and fitting be reduced to an absolute minimum, that above water torpedoes were dangerous and that all water and steam piping be run under the protective deck and fitted with risers where necessary.[17]

Oregon, *after the battle.* (Navy and Army Illustrated)

The Schley-Sampson Controversy

Sampson's attitude to Schley was noticeably cool in the immediate aftermath of the battle and a few days later he sent a confidential message to John Long, the Secretary of the Navy, describing Schley's dilatory approach to Santiago as 'reprehensible'. What is surprising is that if Sampson really believed this, then why did he leave Schley as second in command and in charge of the whole fleet on the day of the battle? Perhaps as a result Long advanced Schley six numbers and Sampson by eight thus promoting both but placing Sampson one ahead of Schley instead, as before the war, one behind. The supporters of Schley, mostly civilians, accused Long of persecuting him, but neither Schley or Sampson, the latter possibly showing the first signs of Alzheimer's Disease, made any public response at that time, but Long under pressure from Congress, made public Sampson's stric-

Gloucester, (Author's collection)

Infanta Maria Teresa, *burnt out main deck.* (Wilson, *The Downfall of Spain*)

Infanta Maria Teresa, *aground.* (Author's collection)

Almirante Oquendo, *burnt out bow.* (Author's collection)

Almirante Oquendo, *stern view.* (Wilson, *The Downfall of Spain*)

Almirante Oquendo, *burnt out stern*. (Author's collection)

Colon, *semi submerged after the battle*. (Author's collection)

tures. There then occurred a dispute between Schley and his navigator, Lt Cdr Hodgson about an exchange taking place when the turn to starboard was ordered, when Schley, being told that *Brooklyn* was on a collision course with *Texas*, is alleged to have said 'Damn the *Texas*, let her look out for herself' words which Schley vehemently denied using.[18] Matters came to a head in 1899 when the third volume of E S Maclay's A *History Of The United*

States Navy was published. The book was important because it was used as a textbook by the Naval Academy. Maclay was fiercely critical of Schley, particularly what he saw as his slow vacillating progress to Santiago, using terms such as 'timidity amounting to cowardice' and 'turned in caitiff flight' and as for the battle, the 'loop' was described as a 'humiliating retreat' summing up his behaviour as 'avoid your enemy for as long as possible and

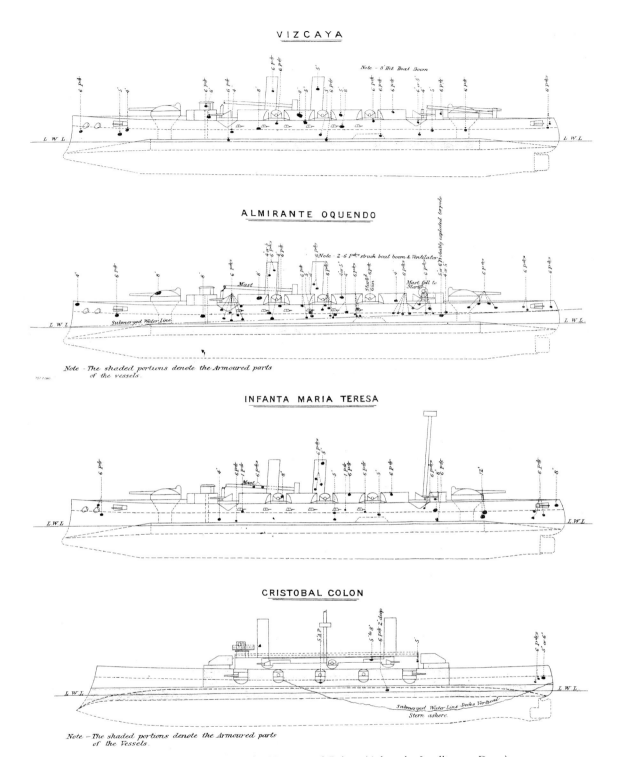

Diagrams showing battle damage to Teresa, Oquendo, Vizcaya *and* Colon. (Admiralty Intelligence Dept.)

if he makes for you, run'.[19] This was too much for Schley who demanded, and obtained, a Court of Enquiry which convened in late 1901; Sampson was now too ill to testify. Two of the three-man board found that Schley had been guilty of failing to act decisively *en route* to Santiago and endangering *Texas* by turning to the east; this was despite good evidence that the two ships were never less than 500 yards apart. The President of the Court, Admiral Dewey, of Manila fame, strongly dissented, not only clearing Schley of all charges but giving him the credit for the victory as he was in command at the time. The controversy dragged on until President Theodore Roosevelt declared the matter closed as further dispute would only damage the Navy.[20]

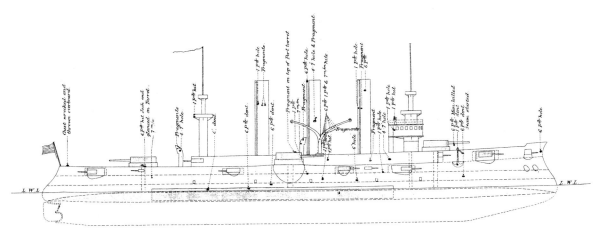

Diagram showing battle damage to Brooklyn. (Admiralty Intelligence Dept.)

Tying up the loose ends

After their deaths Sampson, Schley, Vilaamil and Cervera all had warships named after them. Cervera was court-martialled according to custom and was honourably acquitted. The politicians who sent him on his hopeless mission never faced any charges. Cuba was given independence in 1902 but Puerto Rico, where there had never been an armed uprising and was just about to receive autonomy remains a dependency of the US to this day, something more than a colony but something less than a state. Aguinaldo was captured in 1901 ending the rebellion but the Philippines had to wait until 1946 before they achieved independence. The *Maine* was raised in 1911–1912, finally being scuttled.

Notes

The bibliography of the Spanish-American War is extensive and I have only used a small part. What makes it of particular interest in the Cervera collection of documents and the enormous mass of detail in the two-volume *Secretary of the Navy Reports for 1898*.

[1] F E Chadwick, *The Relations of the United States and Spain*, vol 1, *Diplomacy;* vols 2-3, *Spanish American War*, (Russell and Russell: NY, 1968), *Diplomacy*, pp.262-267, 283-296, 407-511.

[2] H G Rickover, *How the Battleship Maine Was Destroyed*, (GPO: Washington, 1976), pp.1-5, 43-53, 76-78, 95-106.

[3] Chadwick, *Diplomacy;* pp.572-587.

[4] Chadwick, *Spanish American War 1*, pp. 28-46, 154-213.

[5] P Cervera, *The Spanish American War: A Collection of Documents Relating to the Squadron Operations in the West Indies, Office of Naval Intelligence, War Series VII*, (GPO: Washington, 1898), pp.9-80.

[6] *Ibid.*, p.73.

[7] Chadwick, *Spanish American War*, vol 1, pp.262-395, vol 2, pp.79-113; Cervera, *Documents*, pp.115-116.

[8] Cervera, *Documents*, pp.123-127; V Concas, *The Squadron of Admiral Cervera, ONI*,. *War Series VIII*, (GPO: Washington, 1899), p.74.

[9] Chadwick, *Spanish American War*, vol 2, pp.129-163.

[10] Concas, *Squadron*, pp.74-76.

[11] Cervera, *Documents, Oquendo* report, pp.128-130; Chadwick, *Spanish American War* vol 1, pp.141-142.

[12] Cervera, *Documents, Vizcaya* report, pp.130-132.

[13] Cervera, *Documents, Colon* report, pp.127-128; Chadwick, *Spanish American War* vol 2, pp.151-157.

[14] Cervera, *Documents, Furor* and *Pluton* reports, pp.132-134; *Annual Report Of The Navy Department For The Year 1898, Appendix to the Report of the Chief of the Bureau of Navigation*, (GPO: Washington 1898), p.591.

[15] Chadwick, *Spanish American War*, vol 2, pp.176-184; H W Wilson, *The Downfall of Spain: Naval History of the Spanish American War*, (Sampson Low Marston: London, 1900), pp.341-341; H W Wilson, *Battleships in Action*, vol 1, (Sampson Low Marston: London, ca 1926), p.147.

[16] W Millis, *The Martial Spirit* (The Literary Guild: Cambridge Mass., 1931), pp.388-391.

[17] *Annual Reports: Appendix to Bureau of Navigation*, pp.574-592, 601-602.

[18] H D Langley, 'Winfield S Schley and Santiago: A New Look At An Old Controversy', in J C Bradford (ed) *Crucible of Empire* (NIP: Annapolis, 1993), pp.88-91.

[19] E S Maclay, *History of the US Navy*, vol 3, (D. Appleton: NY, 1899), pp.298, 365.

[20] H D Langley, 'Winfield S Schley and Santiago', pp.91-96.

Vizcaya, *two stern views after the battle*. (Author's collection)

AUSTRALIAN COLONIAL NAVIES, 1855-1900

In *Warship 2000-2001* **Colin Jones** examined the premier force of Australian colonial warships in the period before Federation in 1901: the navy of the state of Victoria. In this article he now considers the naval procurement programmes of the other states of pre-federation Australia.

In the period from the granting of local self-government in 1855-56, until 1900, Australia was divided into six separate British colonies. All were responsible for their internal administration, and all raised local defence forces of some sort, but cooperation was minimal. Local naval forces in the colonies other than Victoria were never responsible to formal Defence Departments and remained administratively immature, though all contributed in their own way to the final establishment of the Commonwealth Naval Forces after Federation. They evolved strictly in response to local conditions and are considered here individually.

New South Wales

New South Wales had a record from the earliest colonial days of building ships with some degree of usefulness for naval purposes. The Sydney Naval Yard had built its last vessel, the 150 ton brig *Elizabeth Henrietta*, in 1816, but the subsequent long years of peace had resulted in an abandonment of any warlike pretensions by colonial government vessels. The one change in this policy came during the Crimean War, with the building of the gunboat *Spitfire*.

Spitfire
Gunboat, launched 4/4/1855, by Cuthbert, Sydney
60 tons measurement
62ft bp x 16ft x 5ft 6in
1-32pdr, 56 cwt (proposed)
14 men

It is unlikely that this small ketch was ever seriously considered part of the defence of Sydney. The harbour already had relatively adequate fortress defences, as well as the presence of ships of the Royal Navy, including armed paddle steamers, but she would have proved appropriate for the otherwise undefended estuarine

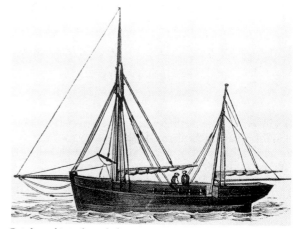

Spitfire, this is the only known representation of the vessel, originally in the Illustrated Sydney News *of 14 April 1855. (Author's collection)*

approach to Brisbane, which was then another town in the same colony. She almost certainly never carried a gun. The *Spitfire* was transferred to Queensland on separation in 1859, while serving as a pilot vessel in Moreton Bay. She was sold out of government service in 1885 and lost in a cyclone in North Queensland as a fishing boat in 1898.

The hydrographer of the Admiralty was provided with the 65 ton schooner *Edith* between 1862 and 1869 for the New South Wales colonial survey.

The task of local naval forces on the coast of New South Wales was mainly to give advance warning to the forts at Sydney of the approach of a hostile force. The existence in Sydney of the home base of the Royal Navy's Australian Squadron made the need for warships for any serious effort at local defence a great deal less urgent than it was perceived to be in the other colonies, and there was a strong feeling that their amateur naval efforts

Avernus and Acheron *take part in manoeuvres on Sydney Harbour at Easter in 1889.* (C. Hancox collection)

would seem somewhat ludicrous in the eyes of the professional British naval officers. Indeed, at least some of the money, which might have been allocated in other colonies to floating defences, was spent instead in New South Wales on the Royal Navy's base facilities, including The Royal Naval House in 1889.

A naval brigade was formed in 1861, the same year that one was established in the state of Victoria, but it was never to mature into a proper professional naval force. This force and the Naval Artillery Volunteers were rarely afloat. It had the same commander for 40 years. The first real New South Wales warships were a pair of torpedo boats, attached to the military forces, for which construction tenders were called in December 1877.

Acheron
Torpedo boat, trials 1/3/1879, by Atlas, Sydney
Avernus
Torpedo boat, by Atlas, Sydney
16 tons
80ft oa x 10ft 3in x 4ft
spar torpedo (pivoted from stern)
200ihp, single screw, 15kts
9 men

The boats originally had a passenger cabin for use as dispatch boats. Initial trials recorded a speed of 14kts, and a higher speed was expected with a smaller screw. In 1887 they were supplied with 14in Schwartzkopff torpedoes, launched from dropping gear. They were sold on 12 November 1902. The *Acheron* was later renamed *Jenner*

for the Quarantine service and both were hulks by the early 1930s.

In particular, New South Wales failed to follow the other colonies in taking up the recommendations of the 1877 Jervois commission which was undertaking a comprehensive review of colonial defence preparedness. Sir William Jervois had suggested a small rigged ironclad of 2500 tons and a speed of 13kts, armed with 2-10in and 1-6in guns (similar to the Portugese *Vasco da Gama*), but colonial politics made this unrealistic, as well as a later suggestion for the purchase of a small cruiser, a sister of the *Protector*, from the Armstrong company. A cheap alternative was to obtain a training ship with some warlike and seagoing capacity and this led to a request for the supply of the corvette *Wolverine*, at the time when she was due to be paid off for scrap.

Wolverine
Corvette, laid down 14/4/1859, launched 29/8/1861, completed 4/1864, by Woolwich Dockyard, London
2568 tons (1710 tons measurement)
225ft x 41ft x 21ft
17-64pdr 71cwt Palliser converted MLR
2-9pdr & 1-7pdr boat guns
1-gatling
1493ihp, single screw, 11.31kts
manned by 266 for exercises in 1885, including 208 naval brigade

The *Wolverine* had an active life in the Royal Navy and

Wolverine flies the colonial flag on Sydney Harbour about 1883. (Author's collection)

Accompanied by some interested holiday sailors, the Wolverine *is cleared for action and engages in target practice in Sydney's Middle Harbour about 1884.* (Author's collection)

was flagship of the Australian Squadron at Sydney after being re-engined, from September 1876. She was transferred to New South Wales on 16 January 1882, but her former commander declared her 'utterly useless for defence purposes', and as such she was an example to other colonial governments of what to avoid. She was stripped for scrapping late in 1886. A change in government saw her retained and she was rigged again in 1889, but she never again carried anything like a full complement of big guns, and in 1888 mounted only 2-16 pounders. Paid off at the end of 1892, she was sold on 28 August 1893 and hulked in Auckland after becoming unseaworthy in 1895.

An important adjunct to the forts at Sydney and Newcastle was the establishment of defensive minefields and to handle these, a dedicated steamer was required.

Lilian
Minelayer, launched 20/3/1886, by D. & W. Robertson, Sydney
104.9 tons gross, 71.4 tons net
102ft oa x 17ft 1in x 5ft 6in
260ihp, single screw, 10kts
5 men

The *Lilian* was built as a coastal trading vessel but was obtained cheaply by the New South Wales government because of the insolvency of her owners on 26 November 1888. She was then fitted out as a minelayer for work at Sydney and Newcastle but was regarded as unsatisfactory in 1890. She was in collision with the vehicle ferry

Barangaroo in 1892 and transferred from military use to act as a government tug in 1898. Renamed *Paterson* about 1919 she was sold about 1960. To assist in military tasks a second steamer was obtained.

Ohm
Inshore minelayer, 1893
33 tons
51ft x 12ft 6in x 5ft 6in
twin screw, 8.5kts

Although following a War Office design, the origin of the *Ohm* is obscure but she was always a subsidiary vessel. Although unserviceable in 1901, she was still in government service on Sydney Harbour in 1919.

The first successful minelaying steamer was built as one of the standard War Office types, the *Sir W Jervois* class.

Miner
Coastal minelayer, commenced 6/1899, trials 28/8/1900, by White, Cowes (y.n. 1088)
160.6 tons
90ft x 18ft x 7ft 11in
329ihp, twin screw, 10.39kts

The *Miner* served in association with Sydney fortress from 1901, was relocated to Port Phillip fortress in 1918 and sold in 1923 as the tug *Minah*. She was stranded in Westernport Bay in 1950 and became a total loss.

Auxiliaries used as gunboats on a more or less regular

The New South Wales Miner *in Sydney Harbour about 1915.* (Postcard)

basis were the hopper barge *Neptune* and the government steamers *Ajax* and *Thetis*. The *Neptune* received the *Wolverene*'s bow chaser for exercises, while the other vessels received 9 and 12pdrs, some of which were field guns. During the 1885 war scare, the 344 ton *Ajax* was fitted with a powerful searchlight as a lookout ship.

New South Wales contributed 30 per cent of the cost of the Australian Auxiliary Squadron from 1891 on the basis of its share of the Australian and New Zealand population. The ship that carried a New South Wales name was the cruiser *Katoomba*. Another of this group, the *Pelorus*, later renamed *Mildura*, was launched at Armstrongs by the wife of the Agent General for New South Wales on 25 November 1889.

Queensland

Queensland separated from New South Wales in 1859, but no consideration was given to naval defence by the new and financially struggling colonial government. The hydrographer was given the use of the schooner *Pearl* for the coastal survey in 1866, and she was replaced by the 160 ton steamer *Llewellyn* for the 1878 season, after which lack of money caused the survey to be suspended.

As with Victoria, Queensland politicians feared the absence from their waters of ships of the Royal Navy. Naval defence was required along a very extensive coast. Townsville, where a fort was provided, was some 800 miles from Brisbane, a huge distance with no railway connection, and all transport by sea. Thursday Island, which was fortified in the 1890s under the intercolonial agreement, was 1500 miles from Brisbane. Nouméa, the nearest French base, though a poor one, was 780 miles from Brisbane. The dangers of the flanking Great Barrier Reef, however, somewhat modified the direction from which a threat might come. The three major Queensland ports at this time, Brisbane, Maryborough and Rockhampton, were river ports, appropriate for defence by gunboats and torpedo boats, though some need was seen for a fast dispatch vessel on the coast. Queensland joined with the other colonies in the purchase of naval vessels following the Jervois report. Jervois had suggested a Rendel gunboat and a fast dispatch vessel, but in the event the choice fell on two Armstrong gunboats, arranged so that they could be used as customs cruisers while disarmed, as well as a Thornycroft torpedo boat. The gunboats were a slightly developed version of the Victorian *Albert*, with a fuller upper deck and a protected conning position.

Paluma
Gunboat, laid down 26/6/1883, launched 6/5/1884, trials 26/9/1884, by Armstrong, Newcastle (y.n. 469)
Gayundah
Gunboat, laid down 26/6/1883, launched 6/5/1884, trials 26/9/1884, by Armstrong, Newcastle (y.n. 470)
412 tons normal

Gayundah on the Tyne before her departure for Australia, 1885. (RAN)

Gayundah in the Brisbane River off the naval stores depot about 1887. The picture is taken from the Botanic Gardens, where police marksmen gathered to enforce the sacking of the ship's commander in 1888. (State Library of Queensland, Oxley Collection)

115ft x 26ft x 9ft 6in
1-8in 11.5 ton BLR 26 cal
1-6in 4.1 ton BLR 26.3 cal
2-1.5in Nordenfelt
1-.45in five-barrel and 1-1in four-barrel machine gun
385ihp, twin screw, 10.57kts
55 men (40 full-time)

The *Gayundah* was the flagship of the Queensland Maritime Defence Force and the *Paluma* was used, unarmed, by the Hydrographer for ten years to complete the coastal survey. As a curiosity, at the persistent request of the Queensland government, the *Gayundah* was granted the right to wear the White Ensign and pennant of Her Majesty's fleet on 2 September 1886. Her visit to Sydney in 1885 had impressed Admiral Tryon, and it was part of his campaign for colonial participation in a new national naval defence effort. It caused some embarrassment on 25 October 1888 when the government had occasion to sack their naval commander and he threatened to take the ship to sea, outside of their jurisdiction. In fact it was shown to be a flag that bestowed a potentially difficult division between colonial and Imperial authority. It was not to be repeated. Of all the colonial vessels, these two were the most active in cruising. The

Paluma was refitting in February 1893 when washed ashore in a flood. The *Gayundah* and *Paluma* were rearmed between 1899 and 1901, both receiving a 4.7in QF aft, and the *Paluma* having her 8in replaced by 2-5in 2.5 ton guns. The *Gayundah* received 2-12pdr QF in place of the Nordenfelts and the *Paluma*, 2 Maxims. The *Gayundah* experimented with wireless telegraphy in 1903, the first by a warship on the Australian Station. They both became units of the Royal Australian Navy and the *Gayundah* fired her only shot in anger while arresting Dutch luggers off the Western Australian coast in 1911. The *Gayundah* had her bow built up in 1914 for better seakeeping, losing her big gun in the process. One of her 12pdr guns was placed aboard the sloop *Fantome* in 1915. The *Paluma* was sold in 1916 and the *Gayundah* in 1922. The *Paluma* worked for the Victorian government as the buoy tender *Rip* until she was scrapped in 1951, and the *Gayundah* was used as a barge until scuttled at Redcliffe, on Moreton Bay, in 1958, where her remains are still visible.

The torpedo boat was a standard Thornycroft design, the same as four already supplied to New Zealand, the only difference being that she had one funnel instead of two.

Paluma stranded in the Brisbane Botanic Gardens between floods in February 1893. The tug in the river is the Advance, *taken over by the Queensland navy as a dispatch vessel during the 1885 Russian war scare, and here preparing for salvage operations. (Author's collection)*

The Queensland Miner *laying a minefield at Lytton in the Brisbane River. (Author's collection)*

A vista of Brisbane from the cliffs above the naval depot in 1889. The Mosquito *lies inshore, and the Royal Navy survey sloop* Egeria *lies in the stream with a bunker barge alongside. The navy office was on the extreme right, behind the floating swimming bath. (State Library of Queensland, Oxley Collection)*

Mosquito

Second class torpedo boat, launched 11/7/1884, trial 25/7/1884, by Thornycroft, Chiswick (y.n. 193)
10 tons
67ft oa x 7ft 6in x 3ft 2in
Spar torpedo
168hp, single screw, 17.21kts
7 men

Dropping gear for two 14in torpedoes was supplied before the boat was shipped to Australia. She was sold in 1910.

At the naval depot at Kangaroo Point there was a training battery. There was also the need for a minelayer for the Brisbane River in support of the fort, but a local design provided for a vessel that could be used for more general service most of the time.

Miner

Coastal minelayer, plans signed 12/3/1886, by Evans Anderson Phelan, Brisbane
65 tons
77ft 10in bp x 15ft x 5ft
single screw, 10kts
5 men

The *Miner* had a passenger cabin for general government use when not in military service. She was lengthened to 92ft 9in in 1893 and was available for an emergency as an examination steamer after the army abandoned minelaying in 1901. Subsequently in use with the dredger fleet, she was scuttled as a breakwater in Moreton Bay in 1953 and demolished about 1991.

A second torpedo boat was provided, a wooden vessel that did not need to be kept out of the water on a slipway.

Midge

Torpedo boat, commenced 10/1887, trial 27/3/1888, by White, Cowes (y.n. 744)
12 tons
56ft 4in oa x 9ft 3in x 4ft 7in
2-1in 2-barrel Nordenfelt

torpedo dropping gear
202ihp, single screw, 17.38kts

The *Midge* passed out of service in 1913 and became a yacht, named *Nola II*.

Auxiliaries comprised a number of government vessels, often usefully distributed in the outports where they could be manned by local units of the naval brigade. These included the 242 ton tug *Otter* and the hopper barges *Bonito*, *Bream*, *Dolphin*, *Pumba* and *Stingaree*. All could be armed as gunboats, the *Otter* with a 64pdr and the barges with a 5in gun. The *Otter* was available also as a dispatch vessel. The hopper barges, built by Walkers at Maryborough in 1887, were altered while under construction to be powered by four boilers instead of two, so that the coal bunkers could be above the boilers to protect them from shot. The boilers proved to be inefficient and were subsequently replaced by two Scotch boilers to the original design.

Queensland contributed an initial 10 per cent of the cost of the Australian Auxiliary Squadron in 1891 and more subsequently. The ship that carried a Queensland name was the torpedo gunboat *Boomerang*. This vessel was damaged on first being put into dock in Sydney in 1891 as it was not realised that its rudder extended below the level of the keel.

The Queensland Maritime Defence Force finished as the second largest of the colonial naval forces on Federation.

South Australia

The seaward approaches to Adelaide, the capital of South Australia, as well as the gulf outports, were difficult to defend by forts, and inappropriate for small vessels, in view of their oceanic environment.

The Hydrographer was given the use of the 99-ton schooner *Beatrice* for the coastal survey from 1862 until 1880. This included work in the Northern Territory, which was ceded to South Australia in 1863.

South Australia joined with the other colonies in the purchases of naval vessels following the Jervois report. Jervois himself, as governor, had attempted to purchase a *La Plata* class monitor from Argentina, but the eventual choice went to a small cruiser scaled up from the basic design of a Rendel gunboat.

Protector
Cruiser, laid down 8/12/1882, launched 27/12/1883, trials 19/6/1884, by Armstrong, Newcastle (y.n. 457)
944 tons normal
185ft oa x 30ft x 12ft 6in
1-8in 11.5 ton BLR 26 cal
5-6in 4.1 ton BLR 26.3 cal
5-'Improved' Gatling
1in steel armour on waterline and conning tower and 2in gun shields
1645ihp, twin screw, 14.15kts
84 men (105 on cruise to China)

Protector in the Tyne, prior to her departure for Australia. (RAN)

The *Protector*, the sole representative of the South Australian Naval Forces, was kept in full commission until the depression of 1893, when her establishment was reduced to 21 officers and men. 4-1.9in 3pdr Hotchkiss QF, a searchlight, and a light armoured splinter deck over the vitals, were fitted during 1890, and at the same time the engines were improved to provide an extra 200hp. If a central pivot mounting for the 8in gun could have been obtained, it was intended to fit two launchers for Whitehead torpedoes. As part of the Australian contribution to the forces sent to China during the Boxer rebellion, the *Protector* was commissioned at Hong Kong as a British warship, wearing the white ensign from 11 September 1900 until 8 January 1901. She served with the fleet around Qinhuangdao, but saw no warlike action. As a unit of the Royal Australian Navy she was rebuilt as a gunboat in 1912, armed with 2-4in, 2-3in and 4-3pdr guns and with her bow built up. She accompanied the submarines to New Guinea in 1914 and captured the 194 ton German steamer *Madang* off Herbertshöhe (near Rabaul). On patrol in violent weather in Bass Strait in 1918 she rolled her funnel out. In 1921 she became tender to Flinders Naval Depot as *Cerberus* and was fitted for a training ship for controlled minelaying. She was sold as a lighter in 1924. Under the name *Sidney*, she was requisitioned by the US army in 1943 but was damaged in collision with a tug and scuttled on Heron Island, at the southern end of the Great Barrier Reef, in 1944 and her remains are still visible.

South Australia built equipment for a controlled minefield, but never allocated a steamer for the work.

South Australia contributed an initial 9 per cent of the cost of the Australian Auxiliary Squadron in 1891 and less subsequently. The ship that carried a South Australian name was the cruiser *Wallaroo*.

Tasmania

Tasmania, as a penal colony, had maintained armed sailing vessels up to 1844, but events had seen the need for them vanish.

For the Derwent estuary on the approaches to Hobart, as for the four major New Zealand ports, a torpedo boat was seen as an appropriate complement to the forts. Launceston, the other major Tasmanian city, was considered to need neither forts nor naval defence because of the difficulties of navigation from the coast. A torpedo boat was obtained for Hobart as part of the general colonial orders following the Jervois report. It was identical to the Queensland *Mosquito*. She was never given a name or a number locally, but retained her yard number for formal identification.

The Tasmanian torpedo boat, probably at Port Adelaide in 1905. As with all the Thornycroft second-class boats for Australia, the funnel is offset to starboard. The paddle steamer in the background has not been identified. (Author's collection)

No 191
Second class torpedo boat, launched 18/12/1883, trial
    24/1/1884, by Thornycroft, Chiswick (y.n. 191)
10 tons
67ft oa x 7ft 6in x 3ft 2in
Spar torpedo
168hp, single screw, 17.21kts
7 men

Torpedo dropping gear was ordered in 1885 to replace the
spar torpedo and a Nordenfelt gun was also supplied.
Operation was very infrequent and in 1900 the boat was
transferred to the books of South Australia, which had a
stock of 10 torpedoes but no boat to make use of them.
She was towed to Adelaide by the *Protector* in 1905. Out
of service by 1910, her hull and slipway were offered for
sale in 1917.

Tasmania never managed to mature its submarine min-
ing defences. It contributed 4 per cent of the cost of the
Australian Auxiliary Squadron. The ship that carried a
Tasmanian name was the cruiser *Ringarooma*.

Western Australia

Western Australia never had its own naval forces, nor did
it build any fortifications for its ports until they could be
subsidised by the other colonies. Even then, the requisite
minelaying steamer was never supplied. The
Hydrographer was given control of the 150 ton 3-masted
schooner *Meda*, specially built in Britain in 1879 for the
colonial survey, in 1880 and she was replaced by the former Victorian gunboat *Victoria* from 1896 to 1902.

Western Australia contributed an initial 1.6 per cent of
the cost of the Australian Auxiliary Squadron in 1891
and more subsequently. The ship that carried a Western
Australian name was the torpedo gunboat *Karrakatta*.

This concludes the brief survey of the ships of the
Australian colonial navies. In 1890 the Colonial Office
stated: 'On account of their position, and of the now considerable population in all these colonies except Western
Australia, there is no British territory so little liable to
aggression as that of Australasia. In view of the armed
forces maintained, and the strong spirit which animates
them, territorial aggression, except on a large scale, is out
of the question.' Theoretically illegal outside their very
limited territorial waters, in many ways the colonial warships were unique, but they were in most cases a focus of
local pride and provided the important stimulus for the
early creation of the Royal Australian Navy.

Sources:
The information is drawn from a large number of mostly
    Australian sources.

Colin Jones is the author of a number of works covering the
    Australian colonial navies, published as follows:
'Queensland Colonial Navy', *The Mariner's Mirror*, November
    1966
Australian Colonial Navies, (Canberra: Australian War
    Memorial, 1986).
'The Voyage of the Colonial Ship Victoria', *The Mariner's
    Mirror*, May 1986.
'The Colour of the Flag', in T Frame, J Goldrick and P Jones
    (eds.), *Reflections on the RAN*, (Sydney: Kangaroo, 1991).
'The Purchase of the Australian Colonial Gunboats', *The
    Mariner's Mirror*, May 1995
'Ruling the Waves', *Warship 1997-1998*.
'The Colonial Minelaying Steamers', *The Log*, February 1998.
'The Colonial Gunboat Spitfire', *Royal Historical Society of
    Queensland Journal*, August 1998.
'The Navy of Victoria, Australia', *Warship 2000-2001*.
'The View from Port Phillip Heads', in D Stevens (ed.),
    Southern Trident, (Sydney: Allen & Unwin, 2001).

'THE WOBBLY EIGHT': THE *KING EDWARD VII* CLASS BATTLESHIPS, 1897-1922

The *King Edward VII* Class Battleships were built by the Royal Navy in response to the increasing armament carried by foreign battleships in the 1890s and yet, as with many ships laid down in this period, none of the class ever engaged an enemy ship. Here **Keith McBride** examines the lengthy discussions behind a design that was shortly to be eclipsed by the '*Dreadnought* revolution'.

From 1892-3 to 1900-01, a period of intense naval building, all British 1st class battleships carried an armament of four 12in guns, in two turrets (actually hooded barbettes) fore and aft, and a secondary armament of twelve 6in guns in casemates on the upper and main decks (US second deck) amidships. Collectively, they were the most powerful ships afloat, and most foreign battleships were inspired by them. The outward similarity concealed many improvements; the last of the *Majestics* brought in all-round loading, the *Canopus* class of 1896-7 brought in Krupp armour and water-tube boilers while the *Formidables* of 1897-88 introduced heavier armour and guns of improved models.

By 1897, foreign navies were beginning to catch up. The French ships of the late 1890s had their 12in guns in two twin turrets, though they were still smaller than British ships and had weak secondary batteries. The Russians were building some good ships alongside a lot of bad ones. Across the Atlantic, the US Navy (USN) had not standardised its ships to the same extent, and had a tendency to make up for small numbers by fitting very (in some cases excessively) powerful armaments. Italy, which was on good terms with Britain and depended to a large extent on British technology, had been suffering from cash problems, and had only built (slowly) two 2nd class battleships in the early 1890s.

The Italian decision of 1896-7 to build two large, very heavily armed ships, which were also, like most Italian ships, very fast, was a reversion to earlier policy and made a great sensation. Nominally, the *Benedetto Brin* and *Regina Margherita* were only slightly larger than the British *Canopus* class, faster, as heavily armoured, and carried the same armament plus four 8in guns. The US *Wisconsin* class of 1897 were heavily armed, though with outdated black-powder main armament, and considerably smaller than British ships. The *Maine* class of 1898 were very much on British lines, but, again, with a smaller displacement and slightly heavier armament.

For 1899 and 1900, the USN planned ships with an even heavier armament and a higher speed of 19kts. At an early stage, an intermediate armament of 8in or a new 7in gun was proposed; at Santiago, 12 and 13in guns scored very few hits, while 8in did well [Ed. See pp.43-44]. The design process was long and controversial, and the ships were not commenced until 1902, but the *Pennsylvania* (later *Georgia*) class caused much concern at the Admiralty. There was a lot of elbowing between the US and Britain at the time. America was moving onto the world stage, and during 1901, the very able First Lord of the Admiralty, Lord Selborne, felt it necessary to circulate a 'Paper' to his cabinet colleagues, warning them that America's ship-building and industrial capacity was now so great that she could out-build Britain if she took a mind to do so.

In February 1899, almost at the end of the financial year, the Admiralty ordered a trial 7.5in gun from Vickers. The calibre was a new one for the RN, the equivalent of the 194mm ('7.6in') of the French Navy. It had the advantage that unlike the 8in used earlier, it could replace the 6in on a 'one for two' basis and that its projectiles could be carried by two men using a grab bar.

Designs for the prototype 7.5in were received about 1 July 1899 and on 5 July Captain E J Jeffreys the Director of Naval Ordnance (DNO), suggested putting studies in hand on the respective merits of turrets and casemates for the new gun. In mid August, Sir William White (DNC) commented that designs, weights and dimensions for casemates were needed, allowing for the usual 120° arc of

HMS King Edward VII in 1912 with white funnel bands. Despite a heavier look, she bears the stamp of the William White era; the class silhouette differs little from that of the Formidables *and* Duncans, *but the upper deck 9.2in turrets show that change is coming.* (Antony Preston)

fire, and that thickness of armour, amounts of ready-use ammunition of this large size, and amount of internal space required, were needed. He felt that upper deck mountings would have to be either turrets or something like them; shields would be quite inappropriate for such large guns.

Testing of the 7.5in was completed about 1 March 1900, and was satisfactory except that muzzle velocity was 2617fps (798mps), not the hoped-for 2700. It was decided to lengthen the gun from 45 to 50 calibres, which added yet more weight. The proposed casemates were much larger than for 6in and restricted the amount of space available in the superstructure and on the main deck. White suggested that turrets on the upper deck were the least objectionable solution. The Controller deliberately delayed action until May 1900 when the weights and dimensions involved were clearer and a choice could made between turrets and casemates for the additional guns. In all this, the number of 12in stayed at four; it was apparently a case of 'Where could you put any more?'

In July, Constructor Deadman, in White's absence (White was frequently ill at this time) asked a number of questions. He was very concerned that the extra guns proposed required a bigger hull, though docking limitations posed problems. He felt that 9in side armour as in the *Formidables* and *Londons*, was necessary; the *Duncan's* 7in was inadequate. All unnecessary weights should be discarded, while the extra men for the extra guns posed severe accommodation problems; the usual space for 15 per cent extra men could no longer be provided. This ruled out one possible weight saver; cutting down the hull one deck aft, as in USS *Maine*, took away too much living space.

Figures worked out in July suggested that a super-*London*, with 8-7.5in housed in upper-deck turrets, plus the usual 4-12in and 12-6in plus 22,000ihp to drive the 425ft x 78ft hull at 19.5 to 20kts, to keep up with the American and Italian ships, would displace 16,948 tons. 25,000ihp would be needed to ensure 20kts. A 22,000ihp 425ft x 77ft super-*Duncan* would displace 15,300 tons. These figures were only rough and ready and more displacement might be needed for stability.

If intermediate changes only were proposed, the resulting vessel would be between the above and the *London* and *Duncan* classes. Up to 265 tons could be saved by various minor omissions, 80 by not providing for an Admiral and 300 tons by cutting down the hull one deck aft; this involved lowering the after 12in guns. A box battery for 8-6in guns would weigh 95 tons, and one extending between the two 12in barbettes, from 150 to 215 tons. If this was to include twelve main deck 6in there would be practically no saving as against casemates. Putting four 7.5in single turrets on the upper deck instead of the usual four 6in casemates would cost 28 to 38 tons, depending on whether the upper deck side was thickened. Four extra main deck 6in would weigh an extra 244 tons, an additional four 7.5in, making eight in four twin turrets, would weigh 504 to 514 tons, and four 6in to make twelve, 618 to 748 tons. Eight 7.5in casemates in a *Duncan* would leave six of them very vulnerable. The Controller pointed out that any secondary armament was liable to be hit by 12in shell, which could penetrate the 6in armour. All that could be done was to localise the effect, 2in closing bulkheads and at least 4in turret bases would be needed.

The 7.5's burster was about twice that of a 6in and the gun should be able to deliver 1.5 to 2 rounds per minute with good gun crews. However, the reputed end-on fire of foreign ships was probably exaggerated. The DNO rejected a proposal to replace the twelve 6in by six more 7.5in (like the Russian *Imperator Pavel*) in main-deck positions, their long muzzles would dip in a roll. The Controller was against having a 2in longitudinal bulkhead in rear of the guns; the weight could be better used on the side. The armour of the 7.5in turrets was limited to 6in by stability considerations, while the foremost main-deck 6in was no worse placed than that in the *Duncan*.

In late August it was advised that a design for the twin 7.5in turrets was being prepared; they were to have hydraulic power. 7.5in AP shell would be effective against 6in Krupp non-cemented (KNC) armour up to 2000 yards, and 7.5in Common Shell against 4.9in KNC up to the same range. It was mentioned that the main purpose of the secondary armament was to silence and destroy that of the enemy. 6in guns would be twice as numerous, would fire twice as fast and score about four times as many hits, but more 7.5in shells would penetrate thin armour and would have twice the effect per shell. Turrets would be the best mountings for 7.5in but the Controller wondered if they would turn after being hit.

It had been decided to provide four of the existing 12in Mark IX guns, as in the *Formidables* and *Duncans*, with 80 rounds per gun. There were to be the usual twelve 6in Mark VII, with 200 rounds each and 25lb charges, using Case 'B' to contain fourteen half charges each, with eighty-six cases at each end of the ship, stowed six layers deep and 15 abreast, plus practice ammunition. The eight 7.5in guns were to have 100 rounds with 50lb charges each, using case 'N'. These weighed 80lb each empty, and 285lbs (129 kg) full. These ammunition stowage problems affected the design's dimensions considerably. To add to the designers' problems, a new less erosive propellant was under consideration which would be about twice as bulky as cordite. This had to be borne in mind and might have required altering the ship's dimensions, gun mountings and turrets.

All this time the concept was of a 17,000-ton 19kt ship, with 4-12in, 8-7.5in housed in turrets, and 12-6in. Displacement might vary two or three hundred tons

either way. The general policy of building these larger and more powerful ships was considered at an informal meeting of the Board of Admiralty on 10 October 1900, and approved. A further meeting was to be held on the Thursday; time was getting short if the design was to be completed and authorised in the 1901-02 Naval Estimates in March 1901. Funds were evidently tight, and the effect of reducing speed to 18kts was raised. Cost was expected to be at least £100,000 more than the *London*. Admiral May proposed a variant with less armament and more armour. A better protected bow was also wanted, and longer 7.5in guns would mean at least five tons more weight per gun.

By 9 November, the 'Heavy Armour' variant, with 4-7.5in and 8-6in, came out at 17,170 tons for 19kts, against 16,140 for a version with 8-7.5in and a ten gun 6in battery; a reduction to 18kts would save about 1000 tons. The gain in the 'heavy armour' versions was 4in bow armour against 2in on 1in, 4in stern armour against 1.5in, and 12in on the 12in gunhouses against 8in. This last would add 130 tons high up. The 6in guns would be in a box battery, in effect a 'terrace' of casemates, instead of separate casemates. Cost would increase by £25-30,000.

Bitter argument continued, and on 8 December, revised characteristics were called for: 18kts speed, 8-7.5in in turrets, 10-6in in a box battery, 10-12pdr, 6-3pdrs for the fighting tops, 4-TT in two rooms, and protection as in the 'ordinary' version. Bow protection was still to be decided, there was to be at least one transverse bulkhead across the battery, and 12in shields to the 12in; this probably refers to the turret faces (US: ports). The ships were to be as short as possible, for manoeuvrability; hence the sacrifice of 2-6in guns in the battery. Deadman forwarded a statement on the new design to the DNO on behalf of White, on 14 December. Ominously, the DNO replied on 1 January that 'all these assumptions are liable to alterations'.

The new propellant was still under consideration and posed serious problems. Charges were longer and bulkier, requiring alternative arrangements in turrets, magazines, hoists and handing rooms, as well as more weight. It was agreed in late January that the 6in were to be fed direct from shell and handing rooms to the main deck, there were to be six 12pdr hoists, the engine-room ventilators had to be re-arranged, which affected boat stowage, the officers' accommodation had to be re-arranged, Belleville boilers were to be used instead of Babcock & Wilcox, and, to reduce topweight, the traditional boat derricks were to be used instead of cranes, despite the faster working of the latter.

For such a ship, with Bellevilles giving 18kts, 420ft (128 metres) length between perpendiculars and 16,000 tons displacement were needed. The absolute minimum length was 410ft. Any more additions to weight would require more length to get 18kts. For stability reasons, 78ft (23.8 metres) beam was needed. By now, the Admiralty knew that the *Pennsylvania/Georgia* was to carry 4-12in, 8-8in, four being in the notorious double-deck turrets, and 12-6in, at 19kts, but White noted on 3 April that 'this disposition involves some serious disadvantages, though it reduces the risk of interfering with the fire of neighbouring guns'.

Long discussions took place over the hull form; one much like the *Formidable* was adopted. There was much criticism of the design's inferiority, on paper, to the American ship. A detailed analysis suggested that the *Georgia* carried far less stores than in Admiralty practice, that the turrets were cramped, that only two thirds of the ammunition was included in the displacement, that she only had half as many boats and that the nominal crew of 703 was not nearly enough to work her. It was felt that an equivalent design to British standards would be at least 16,000 tons, the displacement of the later *Louisiana* class.

Yet again, the Board reconsidered the design, and on 25 April they decided on a maximum speed of 18.5kts, the saving of as much weight as possible by avoiding duplication of services and cutting down the 'Warrant Officers' Stores' to three months' supply. The supply of 6in ammunition was to be 200 rounds (each 100lb plus charge) per gun and was to count against 'legend' displacement, and the 8-7.5in housed in turrets were to be replaced by 4-9.2in. This gun was regarded as an armour-piercer and was a favourite of White's. The change was apparently suggested by Constructor J H Narbeth. Weight of broadside was hardly affected; 2 x 380lb against 4 x 200lb, but the 9.2in required armoured 'carriers', as in many cruisers, high up in the ship; their turrets were also heavier than the twin 7.5in ones, so it was 'back to the drawing-board'

yet again (this was nothing to the Americans' problems with the *Pennsylvania*.) The Engineer in Chief suggested hoisting the 9.2in shells singly through a vertical tube, but this proved impracticable. The side armour above the waterline and within the citadel was to be changed from 9in and 6in to 8in and 7in.

It was decided to omit the stern torpedo tube, and the complement was finally worked out as 735 of whom 190 were in the engine and boiler rooms. 56ft steam pinnaces were retained, though lighter 40ft ones had been suggested. White reported on 14 June 1901 that with 200 tons 'Board Margin' for contingencies, the resulting 18,000ihp 18.5kt ship looked like coming out at 16,700 tons, though he hoped to shave off a few tons. He still needed decisions on the masts, which affected topweight. However, there was no rest for the wicked; at the time many were still suspicious of the water-tube boiler, especially the very anti-Admiralty MP Sir William Joicey. This lobby were so influential that some ships, including 'the new battleships', were given mixed boiler outfits, which proved a great nuisance. Not till late July was approval given to complete the design.

Three ships were authorised under the 1901-02 Navy Estimates, two more under those of 1902-03, and three in 1903-04. The latter trio, *Britannia*, *Africa* and *Hibernia* differed slightly; the *Warrior* class armoured cruisers of that year were designed to have a secondary armament of 50 calibre Mark XI 6in guns, and these guns were duly

HMS Dominion. *Note the very tall pole masts, with topmasts and topgallants. The 9.2in turrets are at a higher level than the 6in case-mated on the main deck. Torpedo nets and booms are clearly visible.* (Antony Preston)

HMS Hibernia in 1909-13 after the addition of extra-tall topmasts for wireless. The sloped face and sides of the forward 12in turret is shown, the after turret is hidden by the quarterdeck. Using a ramp over the forecastle removed from her sister Africa, she could launch a Short S38 'hydroaeroplane'. (CPL)

ordered. It was later decided to replace these by turrets, containing first, twin 6in and then single 7.5in. This rendered the 6in surplus and it was decided to fit some of them in the 1903-04 battleships. This necessitated yet further re-design. Oscar Parkes apparently got hold of a garbled version of this and wrote in *British Battleships* that the 1903-04 ships could have been built as *Lord Nelsons*. Schemes were floated to fit additional 9.2in in the three hulls instead of 6in, but these came to nothing; probably only two or four could have been fitted.

Since there was great pressure to save weight and space, the use of smaller turrets and barbettes in the French or American style was briefly considered, but this would have involved new gun designs and required the use of the dangerous single-stage hoists.

In 1903, the Imperial Japanese Navy had two ships named *Kashima* and *Katori* laid down in Britain and they were delivered in 1906. Though not sisters, they were similar to the *King Edward VIIs*, but carried 4-12in, 4-10in and 12-6in. The extra 6in were in upper-deck casemates, between the wing 10in turrets.

There was a very old tradition that the first '1st Rate' ship completed in a new reign should bear the name of the new sovereign; the new King, to general surprise, took the title of 'King Edward VII' (before his accession, he was usually known as 'Prince Albert'). In giving permission for his name to be used, he specified that the ship to bear his name should always be used as a flagship. Some felt that *Royal Edward* would have been more in accordance with tradition. The other ships of the class

were given 'Imperial' names; the second and third ships were *Dominion* (Canada) and *Commonwealth* (Australia became a Commonwealth on 1 January 1901) *New Zealand* was later renamed *Zealandia* (meaningless to Britons) to free her name for a new battlecruiser.

By the time the *King Edward VIIs* were completed, the 'Dreadnought revolution' was in being, and they were relegated to the category of 'Pre-Dreadnought', which was almost equivalent to 'Pre-Historic'. Hence, they were always regarded as ships that had missed their place in history. Gunnery exercises suggested that the three-calibre armament would be almost impossible to control; though they may have been denigrated to show how superior the *Dreadnought* was.

For a number of years they were an important part of the Home Fleet, and later of the Grand Fleet. Due to the hull form adopted to increase manoeuvrability, they showed a certain reluctance to straighten out after turning; hence their nickname of 'The Wobbly Eight'. They were also known as 'The Behemoths' by analogy with the armoured cruiser *Leviathan*. Once dreadnoughts were available in numbers, their formation speed of 16.5kts hindered the fleet. The solution adopted was to station the eight ships, in two divisions, astern of the dreadnoughts. On deployment, they turned the opposite way to them, then turned in succession sixteen points, and tailed on behind.

At the time of Dogger Bank, they were in the North Sea, and the *King Edward VII* embarked a number of *Blücher* survivors, who looked at the woodwork in her wardroom and said 'My God, how you will burn'. On another occasion 'A battleship of the *King Edward VII* class was placed at the head of each division, in order to indicate the presence of mines'. The *King Edward VII* herself was mined and sunk west of the Orkneys on 6 January 1916; the first occasion she put to sea without an admiral. She lasted over nine hours in a heavy sea, which was very good for a pre-dreadnought. The mine exploded under the starboard engine-room. Her sinking was partly due to a centreline door in the machinery spaces being left open, which flooded them all. The designers thought that if it had been shut, the ship would have listed 14°, water would have come in through the 6in gunports, and, like several other pre-dreadnoughts, she would have capsized rapidly. She did so eventually after four destroyers had got alongside and rescued the entire crew, the brand-new *Musketeer* being badly damaged by projections on the *King Edward*'s side. There were hints that some bulkheads had leaked. In May 1916 the remaining seven sisters, plus *Dreadnought*, now obsolescent herself, were sent to the Swin, in the mouth of the Thames, as a defence against German raids.

Jutland took place soon after their departure (Admiral Scheer unwisely took the *Deutschlands*, equivalent to the *King Edwards*, along, slowing him by 2kts, and costing him the *Pommern* and her 840-man crew), and they continued on routine duties till the end of the war. Most of the 6in were removed or raised to the upper deck, as in many older ships. On 9 November 1918 *Britannia* left Gibraltar for home. Off Cape Trafalgar, she was torpedoed twice by *UB-50*, who was also leaving the Mediterranean for home. Like the *King Edward VII*, and unlike most pre-dreadnoughts, she stood up to the damage well, and floated for over three hours. Her guns fired in anger at the U-boat's periscope; the only action by a *King Edward VII*. The first torpedo set fire to a 9.2in magazine, which burnt without exploding. The survivors were landed at Gibraltar, and were accommodated in the Naval Barracks. When 'Lash-up and stow' was ordered the following morning, some fifty men did not stir from their hammocks; they had been suffocated in their sleep by cordite fumes. The following day news of the Armistice arrived.

The six surviving members of the class were clearly obsolete, and were disposed of over the next few years, prematurely overtaken by evolution. Adding an intermediate armament had taken a great deal of effort, and the results were not spectacular; not one of the 'Wobbly Eight' engaged an enemy ship. The only surface action involving such ships took place in the Black Sea. That fleet was the elite of the Russian Navy, and its five pre-dreadnoughts had two clashes with the *Goeben/Yavuz* [Ed. see pp.117-140]. Honours were even as regards main armament fire, but the numerous Russian 8in and 6in guns did not score a single hit.

Commonwealth's aftermost port 6in is clearly visible, the rest are housed. After 12in and 9.2in turrets and the derricks and davits for the ships numerous boats are clearly visible. Note also the fire control drum on the after side of the mainmast fire control platform. (Antony Preston)

Annex A: KING EDWARD VII CLASS

Name	Builder	Laid down	Launched	Completed	Fate
Africa	Chatham DY	24 Jan 04	20 May 05	Nov 06	Sold for BU 1920
Britannia	Ports Dy	4 Feb 04	10 Dec 04	Sep 06	Torp UB-50 w of Gib 9 Nov 1918
Commonwealth	Fairfield	17 Jun 02	13 May 03	Mar 05	Sold for BU 1921
Dominion	Vickers	23 May 02	25 Aug 03	Jul 05	Sold for BU 1921
Hibernia	Devonport DY	6 Jan 04	17 Jun 05	Jun 07	Sold for BU 1921
Hindustan	John Brown	25 Oct 02	19 Dec 03	Jul 05	Sold for BU 1921
King Edward VII	Devonport DY	18 Mar 02	23 Jul 03	Feb 05	Mined off Dunnet Head 6 Jan 16
New Zealand Zealandia 1911	Portsmouth	9 Feb 03	4 Feb 04	Jul 05	Sold for BU 1921

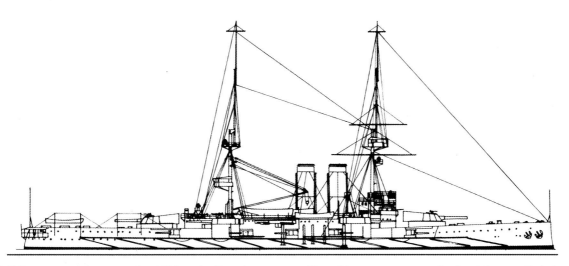

HMS Dominion *as she appeared in 1908, with tall wireless topmasts. She and her sisters were completed with fire control platforms on both masts, recognition of the gunnery revolution but the general layout remained basically nineteenth century. (CPL)*

Annex B: SPECIFICATIONS

Legend displacement:	16,350 tons, actual 15,585 to 15,885 tons, deep load 17,009 to 17290 tons. LBP 425ft, LOA 453ft 9in x 78ft x 25ft 8in (129.54 metres / 138.03 x 7.72)
Speed:	18.5kts on 18,000ihp
Armour:	Belt 9in/8in, Bulkheads 12in/8in, Barbettes 12in, 12 in gunhouses 12in/8in, 9.2in gunhouses 9in/5in,6 in battery 7in,CT 12in, decks 2.5in/1in
Armament:	4-12in 40 calibre Mark IX, 4-9.2in Mark X, 10-6in Mark VII (Mark XI in last three), 14-12pdr, 14-3 pdr, 4-18in submerged TT
Complement:	777

THE ROYAL ROMANIAN NAVY AT WAR, 1941-1944

From 1941 until 1944, the Royal Romanian Navy played an integral role in Axis operations against Soviet forces in the Black Sea littoral. Here **Pierre Hervieux** investigates the important, yet often ignored, role played by the Romanian Navy, which had the unique distinction, in the Second World War of being the only Navy to have fought over three years without losing a single unit of its main force.

When the Second World War spread to the Black Sea on 22 June 1941, the Romanian Navy could be considered very small compared with its Soviet opponent. Here are the respective forces of the two navies on that day:

	Romanian Fleet	Soviet Fleet
Battleships	0	1
Modern Cruisers	0	2
Old cruisers	0	4
Flotilla leaders	0	3
Modern destroyers	2 (*Regele Ferdinand*) (*Regina Maria*)	8
Old destroyers	2 (*Marasti*) (*Marasesti*)	5
Torpedo boats	3 (one with torpedo tubes: *Sborul* two without : *Naluca* and *Smeul*)	2
Submarines	1 (*Delfinul*)	44
Motor Torpedo Boats	3 (*Viforul, Vijelia, Viscolul*)	60 (+ 16 for training, liaisons, etc.)
Minesweepers	0	15 (+ 24 auxiliary minesweepers)

The Soviet superiority was therefore enormous, nevertheless the Romanian Navy was quite active. In addition to the above-mentioned warships it had the following units available:

3 old gunboats (ex-First World War French units) employed as anti-submarine escorts: *Stihi Eugen*, *Dumitrescu* and *Ghiculescu*.

3 minelayers: the modern and specially built *Admiral Murgescu*, the old converted merchant ships *Regele Carol I* (1898, 2369 tons) and *Aurora*.

1 submarine tender: *Constanza*.
1 training ship: the *Mircea*.

The Romanian Navy Headquarter's dependence on the Headquarters of the German Navy varied during the war according to:

The general military situation and operational interests of German Naval Headquarters in the Black Sea.

The importance of the operational command to which missions were entrusted in this naval operational zone.

The percentage of the German naval and littoral forces brought to the Black Sea.

The measure in which the German Command was interested in the Romanian Sea and River forces with regard to operations in the Black Sea.

The first phase for the Romanian Navy went from 22 June to 8 August 1941, when the main task of the naval forces was to defend the coast. Officially, for, in secret, the minelayers *Amiral Murgescu*, *Regele Carol I* and *Aurora* laid a 1000-mine barrage, five miles off the coast between Cape Midia and Tuzla, from 16 to 19 June 1941, to protect the approaches and the surroundings of Constanza harbour.

On the evening of 25 June, a Soviet naval force sailed from Sevastopol, comprising an assault group with the flotilla leaders *Kharkov* and *Moskva*, followed by a covering force with the heavy cruiser *Voroshilov*, escorted by the destroyers *Smyshleny* and *Soobrazitelny*. Their aim was to reconnoitre in strength the defensive system of the Romanian naval base of Constanza, and to destroy the petrol and oil supplies which were stored at La Pallas. Simultaneously, with a diversionary attack by aircraft of the Soviet Naval Air Force, the *Kharkov* and the *Moskva* opened fire with their 130mm guns on oil tanks and railway installations near Constanza in the early morning of

The Romanian auxiliary cruiser Regele Carol I (*ex passenger ship, 1898, 2400 tons*) *during the First World War. She was transformed into a minelayer (200 mines) and armed with 2-102mm, 2-20mm AA guns.* (Author's collection)

26 June. The shelling from the two ships was accurate and effective, although the distance was about 20km; 350 130mm shells were fired in ten minutes. Fires started, an ammunition train blew up and considerable damage was inflicted, but the supplies of oil were not destroyed. At 04:16, as they were beginning to withdraw from the bombardment, the two Soviet destroyers came under fire of the German 210mm railway battery Bismarck and the 280mm battery Tirpitz, respectively to the north and south of Constanza (since March 1941 for the latter), and also the fire of the Romanian destroyers *Regina Maria* and *Marasti* which were hidden against the high coast behind them and proved a difficult target for the two Soviet flotilla leaders, who were themselves clearly silhouetted against the dawn. The exchange of fire, between the destroyers, took place between 11,000 and 16,000 metres. *Moskva*, in the lead, was soon bracketed by German and Romanian fire and, shortly afterwards, her main mast was brought down by a hit.

Soviet prisoners picked up by the Romanians after the action indicated that they thought the damage was caused by a small-calibre shell, implying that it came from one of the Romanian destroyers. The two Soviet destroyers reached the outer edge of what was believed to be the possible mined area and the *Kharkov* signalled the *Moskva* to proceed at full speed on a direct course. A minute later the *Moskva* had acknowledged the *Kharkov's* signal, and had reached about 36-37kts when a heavy explosion occurred beneath the vessel, blowing up a fuel tank, which caused the *Moskva* to break in two at the first boiler room and sink in four or five minutes, 69 survivors being picked up, 41 by five German Heinkel He 59 float-

planes from 8 Seenot in ten missions, 26 by the Romanian motor torpedo boats *Viforul* and *Vijelia* and two swam ashore.

What was the cause of her loss? I left the debate open in *Warship 1991* (my article having been written in 1990) but, after 1990, with the post-*glasnost* era, more information about Soviet submarine attacks became available to western naval historians and it is now possible to present more accurately what probably happened. There were two submarine attacks on two Soviet destroyers, the first one at 06:43, in 44°04N/29°09E, east of Constanza, one torpedo being fired at the *Kharkov* by the only submarine in the area, the Soviet *Shch-206* (Captain Karakui). The second attack took place at 07:00 and two torpedoes were fired, by the same submarine, at the *Soobrazitelny* in 44°04N/29°14E. Both destroyers were missed and the latter made a depth-charge attack against the submarine and her stern was seen briefly afterwards on the surface, and oil bubbles were also seen. But there was no proof that the submarine was really sunk and, according to recent Russian information (1996), the *Shch-206* was still operating after 26 June and was depth-charged and sunk on 9 July, by the Romanian torpedo boat *Naluca* and the Romanian motor torpedo boats *Viscolul* and *Vijelia*, at about 8 miles off Mangalia.

During the Soviet air raid over Constanza, on 26 June, the Romanian minelayer *Amiral Murgescu* claimed to have shot down two Soviet aircraft. The mouth of the Danube had also to be defended, for it was where the Romanian river monitor fleet faced its Soviet counterpart. The Romanian Danube Flotilla's main units were the seven monitors:

Ion C Bratianu
Lascar Catargiu   680 tons, launched in 1907-08,
Alexandru Lahovari   main armament: 3-120mm
Mihail Kogalniceanu

Basarabia   550 tons, 1915, 2-120 mm
Bucovina

Ardeal   450 tons, 1904, 2-120 mm

Between 23 June and 8 July the Soviet monitors *Rostovtsev* and *Zhemchuzhin* (385 tons, 1932, 2-130mm) accompanied by *Zheleznyakov* (263 tons, 1936, 2-102mm) together with four BKA armoured motor gunboats, held up attempts by Romanian monitors to advance down the Danube across the Pruth estuary. The Soviet monitors *Udarny* and *Martynov* (385 tons, 1932, 2-130mm) with twelve BKAs supported small landings of infantry troops on the southern bank of the Kilia arm. Nevertheless, the Soviet river flotilla of the Danube was trapped on the front line and found itself in a difficult situation. It had to be supported by the destroyers *Kharkov*, *Smyshleny* and *Besposhchadny*, coming from Sevastopol, between 23 and 25 June. No action took place between the major Romanian and Soviet combat ships, but in addition to supporting several landing operations, they also shelled enemy positions and laid and swept mines. Finally, the Soviet Danube flotilla was obliged to evacuate the river and, on 18 July, after having forced the passage between the Romanian coastal defence batteries of Periprava and Vilkovo, the five monitors and sixteen BKA armoured motor gunboats retreated to Odessa, under the protection of the light cruiser *Komintern*, the destroyers *Kharkov*, *Bodry*, *Shaumyan*, 2 gunboats, 10 motor torpedo boats and 6 armed motor boats. During that retreat a certain number of armoured motor gunboats and other small craft were lost: there were original-ly 23 BKAs (29 tons, 1-76mm, 3 AA machine guns) in the Danube Flotilla and seven were lost before it evacuated the river, five having been identified:

MBKA 114 sunk or scuttled on Lake Kagul (Danube) on 8 July 1941
MBKA 134 sunk by Romanian gunfire near Periprava (Danube) on 8 July 1941
MBKA 232, 233, 234 (one sunk by gunfire off Reni on 29 June 1941, one sunk by gunfire near Vilkovo on 18 July 1941, one fate unknown, (scuttled?))

On 15 July a Soviet air attack sank the auxiliary Romanian minelayer *Aurora* in the harbour of Sulina and minelaying operations had to be suspended temporarily, until the advance of Romanian land forces drove away the Soviets from their nearest air bases. Later in the war, six other light vessels, including tugs, were employed in laying inshore mine barrages. On 21 July an SB-2 Soviet bomber claimed wrongly to have sunk the Romanian monitor *Ardeal* on the Danube! On 5 August the auxiliary minelayer *Regele Carol I* had several men wounded during Soviet air raids on Constanza, but she was not seriously damaged, whilst the *Amiral Murgescu* claimed three more Soviet aircraft shot down. Her 102mm gun shields had been taken off to allow the two guns to shoot against aircraft. To replace the lost *Aurora*, another auxiliary minelayer was commissioned in the Romanian Royal Navy. It was a much bigger unit, the ex-passenger vessel *Dacia* (1907, 3418 tons), armed with three 102mm guns and able to carry 200 mines.

Between 22 and 27 June 1941 *Delfinul* (Captain Voinescu), the one and only Romanian submarine, participated in a mission as a forward picket, 30-60 miles east-north-east of Constanza. She saw signal lights, but could not identify them and had no contact. The Romanian Navy was concerned by the risk of losing her

The Romanian monitor Lascar Catargiu *in 1934 on the Danube.* (Author's collection)

The Romanian submarine Delfinul *during her first war patrol at the end of June 1941.* (Author's collection)

and, preferring to maintain the threat on the Soviet Navy in immobilising useful escorts and aircraft, successive *Delfinul* commanders received restrictive orders; they were not allowed to attack escorted merchant vessels. Between 10 and 19 July, during her second mission, she met Soviet submarines on the surface without any consequence and sailed home on the next day. On 3 August, whilst being moored along the submarine tender *Constanza*, in the harbour of the same name, her conning tower was damaged by splinters from a bomb dropped by a Soviet aircraft.

The second phase for the Romanian Navy went from 8 August 1941 to 28 July 1942, when the main task of the naval forces was to protect the transport on the western coast, between Odessa and the Bosphorus, and various operations in connection with this. As the front went deeper into the Ukraine, and the transport difficulties became great, the German Command decided to use naval transport. To this end the Admiral commanding the Southern Group of the German Navy interceded with the Romanian Government, the main duty of the Romanian naval forces being the sea-transport of supplies for the German and Romanian armies.

Between 12 and 20 August *Delfinul* accomplished her third mission, without any result. Her purpose was to attack Soviet ships evacuating the harbour of Odessa. On 20 August at 12:08, as she was sailing home on the surface four miles east of Constanza, the Soviet submarine *M-33* (Captain Surov) launched one torpedo at her but missed.

In the meantime, on 15 August at 09:30, the Soviet submarine *Shch-211* (Captain Devyatko) had attacked the Romanian cargo ship *Peles* (5708 tons) and the Italian tanker ship *Superga* (6154 tons), under Bulgarian escort, launching two torpedoes at each of them, but the precious tanker was missed. *Peles* was damaged, in 42°46N/27°59E, north of Cape Emine and, after an

explosion, sank the next day. She was the first loss for the small Romanian merchant navy, which comprised 35 ships representing 111,678 tons in 1939. The next day, at 13:25, the *Shch-211* launched one torpedo at the Romanian cargo ship *Ardeal* (5695 tons), north of Cape Emine, but she was missed. Also on 16 August, the Romanian motor torpedo boats *Viscolul*, *Vijelia* and *Viforul* were involved in an operation against Soviet supplies between Sevastopol and Odessa, but it was unsuccessful, for the Soviet escort forces in that area were far too strong: the light cruiser *Komintern*, two destroyers, four gunboats, forty motor torpedo boats and seven auxiliary minesweepers were at sea off Odessa and Otchakov!

In August, Soviet submarines were particularly active in laying minefields. On 2 August the *L-5* (Captain Zhdanov) laid eleven mines, 6 miles south-east of Mangalia. This minefield was found by Romanian minesweepers on 18 September and two mines were swept. At the start of the war the Romanian Navy did not have any minesweepers, but fishing vessels were quickly requisitioned, equipped and used as auxiliary minesweepers. On 12 August the Soviet submarine *L-4* (Captain Polyakov) laid twenty mines, 8 miles south-east of Mangalia and the minefield was not reported. Four days later *L-5* laid eleven mines again, this time 4.5 miles east of Mangalia. This minefield was reported the next day when four mines were swept, seven more on 9 September and four more later. On 19 August *L-4* laid twenty mines, 4 miles east of Cape Olinka, six mines were swept on 11-12 December 1941, but the German landing craft *F-130* (155 tons) hit one of the fourteen left on 29 April 1942. She did not sink, being only damaged and grounded, and was salved and repaired. On 24 and 28 August *L-4* and *L-5* laid twenty mines each, the former 6 miles east of Cape Olinka and the latter 3 miles east of Mangalia, where two mines were swept in September.

From 3 to 19 September *Delfinul* accomplished her

Dacia, *Romanian auxiliary minelayer, in September 1941 as she leaves Constanza in company with the* Murgescu.
(Author's collection)

Built in Britain by Vosper, the Romanian motor torpedo boat Viscolul *survived the war. In this picture, taken in 1941, she is armed with 2 quadruple light machine guns, 2 TT and 6 depth charges.* (Author's collection)

fourth mission with a new Captain, Commander Lungu. On 9 September the old Soviet light cruiser *Komintern* was missed as she was zigzagging behind the cover of rocks off Cape Ortschanok. A coastal shelling was cancelled because of bad visibility.

On 7 September, at 14:41 (Soviet time exceptionally), the Soviet submarine *S-34* (Captain Khmelnitskii) reported having launched one torpedo at a Romanian destroyer but missed. In reality, it was the gunboat *Dumitrescu*, which was sailing at 3 miles east of Cape Shabla. On 5 October, at 10:35, off Cape Tuzla, the Romanian destroyer, *Regina Maria* was escorting the minelayers *Amiral Murgescu* and *Regele Carol I*. She observed two torpedoes which missed. They had been launched by the Soviet submarine *L-4* (Captain Polyakov). Between 8 and 16 October four mine barrages and one partial barrage were laid, to protect Axis sea traffic off the Bulgarian coast. The Romanian minelayers involved were the *Amiral Murgescu*, *Dacia* and *Regele Carol I* who were under the command of Captain Niculescu and, as a German adviser, *Kapitän* von Davidson. The escort comprised the Romanian torpedo boats *Naluca*, *Sborul*, *Smeul*, the Romanian gunboats *Dumitrescu*, *Ghiculescu* and, for a time, the Bulgarian torpedo boats *Derzky*, *Khabri*, *Smeli* and, in the approach and the departure, Romanian destroyers. Shortly after having sailed from Varna, on 10 October, the *Regele Carol I* hit a mine laid by the Soviet submarine *L-5* on 13 September or by *L-4* on 18 September, two to three miles east of Cape Galata. There were 150 mines on board and the ship sank 13 minutes later with 21 crew members; the German and Bulgarian liaison staff and most of the crew were rescued.

It was a serious blow for the small Romanian Navy, but the Soviet submarines paid dearly for the mines laid by the Romanians between 8 and 16 October:

On 18 October the *Shch-212* was damaged.
Between 18 and 21 October the *M-58* was sunk off Constanza.
Between 28 October and 1 November the *M-59* was sunk off Sulina.
On 3 November the *M-34* was sunk off Constanza.
On 12 November the *S-34* was sunk in the Bay of Burgas.
On 16 November the *Shch-211* was sunk off Varna.
The *Shch-205* was damaged on unknown date and place.
The *L-24* was sunk as late as between 15 and 29 December 1942 off Szabla.
Making a total of six Soviet submarines sunk and two damaged.

On 15 October, south of Constanza, the Romanian torpedo boat *Sborul* reported having been missed by a submarine's torpedo, but there was no submarine in the area! On 16 October Romanian troops entered Odessa. During the Soviet evacuation of Odessa harbour, a mine barrage was laid by the Soviet destroyers *Bodry* and *Smyshleny* in the area of Ilyichevka. Part of it, consisting of 32 mines, was cleared on 21 October by motor minesweepers of the German Danube Flotilla but, the day before, the Romanian *Dredger B* (80 tons) and *Dredger D* (80 tons) had been sunk by Soviet mines. The Hungarian cargo ship *Ungvar* (1031 tons) and the Romanian motor torpedo boats *Viforul* (1939, 32 tons) and *Vijelia* (1939, 32 tons) on 9 November, in 46°11N/30°41E, and, on 2 December, the Romanian cargo ship *Cavarna* (3495

The Romanian destroyer Regina Maria *in 1941 with her early camouflage. Her 76mm AA is still on board between the 2 funnels.* (Bundesarchiv)

Regina Maria *in 1942. The 76mm AA gun has been replaced by 2-20mm AA guns.* (Drüppel)

tons) and the German cargo ship *Cordelia* (1357 tons) were sunk by mines in another part of it. On 6 November, at 07:46, the Soviet submarine *S-33* (Captain Alekseyev) launched two torpedoes at the Romanian destroyer *Marasesti*, off Mangalia and, again in the same area, at 13:34, but the four torpedoes all missed! On 17 November the Soviet submarine *L-6* (Captain Bul) laid a mine barrage of 20 mines in Ak Mechet Bay, one of them being possibly responsible for the loss of the Romanian barge *Danubius* (550 tons) on 20 June 1942.

In the meantime the Romanian submarine *Delfinul*, with a new Commanding Officer, Captain Costachescu, sailed for her fifth mission, on 2 November 1941, to attack the Soviet supply traffic between the Caucasus and Crimea, and also to attack Soviet ships evacuating the Sea of Azov. On the next day there was a surface encounter, in bad visibility and without any result, between the *Delfinul* and a Soviet submarine, possibly *M-34*. On 5 November, at 08:05, the *Delfinul* saw an unescorted Soviet cargo ship and, at 08:45, from a distance of about 800 metres, she launched one torpedo which hit her. It was quickly followed by another explosion and the ship sank, 4 miles south of Yalta; she was the *Uralets* (1927, 1975 tons). Later on, between 10:30 and 18:40, the *Delfinul* was depth-charged by Soviet anti-submarine ships and about 85 explosions were counted by her crew. She then moved south and took shelter near the Turkish coast, returning slightly damaged to Constanza on 7 November. *Delfinul* sailed on 30 November for her sixth mission, which had to be stopped, off the Bosphorus, because of poor mechanical state and bad weather, being back home on 3 December. It was the same for her seventh mission, from 6 to 13

December, but this time the operation was cancelled off Batumi and two Soviet submarines were avoided on her way back to Constanza. Because of her mechanical problems, the *Delfinul* would only be back in operation in May 1942.

On 1 December at 08:12, the Soviet submarine *D-4* (Captain Izraelyevich) launched three torpedoes at the Romanian cargo ship *Cavarna* and missed her, east of Cape Kaliakra, the escorts dropping 34 depth-charges. As mentioned above, the cargo ship was sunk the next day by a Soviet mine. On 17 December two Romanian ships were attacked by unidentified Soviet submarines. At 06:16, 15 miles south-east of Bugaz, the destroyer *Regele Ferdinand* reported two torpedoes which missed her, and she counter-attacked with depth-charges. It was not the *Shch-203*, who had left the area earlier. Off Cape Emine, the cargo ship *Oituz* (1905, 2686 tons) was torpedoed and damaged, certainly not by the *Shch-211*, which had been sunk on 16 November.

At the end of February 1942 the Romanian minelayer *Amiral Murgescu* participated in a defensive minelaying operation, off Sulina, at the mouth of the Danube, in company of a new minelayer, the *Romania* (1905, 3200 tons) who was an ex-passenger ship and could carry 200 mines. She also had been the first Romanian seaplane tender during the First World War. On 12 March the Soviet submarine *Shch-210* (Captain Zelbst) was sunk on the Romanian mine barrage S15 off Szabla.

On 20 April, after the ice melted, Romanian and German convoy traffic began between Constanza and Ochakov. The merchant ships used were the Romanian *Suceava* (6876 tons), *Ardeal* (5695 tons), *Carpati* (4336 tons), *Sulina* (3495 tons), *Oituz* (2686 tons), *Danubius*

(1489 tons), the Bulgarian *Zar Ferdinand* (1994 tons), the German *Arkadia* (1756 tons), *Salzburg* (1742 tons), *Le Progres* (ex-French, 511 tons), the Hungarian *Kolozsvar* (1200 tons), *Kassa* (1022 tons), *Tisza* (961 tons) and *Budapest* (485 tons). They were escorted by the Romanian destroyers *Regina Maria*, *Marasesti*, *Maresti*, the Romanian torpedo boat *Smeul*, the Romanian gunboat *Dumitrescu* and the German Danube Flotilla. Odessa harbour being used again after its capture, Romanian minelayers laid flanking mine barrages in May to protect Odessa Bay against Soviet submarines. The operation was completed on the nights of 22-23 and 24-25 June, 200 German mines being laid each time. One of those barrages, S33, was responsible for the loss of two Soviet submarines: M-33 (Captain Surov) on 24 August, in 46°20N/30°54E, and M-60 (Captain Kudriavcev) on 26 September, which was sunk only 150 metres from M-33 (both wrecks were discovered in 1951). The ships which took part were: *Amiral Murgescu* and *Dacia*, escorted by the destroyers *Regele Ferdinand*, *Regina Maria* and *Marasesti*, the gunboats *Dumitrescu*, *Ghiculescu* and *Stihi Eugen*, the torpedo boat *Smeul* and the German motor minesweepers (R-Boote) of the Danube flotilla.

In the meantime the Romanian submarine *Delfinul* had sailed on 18 May for her eighth mission, to attack Soviet supply traffic to Sevastopol. It was completely uneventful, apart from a few aircraft alerts, one being particularly dangerous, on 27 May, with four bombs falling near the *Delfinul*. On 29 May, at 09:25 (all times given are as reported by the attacked ships), the Romanian cargo ship *Sulina* (3495 tons) was attacked by the old Soviet submarine A-3 (Captain Tsurikov) who launched two torpe-

does and sank her, in 46°31N/30°52E. Another old Soviet submarine, the A-5 (Captain Kukuy) launched one torpedo at the Romanian cargo ship *Ardeal* (5695 tons, always given in GRT for merchant ships), in the same area (46°32N/30°56E), on 11 June at 14:10, but the *Ardeal* was only damaged and beached, being salvaged and repaired later.

The ninth and last mission of the *Delfinul* was in connection with the final German-Romanian assault on Sevastopol, for attacking Soviet transports evacuating or reinforcing the surrounded harbour. On 30 June the Soviet Command gave orders to evacuate Sevastopol, but the evacuation could only be carried out on a small scale with little ships and submarines because of intensive Luftwaffe activity. Consequently, after sailing on 25 June, *Delfinul* did not find any interesting target. She also was attacked several times by Soviet aircraft and anti-submarine ships. On 27 June she was bombed and depth-charged for eleven hours, 240 explosions being reported. The next day *Delfinul* was surprised on the surface by a Soviet aircraft which missed her with a bomb, but managed to machine-gun the conning tower before being submerged, the damage being superficial. On 1 July, early in the morning, *Delfinul* was seen by an aircraft and, during the next thirteen hours of daylight, 268 bombs and depth-charges were dropped against her. She was very lucky to have survived over 500 explosions! After Sevastopol finally fell, *Delfinul* was recalled to Constanza on 2 July, where she arrived the next day. As her mechanical condition remained unreliable ('helped' perhaps by the Romanian underground movement?), it was decided to use her only for training the future crews of the forthcoming new submarines *Marsuinul* and *Rechinul*.

Romanian torpedo boats in 1942. Foreground the Naluca *or* Smeul, *behind the* Sborul. *(Drüppel)*

Aboard the Murgescu *in 1942, fully loaded with 135 mines in five rows.* (Author's collection)

The third phase for the Romanian Navy went from 28 July 1942 to 5 April 1944. After the fall of Sevastopol (2 July 1942), thanks to the progress of the German and Romanian armies to the east, the strategic situation in the Black Sea underwent another change. Up to Spring 1942, the task of the Romanian naval forces was to protect the transports on the Western coast of the Black Sea, as well as local operations in connection with this duty. On 28 July 1942, the Admiralty Command of the Southern Group of the *Kriegsmarine* made representations to the Romanian government and secured a greater control over the Romanian naval forces, to develop operations in the Black Sea:

Offensive operations in the Eastern Basin of the Black Sea, to support directly, or indirectly, the army's operations.
To open and use the naval communications between the ports on the Western coast of the Black Sea and those in the Crimea and the Asov Sea.

On 5 August, at 02:53, the Soviet submarine *Shch-205* (Captain Sukhomlinov) launched three torpedoes and claimed to have sunk a cargo ship of 8000 tons. In reality it was the small German tanker *Le Progres* (511 tons) who was escorted by two Romanian gunboats and was missed in 44°34N/29°28E. The Soviet submarine *Shch-208* (Captain Bielanov) was sunk by a Romanian mine, 5 miles off Zmiejnyj, between 26 August and 30 September 1942.

On 5 September, at 04:08, the Romanian cargo ship *Suceava* was missed by two torpedoes launched by the Soviet submarine *M-35* (Captain Greshilov), east of

Dacia in Constanza *in 1942.* (Author's collection)

The destroyer Marasesti *during the winter of 1942.* (Author's collection)

Budaki, as she was escorted by two gunboats. Two days later, two miles north-east of the Bosphorus, at 19:23, the Soviet submarine *Shch-207* (Captain Panov) missed the Romanian destroyer *Regele Ferdinand* with two torpedoes and, eight minutes later, the Romanian destroyer *Marasti* with four torpedoes, as they were picking up the escort of the Italian tankers *Albaro* and *Celeno*. They dropped depth-charges, but the Soviet submarine got away. On 16 September the Soviet submarine *L-5* (Captain Zhdanov) laid 20 mines, seven miles east-north-east of Burnas. Much later, on 6 November, the small Romanian tugboat *Oitul* (or *Oituz?*) (95 tons) hit one of them and sank, in 45°47N/30°19E. On the same day at 05:05 the German auxiliary anti-submarine vessel *Lola* and the Romanian destroyer *Regele Ferdinand*, in 44°11N/32°42E, reported two torpedoes which missed. It seems that the Soviet submarine *L-4* (Captain Polyakov) did not fire any torpedoes, but she was located and attacked with 26 depth-charges. On 21 September, at 09:10, the Soviet submarine *M-35* (Captain Greshilov) launched one torpedo at the Bulgarian cargo ship *Varna* (2141 tons) which was escorted by the Romanian torpedo-boat *Naluca*. It was in 45°54N/30°22E, and she was missed. Captain Greshilov estimated her as being an 8000 ton cargo ship, and claimed to have sunk her!

The *Naluca* was again attacked on the morning of 28 September, south-east of Sulina, by the Soviet submarine *M-120*, who launched two torpedoes and missed her. On 1 October, at 14:15, the German cargo ship *Salzburg* (1742 tons) was attacked by the Soviet submarine *M-118* (Captain Savin) which launched two torpedoes and sank

her, south-east of Shagany, in 45°54N/30°19E. She was carrying about 2000 Soviet prisoners of war, only 34 were rescued. The *Salzburg* was part of a Romanian convoy and *M-118* was soon after located by a German Blohm und Voss BV138C flying boat, and the Romanian gunboats *Stihi Eugen* and *Ghiculescu* were sent to the scene, the latter sinking *M-118* shortly after. On 6 October, at 22:42, the Romanian tugboat *Mina Daniel* (293 tons) was attacked by the Soviet submarine *M-31* (Captain Rastochil), north of Sulina, who launched two torpedoes and sank her in 45°47N/30°19E. On the next day, in the same area, the Romanian cargo ship *Sulina* was missed by two torpedoes launched by the Soviet submarine *Shch-216* (Captain Karbovskii). But, on 10 October, at 19:44, the same submarine launched three torpedoes at the Romanian cargo ship *Carpati* (4336 tons) and sank her in 45°o1N/29°47E, eight miles north-east of Gheorghe Mouth. On 14 October, at 12:43, the Romanian destroyer *Regele Ferdinand* evaded two torpedoes launched by the Soviet submarine *M-32* (Captain Koltypin), south of Cape Burnas, and the Romanian torpedo-boat *Smeul* dropped depth-charges.

On 4 November, at about 11:00, north-east of Sulina, the Romanian hospital ship *Bessarabia* (ex-passenger ship, 1938, 6672 tons) had observed the conning tower of a submarine. She was the Soviet *M-31* (Captain Rastochil) which had launched two torpedoes at her and missed. On 5 November the Romanian minelayers *Amiral Murgescu* and *Dacia*, escorted by the destroyers *Regele Ferdinand*, *Regina Maria* and *Marasti* laid anti-submarine mines off the island of Serpilor, off the main mouth of the Danube at Sulina. The purpose was to protect the constant river and coastal traffic on their way to the front. When not used as minelayers, the *Amiral Murgescu* was employed as a convoy escort and the *Dacia* as an armed merchant cruiser.

On 14 November, at 16:44, twelve miles north-north-west of the Bosphorus, the German tanker *Ossag* (2793 tons) was attacked by the Soviet submarine *L-23* (Captain Fartushnyi), which launched three torpedoes and damaged her, in 41°48N/29°02E, after she was met off the Bosphorus by the Romanian destroyers *Regele Ferdinand* and *Regina Maria*. The tanker was towed into the Bosphorus by a Turkish tug. Between 11 and 14 December there was a sortie against the Romanian coast by two Soviet minesweeper groups, under the command of Rear-Admiral Fadeev. The first group included the minesweeper T-407 *Mina* and T-412 *Arseni Rasskin*, and the 2nd group the minesweepers T-406 *Iskatel* and T-408 *Yakor*. Cover was provided by the destroyer *Soobrazitelny*. The 1st group attacked a German convoy, between Gibrieni and Burgas, comprising the Romanian cargo ship *Oituz* and the Bulgarian cargo ship *Zar Ferdinand*, the Romanian torpedo-boat *Smeul* and four German R-Boote motor minesweepers of the 3rd Flotilla (Lt Cdr Klassmann), but was driven off by the motor minesweepers feigning a motor torpedo boat attack whilst the *Smeul* covered the cargo ships in smoke. On 17 December at 13:48 the Soviet submarine *M-62* (Captain Malyshev) launched two torpedoes at the Romanian cargo ship *Durostor* (1309 tons), in 45°53N/30°32E, but missed her. The *Durostor*, with four escorts, did not observe the attack. On 26 December, at 10:48, the Romanian cargo ship *Danubius* and the Hungarian cargo ship *Tisza* with four escorts, were attacked by the Soviet submarine *M-111* (Captain

Iosseliany), east of Cape Burnas, who launched two torpedoes at one of the two cargo ships, but missed.

On 8 March 1943 at 17:10. South-west of Tarkhankut, the German tanker *Wolga-Don* (965 tons) was escorted by two Romanian gunboats when the Soviet submarine *Shch-215* (Captain Greshilov) launched three torpedoes at her, but they missed. On 27 March at 13:55, two cargo ships, the Romanian *Suceava* and the German *Charkov*, were escorted by two Romanian destroyers and three German motor minesweepers. That convoy reported a submarine attack. The Soviet submarine *L-23* (Captain Fartushnyi) was in the area but did not report any attack.

From April, patrol lines of Soviet submarines (*S-33*, *Shch-209*, *M-35* and *M-112*) were formed in the open sea against Romanian and German convoy traffic between Constanza and Sevastopol. On 17 April at 00:30, the German cargo ship *Arkadia* was sailing 65 miles east of Olinka, escorted by two Romanian destroyers and three German motor minesweepers, when the Soviet submarine *M-35* (Captain Prokofev) tried to attack her, but the attack was aborted and twelve depth-charges were dropped. On 20 April the biggest Romanian cargo ship, the *Suceava* (6876 tons) was sailing, escorted by the Romanian destroyer *Regina Maria* and three German motor minesweepers, but the Soviet submarine *S-33* (Captain Alekseyev) launched three torpedoes at her, and she sank, at 01:28, in 44°52N/31°22E. At the end of April the Romanian minelayers *Amiral Murgescu* and *Romania* laid several floating barrages off Sulina and in the Bay of Odessa. On 9 May, the German cargo ship *Charkov*, escorted by one Romanian gunboat and two German motor minesweepers reported two prematures and one torpedo which missed, in 45°12N/32°42E. The Soviet submarine *L-6* (Captain Gremyako) was in the area but reported no attack. On 1 June, at 15:06, the

The destroyer Marasti *in 1943. (Author's collection)*

Soviet submarine *D-4* (Captain Trofimov) launched four torpedoes at the Romanian destroyer *Marasti*, but all missed. This happened off the Crimea, on the Constanza-Sevastopol route, when the destroyer was escorting the Italian tanker *Celeno* (3741 tons) in company of another Romanian destroyer, two German motor minesweepers and the German A/S vessel *Schiff 19*. In the evening, at 19:05, *Celeno* was again attacked by the same Soviet submarine, which launched two torpedoes at her, south-west of Yevpatoriya in 45°06N/32°52E, but they missed.

On 7 July the Soviet submarines *S-33*, *Shch-201* and *Shch-203* operated against a convoy consisting of three merchant ships, including two cargo ships, the Romanian *Ardeal* and the Bulgarian *Varna*, escorted by the Romanian destroyers *Marasti*, *Marasesti* and the Romanian gunboats *Stihi Eugen* and *Ghiculescu*. *Shch-201* (Captain Paramoshkin) missed a gunboat with two torpedoes and the *Varna* with four, in 45°00N/32°37E at 03:36. The destroyer *Marasesti* claimed erroneously to have sunk a Soviet submarine with depth-charges on that occasion. On 18 July at 09:04, the Romanian barge *Dunarea-1* (505 tons) was sunk by one torpedo launched by the Soviet submarine *M111* (Captain Iosseliani), off Feodosiya in 44°59N/35°32E. On 24 July at 08:55, the German tanker *Podromos* (ex-Greek), escorted by the Romanian gunboats *Stihi Eugen* and *Ghiculescu*, reported one torpedo which missed, in 44°52N/30°30E, but there was no submarine in the area. On 30 August, when being escorted by two Romanian destroyers, two German submarine-chasers and two German motor minesweepers, the German tanker *Thisbe* (1782 tons) was hit by two torpedoes out of four launched at her by the Soviet submarine *Shch-215* (Captain Greshilov), at 18:36, and sank in 41°22N/29°08E. On the night of 13-14 September, the Romanian minelayers *Amiral Murgescu*, escorted by the destroyers *Regele Ferdinand* and *Marasesti* laid mines in the approaches to Sevastopol harbour, off Cape Khersonesskiy. Five miles south of Yevpatoria, on 22 September at 03:19, the Soviet submarine *S-33* (Captain Alekseyev) launched three torpedoes at the German cargo ship *Burgas*, in 44°38N/31°39E, escorted by the Romanian destroyer *Regele Ferdinand*, and missed her.

On 19 October at 22:39, the Romanian cargo ship *Ardeal* and the Hungarian cargo ship *Kassa* were attacked by the Soviet submarine *Shch-201* (Captain Paramoshkin) which launched four torpedoes without any hit, in 45°04N/32°28E; they were escorted by two Romanian destroyers and five German motor minesweepers. On the night of 9-10 November the minelayers *Amiral Murgescu* and *Romania*, escorted by the two 'R' class destroyers, laid more mines in the approaches to Sevastopol. The same two minelayers extended the minefield, escorted by the destroyers *Regele Ferdinand* and *Marasesti*, between 14 and 16 November. On 17 November, north-west of Yevpatoria, the Soviet submarine *D4* (Captain Trofimov) fired two torpedoes at the German A/S vessel *Rosita* and then, at 08:16, two were fired at the Romanian cargo ship *Danubius*; all missed. On 23 November, escorted by the Romanian minelayer *Amiral Murgescu*, the Romanian destroyer *Marasesti* and the German motor minesweepers *R165*, *R197* and *R209*,

The torpedo boat Sborul *in the floating dock at Constanza during 1943.* (Author's collection)

the German cargo ship *Santa Fe* (4627 tons) was attacked by the Soviet submarine *D4* (Captain Trofimov), which launched four torpedoes and sank her at 05:50 in 45°05N/33°16E south of Yevpatoriya. West of the Crimea, on 25 November, at 17:09, the Soviet submarine *L-6* (Captain Gremyako) launched four torpedoes and claimed to have sunk a cargo ship of 6000 tons. It was the small German tanker ship *Wolga-Don* (965 tons) which was escorted by the Romanian gunboats *Dumitrescu* and *Stihi Eugen*, the German submarine-chasers *UJ2301*, *UJ2309* and the German MMS *R205*. She sank in 45°07N/32°08E. On 4 December, off Tarkhankut, a cargo ship, escorted by a Romanian destroyer and three patrol vessels, was attacked by the Soviet submarine *Shch-209* (Captain Sukhodolskii), at 11:04. Two torpedoes were launched but missed.

During the winter of 1943-44, the minelayer *Romania* was also used as an accommodation ship for the German S-Boot flotilla operating from Sevastopol and Odessa. In the Black Sea, on 20 May 1943, the Italians had transferred their seven remaining MAS motor torpedo boats to the *Kriegsmarine*: MAS 566-570, 574 and 575. They were renumbered *S501-S507* and, early in 1944, they were transferred to the Royal Romanian Navy, minus the *S505* (ex-MAS 570), lost in the meantime. In 1943, four Dutch-built MTBs (TM52 class) were handed over by the Germans to the Romanian Navy. Unlike the six ex-

Another view of Sborul *in 1943.* (Author's collection)

German/Italian MTBs which were scuttled in August 1944, they were seized intact by the Soviets, and became *TKA951-954* and *TKA955* (ex *Viscolul*).

The five Italian midget submarines *CB1-CB4* and *CB6* were transferred to the Romanian Navy on 30 November 1943. Only two could be made serviceable and, although they made practice dives in Constanza harbour in 1944, neither became fully operational.

No information is available covering the first three months of 1944 as far as the Romanian Navy is concerned. The German-Romanian forces in the Crimea were successfully maintained by sea throughout the winter of 1943-44, but then the Crimea became isolated. During the Soviet offensive north of the lower Dnieper, Nikolaev had to be evacuated on 11 March and, after the blowing up of harbour and dockyard installations, was captured on 28 March. Soviet forces then drove the German and Romanian armies across the Lower Bug past Odessa to the Dniester. The attempt to encircle strong German and Romanian forces in Odessa failed, because 9300 wounded, 14,845 troops and 54,000 tons of mobile supplies could be evacuated from Odessa by sea. Eighteen sea-going ships in 26 missions, nine towed vessels in 27 missions, fifteen tugs in 33 missions and twenty-five naval ferry barges in 76 missions were used. In March, 45,000 tons of supplies and a German infantry division were brought to the Crimea by the sea route, evacuating and reinforcing involved German, Romanian, Hungarian and Bulgarian ships and boats (the deployment of Soviet submarines achieved no result).

The minelayers *Amiral Murgescu*, *Dacia* and *Romania* made several round trips between them, as the Red Army closed in on Sevastopol. The 4th phase for the Romanian Navy went from 5 April 1944 to 13 May 1944, when the situation on the front brought the front line back to its initial position, and the strategic problems took another form. Besides the army supply problem, a new situation had to be faced: the evacuation of troops and materials from zones which succumbed quickly to the blows of the Soviet forces. Romanian submarines were used to protect the evacuation from the Crimea, helping the German submarines to keep a watch on the Soviet bases on the Eastern coast of the Black Sea. By early April, when the Red Army finally broke into the peninsula and Sevastopol became encircled, up to eight convoys a day were used to evacuate 29,000 Romanian and 13,400 German troops out of Sevastopol, and also for extensive supply missions between 17 April and 4 May. The following cargo ships were used: the Romanian *Oituz* (2686 tons), *Ardeal* (5695 tons), *Alba Julia* (5700 tons), *Danubius* (1489 tons), *Durostor* (1309 tons), the German *Helga* (2200 tons), *Gieserich* (712 tons), *Totila* (2773 tons), *Teja* (3600 tons), the Hungarian *Budapest* (485 tons), *Kassa* (1022 tons), *Tisza* (961 tons) as well as the German tanker ships *Prodromos* (877 tons), and *Ossag* (2793 tons). There were also KT ships, many tugs and ferry-barges of German Landing Flotillas. The escort was under the overall command of the German Admiral Black Sea, Vice Admiral Brinkmann, and the Romanian naval forces were under the command of Rear Admiral Marcellariu. The following Romanian ships were employed: the destroyers *Regina Maria*, *Regele Ferdinand*, *Maresti*, *Marasesti*, the gunboats, *Ghiculescu* and *Stihi Eugen*. The German ships numbered 25 Uj submarine-chasers, 14 R-Boote and 13 S-Boote.

On 13 April at 09:25, in 43°47N/31°05E, a convoy with three ships and four escorts was attacked by the Soviet submarine *S31* (Captain Belorukov) which launched four torpedoes and missed the Romanian cargo ship *Ardeal*. On 18 April, a convoy, including two cargo ships and four escorts, was attacked three times by Soviet submarines. First, at 07:08, the Hungarian cargo ship *Kassa* was missed by three torpedoes from L-6 (Captain Gremyako) in 44°38N/32°13E, then the Romanian cargo ship *Alba Julia* was missed by torpedoes from the same submarine, at 11:06, in 43°28N/31°32E and, finally, at 23:32, the same cargo ship was again missed, this time by two torpedoes from L-4 (Captain Polyakov) in 43°25N/31°28E. *Alba Julia* was a lucky ship. She had already been missed twice, in the Aegean, by Allied submarines before: on 16 November 1942 by the Greek *Triton* (claimed sunk on that occasion by the German anti-submarine vessel *Uj-2102* and the German destroyer *Hermes*) and on 5 May 1943 by the British *Parthian*! But on 18 April her luck ran out for, shortly after the submarine attacks, she was set on fire by Soviet bombers, and lost. However, there is still some mystery about her, for another source says that she was only damaged. On 22 April, at 11:14, the Romanian cargo ship *Ardeal* was missed by two torpedoes launched by the Soviet submarine M62 (Captain Malyshev), in 43°42N/31°10E, as she was escorted by the German submarine-chaser *Uj-105* and the German motor minesweeper *R166*. At 18:15 she was again missed by two torpedoes from another Soviet submarine, M111 (Captain Khomyakov) in 43°45N/29°45E.

When the war started, the Romanian Navy was completing two new submarines, *Rechinul* and *Marsuinul* which had been launched on 5 and 25 May 1941 respectively. They were handed over to the Navy on 9 May and 4 October 1943, and they came under the command of Captains Corneliu Lungu and Grigore Ciolac. A long series of trials and torpedo firing tests were carried out by the two submarines and, being at last ready, *Rechinul* sailed for her first mission on 20 April 1944 to harass the Soviet ships trying to attack German and Romanian shipping evacuating the Crimea. On 26 April *Rechinul* received a secret order, Turkey was then under strong pressure from the Allies to declare war on Germany. *Rechinul* had to check which ports were the most used by Turkish merchant ships, in order to attack them and inflict the maxi-

mum losses in case of war. Two days later, Turkey declared by radio that she wanted to stay neutral, so the secret order was cancelled and the Batumi/Novorossisk area was again the target. Soviet aircraft attacked the *Rechinul* several times without any result, and it was the same against the Soviet shipping, so, as the evacuation of the Crimea was over, she was recalled on 13 May and was back in Constanza on 15 May.

The evacuation of the Crimea had involved Romanian, German and Hungarian merchant ships, and Romanian and German warships. Despite continual and very strong Soviet air attacks, and massive deployment of submarines, they were able to evacuate 37,500 men by 13 May, including 25,677 troops and 6011 wounded in the last three days.

On 11 May at 12:00, a convoy, escorted by the Romanian gunboat *Dumitrescu* and the German submarine-chaser *Uj-105* (ex *KT-24*), was attacked by the Soviet submarine *Shch-201* (Captain Paramoshkin) which launched two torpedoes and missed, in 44°14N/30°58E. On the same day, at 19:45, the Romanian minelayer *Dacia* was missed by two torpedoes, launched in 44°13N/32°03E by the Soviet submarine M62 (Captain Malyshev). The *Shch-201* and the M-62 respectively claimed to have sunk a landing craft and a minelayer. The latter submarine also claimed to have torpedoed and sunk the Romanian cargo ship *Durostor* (1917, 1309 tons), but that ship was damaged by air attack and sank afterwards in 44°37N/31°57E.

On 11 May the Romanian minelayers *Amiral Murgescu*, *Dacia* and *Romania* were amongst the last ships to evacuate troops from the Khersonesskiy Cape, escorted by the destroyers *Regele Ferdinand*, *Regina Maria* and the gunboats *Stihi Eugen* and *Dumitrescu*. On the morning of 12 May the *Romania*, loaded with troops, was bombed and sunk by enemy aircraft with heavy loss of life, two miles from the Khersonesskiy Cape. Despite heavy air attacks and land artillery fire, *Dacia* and *Amiral Murgescu*,

Torpedo boat Naluca *in 1943.* (Author's collection)

The gunboat Dumitrescu (*ex-French* Impatiente) *in 1943.* (Author's collection)

with 800 troops on board, managed to reach the open sea, escorted by the destroyer *Regina Maria*, and reached Constanza safely. The following merchant ships were sunk by Soviet air attacks: the German *Gieserich, Totila, Teja, Helga, Prodromos* and the Romanian *Danubius*, as well as five German submarine-chasers, three auxiliary vessels, five tugboats, twelve lighters and other small craft. Of the troops embarked on the sunken transports, 8100 could not be rescued. In all, 130,000 German and Romanian troops were evacuated by sea and 21,457 by air between 12 April and 13 May, 78,000 having been left behind as prisoners or dead.

The evacuation of the Crimea was a big success for the Romanian and German ships and boats which took part in it, for it was achieved despite vastly superior Soviet military power, on land, in the air and at sea. Against eventual Soviet surface raids along the Romanian coast, the last minelaying operation of the war was accomplished by the minelayers *Amiral Murgescu* and *Dacia*, south-east of Sulina, on the night of 25-26 May, the barrage supplementing the existing one. They were escorted by the destroyers *Regina Maria* and *Marasesti*, the torpedo boats *Sborul, Smeul* and the motor torpedo boats *Viscolul* and *Vedenia*.

On 11 May at 22:00, the other new submarine, the *Marsuinul*, sailed from Constanza for a cruise along the Turkish coast, between Eregli and Trabzon, to replace *Rechinul* off Batumi. At 02:30 there was an uneventful encounter with a Soviet submarine. At 06:30 an aircraft appeared, and *Marsuinul* dived. No recognition signals were exchanged, and the *BV138* called for German-commanded Croatian submarine-chasers. A series of attacks was launched from 08:30 until 20:00, about 420 depth-charges having been dropped. She then sailed for the Caucasus coast, where she was depth-charged several times the same day, then spending a full day off the

Turkish coast. On 17 May *Marsuinul* returned to the zone, off Batumi, but she was soon detected and depth-charged, between 04:00 and 12:00, sailing again consequently to the Turkish coast. But the Soviets were now fully alerted and, on 19 May she was again detected and 43 depth-charges were dropped on her. The next day she was seen by a Soviet submarine, who missed her with one torpedo and then called for submarine-chasers, who dropped 31 more depth-charges. On 21 May she was again attacked with 43 depth-charges, and then returned to Batumi. On 23 May, at 04:55, there was a distant and inaccurate depth-charging. From 07:55 *Marsuinul* had to endure a close depth-charging for the rest of the day, but at 20:25, being recalled to Constanza, she returned home, and surfaced off that harbour on 26 May. She was then attacked by a Soviet aircraft, which dropped six bombs without any result. *Marsuinul* submerged and only entered Constanza the next day. It is astonishing how lucky she was to have escaped so many depth-charges, friendly or not!

The 5th and last phase for the Romanian Navy went from 13 May to 23 August 1944, when the main task of the naval forces was to defend the coast, after the front on the Dniester and in northern Moldova and Basarabia was consolidated. But in this period the Romanian naval forces, after their efforts in connection with the Crimea evacuation, had a very small operational capacity. Consequently, the Romanian Navy relied on its coastal flanking barrages, waiting for eventual surface Soviet attacks, but after the Luftwaffe victory of 6 October 1943, when three modern Soviet destroyers were sunk, Stalin forbade the employment of surface warships, destroyers and bigger units.

On 15 June, *Rechinul* sailed for the last mission of a Romanian submarine in World War II and also for the

The minelayer Murgescu *in Constanza harbour, during the winter of 1943.* (Author's collection)

Romanian gunboat Ghiculescu (*ex-French* Mignonne) *in winter of 1943. On 1 October 1942 a German Blohm und Voss BV 138c flying boat located the Soviet submarine M-118, which was then sunk by* Ghiculescu *(armed with 2-37mm in this photo).* (Author's collection)

The Romanian submarine Rechinul *leaving Constanza for her first patrol on 20 April 1944. The camouflaged vessel in the rear right background is the auxiliary* Romania *used as a base ship for German S-boats.* (Author's collection)

largest, 45 days. Strangely enough, probably for political reasons, it seems that she did not have any orders to attack Soviet ships! Only for reporting the movements of Soviet warships above destroyer size, off the Caucasus coast, between Anapa and Tuapse, from where a possible seaborne invasion was expected to be launched against the Romanian coast. *Rechinul* only once spotted a major group of exercising Soviet warships, but she was attacked

several times by Soviet submarine-chasers and aircraft. On 28 June, 5-19 and 24 July she was depth-charged, but suffered only minor leaks on the first date. She returned to Constanza on 29 July, arriving there at 22:15.

In the second half of August, the Soviets began their final strong land attack on Romania. On 20 August, 62 bombers and 80 fighters and ground-attack aircraft of the Soviet Black Sea Fleet, after dropping smoke bombs to

Regina Maria *off Sevastopol in 1944 displaying another pattern of camouflage.* (Author's collection)

The destroyer Regele Ferdinand *headed for Sevastopol in 1944.* (Author's collection)

counter AA fire, attacked the harbour of Constanza. The Romanian torpedo boat *Naluca* (1914, 270 tons), the German submarine *U-9*, three German MTBs *S42, S52, S131*, the German motor minesweeper *R37*, and many smaller vessels were sunk. The Romanian destroyers *Regele Ferdinand* and *Marasesti* were damaged, the former more seriously, requiring extensive repairs, with 47 officers and crew killed. Also damaged were the gunboat *Stihi Eugen*, the minelayer *Dacia*, the German submarines *U-18* and *U-24*, the German MTBs *S28, S45, S47, S49* and *S51* and other vessels. After the air bombardment, the submarines *Marsuinul* and *Rechinul* moved to Turnul Magurete up the Danube. On 22 August, the minelayer *Amiral Murgescu* was heavily bombed in Constanza harbour, but she was not seriously damaged.

Light units of the Soviet Danube Flotilla supported, on 23-24 August, the crossing of the Dniester/Liman by elements of the Soviet Army and, in the following days, they entered the Danube Estuary. In the night of 23-24 August instructions were given to the naval units of Romania to cease fighting against the Soviet forces. Nonetheless, on 24 August the Soviet Air Force sank the monitor *Kogalniceanu* at Valcov. The crew, while trying to save themselves, were machine-gunned by Soviet PT-boats which had penetrated Stary Stambul. A second Romanian monitor, the *Catargiu*, was sunk on the same day, at about the same place, in the Danube Estuary, also by Soviet aircraft. On 24-25 August the *Kriegsmarine* evacuated the harbour of Constanza, scuttling the non-operational warships: submarines *U18* and *U24*, MTBs *S27, S49, S72, S149* and four submarine-chasers.

On 26 August six German Uj submarine-chasers were scuttled off Kaliakra. On 29-30 August the German warships remaining in the Romanian/Bulgarian theatre were scuttled off Varna, outside Bulgarian territorial waters.

Among the approximately 200 craft were three S-Boote, thirteen R-Boote, three Uj submarine-chasers, five AF gun ferries and ferry barges. Some of the units in the Sulina area, together with vessels of the Danube Flotilla, particularly ferry barges, went up the Danube, two Uj submarine-chasers being scuttled at Prahovo on 5 September, whilst the three last U-boats *U19*, *U20* and *U23* were scuttled by their crews less than a week later, near Erekli on the Turkish coast.

In the meantime Romanian Naval Forces had ceased fighting the Soviets in the evening of 23 August 1944 and, at the beginning of 24 August 1944, the Romanian Army, Air Force and Navy found themselves at war with German Forces.

On 30 August Soviet warships entered the harbour of Constanza. They comprised 6 armoured motor gunboats, 26 motor torpedo boats and 5 patrol boats, minesweepers being also transferred. The Soviet Command notified the Romanian Authorities at Constanza that, in the future, no Romanian vessels would be allowed to move within that zone without Soviet approval.

On 2 September the Soviet Naval Command ordered that the Romanian minelayer, *Amiral Murgescu*, escorted by four anti-submarine Soviet vessels, should put to sea at 2 o'clock the same day, and sail to the point 43°51N/29°15E, where she would be joined by five Soviet vessels on their way from Odessa, and which were to be escorted into the port of Constanza. The mission was executed, but one of the Soviet minesweepers was sunk at the point of joining, by an unknown cause. Out of about 300 men, only 36 were saved as there were many troops on board. The Romanians were accused of complicity and treachery, heavy threats were made against them, and an investigation was ordered by the Soviets. The Romanians were suspected and retaliation was expected, which happened very quickly. The Romanians, in reality, were not at all responsible for the loss of the Soviet minesweeper *Vzryv* (1939, 441 tons). The culprit was the German submarine *U-19* (Captain Ohlenburg) who had launched a 'farewell shot' before scuttling herself a few days later!

On the same day, 2 September, in the harbour of Calarasi, by the demand of the Soviet commander, the wounded Romanians in the hospital ships *Rufcu* and *Brancoveanu* were disembarked, the ships remaining at the disposal of the Soviet command. On 3 September the Soviet Army placed guards on all the vessels in the harbour of Giurgiu. On the morning of 5 September, at 04:30, Soviet troops had disarmed all the Romanian ships in Constanza harbour, putting Soviet crews on board. The non-commissioned officers and men with special duties, such as mechanics and telegraphists had been kept on board some of the vessels. The rest were set free with the advice to go home, as well as the officers. Commander A Dumbrava, Leader of the Destroyer Squadron, committed suicide the very moment his vessel was disarmed, and Lieutenant T Nicolae was severely wounded by the Soviets.

The Royal Romanian Navy had the unique distinction, in the Second World War to have been the only Navy to have fought over three years without losing a single unit of its main force (four destroyers and three submarines)!

This article covers only the activities and successes of Romanian merchant ships and warships, the lack of space preventing the many actions of the *Kriegsmarine*. An exception is the tiny navy Royal Bulgarian Navy, which deserves a few lines for, despite limited number of warships, managed to sink one Soviet submarine. The *Shch-204* (Captain Gricenko) was indeed sunk by depth-charges from the patrol boats *Belomorec* and *Chernomorec*, on 6 December 1941, 20 miles off Varna. It proves that the very few available Bulgarian warships were active in escorting convoys with their German and Romanian allies.

Some details about changes of armament on Romanian warships

In August 1944 the destroyers *Maresti* and *Marasesti* were capable of steaming only 18-20kts, but their AA gun armament had by then been improved to 4-37mm (1x2, 2x1), 5-20mm (1x4, 1x1) and 2-13,2mm (2x1), in addition to 4-120mm guns (2x2) which could not be used against aircraft. The gun armament of the torpedo boats *Sborul*, *Naluca* and *Smeul* comprised 1-66mm, 1-37mm AA and 1-20mm AA, with variants.

The gun armament of the *Ghiculescu* class gunboats comprised 1-88mm AA, 1-37mm AA and 1-20mm AA, but there were also other variants.

Being short of minelayers, the Romanian Navy decided to transform the gunboat *Lepri Remus* (ex-French *Chiffonne*, 1917, 400 tons). But she was accidentally sunk, on 11 January 1941, after having been fitted with mine rails. Her unsuitability led to her loss from an explosion during trials in the Danube.

During the war one 120mm gun was landed, two 20mm AA guns replaced the 76mm gun and two more 20mm and two 40mm AA guns were also added in the destroyers *Regele Ferdinand* and *Regina Maria*, with variants, (see photos).

Correction to 'German Type II Submarines at War', Warship 2000-2001

Pages 30 and 33: Now another date has been given for the sinking of *U-144* by the *Shch-307*, 10 August 1941 at 58°58N/21°24E.

The motor torpedo boat Vantul *in 1944. She was one of the four ex-Dutch units of the TM52 class transferred by the Germans in 1943.* (Author's collection)

THE SWEDISH TORPEDO CRUISERS

In this article **Dan Harris** examines the two classes of 'torpedo cruisers', which were built between 1895 and 1899 to a purely Swedish design. Although obsolete by 1910, they saw active service in the First World War, patrolling coastal waters, implementing Swedish neutrality and carrying out escort duties.

The Swedish Board of Admiralty's 1879 construction committee recommended the building of a series of lightly-armed vessels for scouting purposes, and to support torpedo boat groups. However, the Board did not have the financial resources and was unable to recommend implementation of the committee's proposal. The Board was probably aware of the discussions about different types of warships at the 1880 meeting of the British Institute of Civil Engineers. At that meeting, William Armstrong proposed that fleets have light, speedy, heavily-armed vessels that would be effective against armoured ships, and support torpedo boat actions. Armstrong held that such vessels should have armoured decks. Four years later, the British Admiralty authorised the building of a series of 810-ton torpedo gunboats,

armed with three 45cm (18in) TT and two 12cm (4.7in) guns. Triple expansion engines and twin screws were to give a maximum speed of 18kts.

In 1892, the Swedish Naval Defence Committee, knowing of developments in Britain, recommended the building of two types of 'torpedo cruisers'. The larger type was to patrol open coastal waters, attack and drive off enemy unarmoured vessels, carry out special scouting, and capture enemy merchant vessels. The smaller were to patrol inner waters and drive off or destroy enemy scouts and torpedo boats. In additions, this class was to act as signal repeaters for the main fleet, when smoke obscured the flagships' signals to other vessels in the line. No funds became available to build the larger vessels. Nonetheless, in 1895, parliament authorised the design of the smaller

Swedish Torpedo Cruiser Örnen. (Sjöhistoriska Museet)

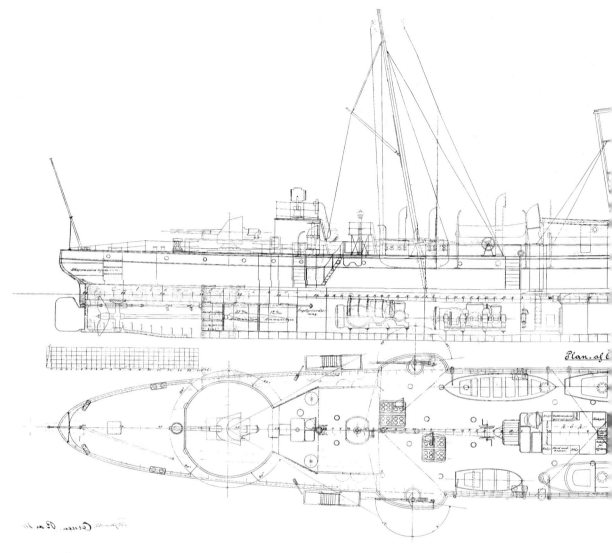

Plan and section of Örnen. (Krigsarkivet, Stockholm)

vessels. In 1896, parliament released funds for the construction of five vessels of the smaller torpedo cruiser class over the following four years.

The Navy Board proposed that the design for those new vessels be put up to open competition, with a prize for the best design. The Navy's Chief Engineer, G W Svenson (1828-1906), vigorously opposed that plan. Svenson had qualified as a ship constructor at the age of 21. Subsequently, he had been employed by the Motala, Nyköping and Oscarshamn Engineering companies. He joined the Navy's Engineering Branch in 1868, which enabled him to visit Britain, Denmark, and Germany. He designed the *Blenda* class gunboat built in the 1870s. On becoming head of the Engineering Branch in 1875, Svenson became responsible for the design of the first armoured coastal defence vessel, the *Svea*. The Board insisted that Svenson design a purely Swedish torpedo cruiser, and not one based on a foreign prototype. It is unlikely that the Chief Construction knew nothing of the British 800-ton gunboats built in 1893.

The Board decided that the new 810-ton torpedo cruisers were to have a maximum speed of 20kts. The dimensions, armament and machinery of this new class of warship were as follows:

Length: 96.2 metres
Beam: 8.2 metres
Draft: 3.2 metres
Tonnage: 810

The vessels' decks were to be of armoured steel.
The armament was to comprise the following:
One underwater bow TT for 38cm torpedoes (the torpedoes had a speed of 24kts and a range of 800m)
The torpedo room or magazine was to be lined with wood and have space for two torpedoes and warheads
2-12cm guns, one on the forecastle, the other on the stern
5-57mm QF
2 searchlights of Siemens type (to be supplied by Breguet of France)
40 cutlasses, 50 carbines and 30 revolvers

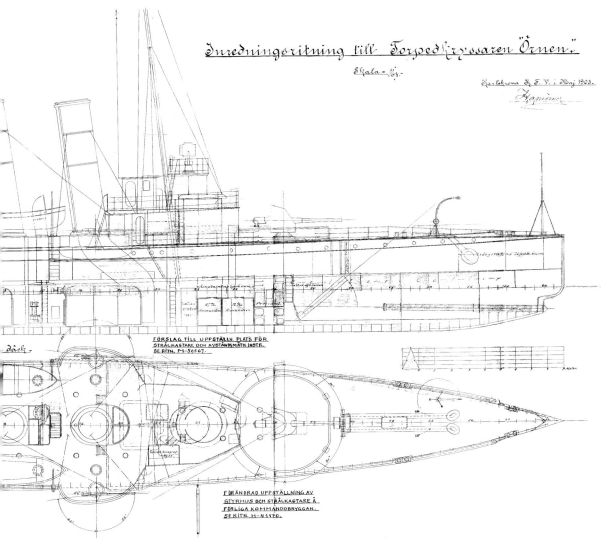

Propulsion was by two 4000hp triple-expansion engines; four fire-tube boilers provided the steam. The bunkers could hold 100 tons of coal. The complement was 104 men, including five officers. Svenson proposed horizontal engines instead of vertical. He held that horizontal engines would be less exposed to damage by shells penetrating the engine room. The vessels were to have two signalling masts.

The Board noted that Svenson's draught for the torpedo cruiser had a flat, or so-called sailing ship stern. It rejected the constructor's proposal and ordered him to submit new draughts having a rounded stern. At that first meeting with Svenson, one of the admirals outlined the cruiser stern by pressing his thumbnail on the stern section of Svenson's draught.

The first of this new class of vessels' name was originally Örn (Eagle). In 1895, Norway and Sweden were united under one sovereign, King Oscar II. The two navies had agreed not to duplicate ships' names. Since the Norwegian Navy already had a vessel called Örn, the Board agreed to the name being changed to Örnen (The Eagle). King Oscar II then signed the revised draughts

that enabled negotiations to begin with contractors for the hull and machinery.

On 7 August 1896, the Naval Administration Board entered into a contract with Motala Verkstad, a general engineering concern with plant at Motala on Lake Vätter, to build Örnen. Motala Verkstad, founded in 1822, was a builder of locomotives, and ships machinery. It, in turn, made a contract with its wholly-owned subsidiary, Lindholm's Varv Göteborg for the construction of Örnen. The specification, terms and conditions of the contract between Motala and its subsidiary were the same as those in the original agreement with the naval board.

The contracts stipulated that delivery be made within eleven months. An additional clause required the builders to provide suitable accommodation for the Board's overseers in Motala, and Göteborg. The construction contract stipulated the hull was to comprise seven watertight compartments. It required the whole of the underwater body to be covered with 12-19mm nickel steel armour. The deck was to comprise 15mm plate, the keelson under the engine and boiler rooms of 12mm and 11mm plate. The hull plating was to be from 12mm

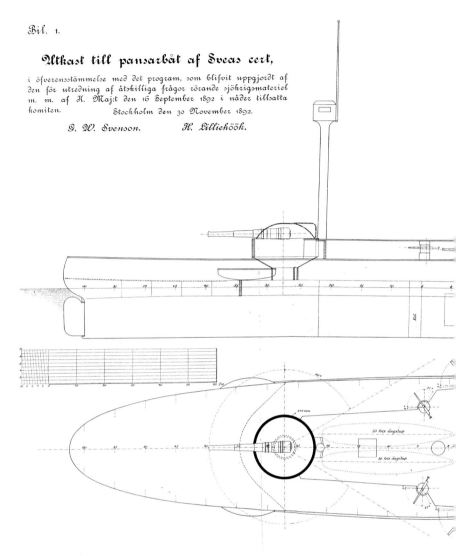

Bil. 1.

Utkast till pansarbåt af Sveas cert,

i öfverensstämmelse med det program, som blifvit uppgjordt af
den för utredning af åtskilliga frågor rörande sjökrigsmateriel
m. m. af K. Maj:t den 16 September 1892 i nåder tillsatta
komiten.   Stockholm den 30 November 1892.

G. W. Svenson.   H. Lilliehöök.

to 40mm thick over the engine and boiler rooms. It was then to diminish to 11mm. 40mm plate was to cover the steering machine area. Steel for the wheelhouse was to be 40mm thick, its roof of 12mm plate. The decks were to be covered with pine planking. All other steel was to meet British Lloyd's Registry's standards for merchant vessels.

Two 4000ihp triple expansion horizontal engines drove the two propellers. The diameters of the cylinders were 588mm, 878mm and 1311mm respectively. The stroke was 519. Other reasons for horizontal engines were that these would be below the armoured area, and thus protected. Four locomotive-type boilers with iron tubes, 12kg per cm^2 over atmosphere pressure, in two compartments, provided steam for the main engines, condensers, circulation and bilge pumps. In addition, the boilers supplied steam to the British-made steering engine placed aft of the engine rooms. Pipes supplying steam to the steering engine were to be below the water line. The rudder stock was to be of forged steel covered with 6mm thick plate.

The designed speed was 19kts. The contract contained penalty clauses should that speed be unachieved. The

contract also stipulated that the Board was to have a special representative on board in the engine room during the trial runs. *Örnen* was to make two trial runs with forced draft, each for four hours. The Board stipulated that the fuel for the trials be supplied by the Nixon Steam Navigation Coal Co.

Lindholm laid down *Örnen*'s keel in 1895, although the final contract between the Crown and Motala had not been signed. In August 1896, Lindholm launched *Örnen*. The trials took place in May 1897 where the maximum speed attained was 20.2kts. The navy took delivery the same month. Together with the armoured coast defence ship *Oden*, and torpedo boat *Galor*, *Örnen* formed part of the 1897 Stockholm Art and Industry exhibition.

When the reports of *Örnen*'s acceptance trials were available, *The Journal of the Royal Academy of Naval Sciences* in the 1898 issue published the following: '*Örnen*'s turning circle with the rudder hard over at 14 knots, and both engines at full ahead was 560 metres. In comparison, the Japanese British-built *Yashima*, 113m long with a large balanced rudder and improved stern, had a turning circle of less than $1\text{-}1/2$ times her length

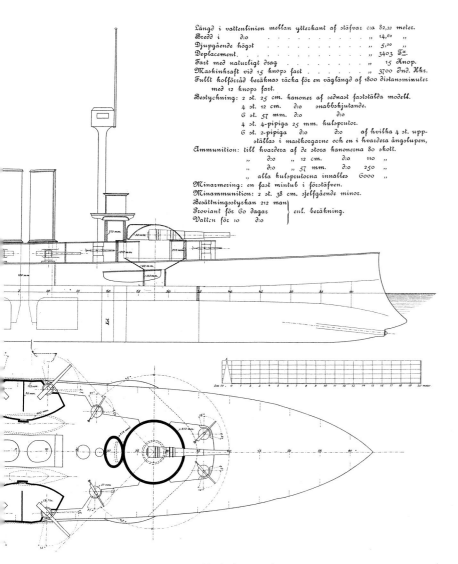

Längd i vattenlinien mellan ytterkant af stäfvar c:a 82,39 meter.
Bredd i d:o . . . . „ 14,62 „
Djupgående högst . . . . „ 5,20 „
Deplacement . . . . „ 3403 T̃.
Fart med naturligt drag . . . . „ 15 Knop.
Maskinkraft vid 15 knops fart . . . . . „ 3700 Ind. Hkr.
Fullt kolförråd beräknas räcka för en väglängd af 1800 distansminuter
    med 12 knops fart.
Bestyckning: 2 st. 25 cm. kanoner af sednast faststälda modell.
    4 st. 12 cm. d:o snabbskjutande.
    6 st. 57 mm. d:o d:o
    4 st. 4-pipiga 25 mm. kulsprutor.
    6 st. 2-pipiga d:o d:o af hvilka 4 st. upp-
        ställas i masthorgarne och en i hvardera ångslupen,
Ammunition: till hvardera af de stora kanonerna 80 skott.
    „ d:o „ 12 cm. d:o 110 „
    „ d:o „ 57 mm. d:o 250 „
    „ alla kulsprutorna innalles 6000 „
Minarmering: en fast mintub i förstäfven.
Minammunition: 2 st. 38 cm. sjelfgående minor.
Besättningsstyrkan 212 man|
Proviant för 60 dagar } enl. beräkning.
Vatten för 10 d:o |

Plans of Svea. (Krigsarkivet, Stockholm)

with helm hard over, at about 340 metres'. The Journal suggested that Örnen's large turning circle would make the underwater bow torpedo tube difficult to use. The *Journal* held that the stern's design was the cause of Örnen's large turning circle. It also held that Örnen's speed was too low for scouting: 'Foreign vessels for that purpose had speeds of almost 30 knots'.

Örnen lasted until 1947. During the 1905 dissolution of the Norwegian and Swedish union, Örnen and her sisters were stationed on the west coast. In the event that negotiations failed, the plans were for these vessels to attack Norwegian coastal batteries in the Oslo Fjord.

In December 1905, revolts against the regime and general strikes broke out throughout Russia. At that time about one hundred and fifty Swedish subjects engaged in commercial activities resided in Riga. That community, alarmed by the disturbances, requested the Swedish government to arrange for its evacuation. The crown dispatched the coastal steamer *Sophia*, and Örnen as escort, to Riga to bring Swedish citizens to safety. Some days after

the two ships' arrival, the situation in Riga stabilised, finally only forty took passage in *Sophia* to Sweden.

During the First World War, Örnen carried out continuous neutrality patrols in the Baltic. As a result of that service, Örnen needed extensive refits. In 1919, the naval command believed that available funds could be put to better use. Consequently, Örnen was laid up, and subject to minimum maintenance. Nonetheless, in 1925, the naval administration had new boilers installed and the TT removed. Örnen became a cadet training vessel during the summers of 1926-1946. Many cadets experienced stoking coal-fired boilers during those years. In 1940, four double 25mm and two 20mm anti-aircraft guns replaced the two 57mm. In addition, rails for twenty mines were fitted. Finally in 1947, the naval command struck Örnen off strength and it was sunk as a target in 1950.

In 1896, the Naval Administration Board ordered the second vessel in the Örnen-class from Kockums' yard in Malmö. The original name was to be *Tärnan* (Sea Swallow). Prior to launch, it was changed to *Jacob Bagge*.

Psilander at sea between 1900 and 1905. (Sjöhistoriska Museet)

He was the commander of the Swedish force that defeated the Danish fleets off Bornholm and Landsort in 1563. A year later, in a third engagement with the Danes and Lubeckers that ended in a draw, Bagge's flagship *Makalos* blew up and he was captured by the enemy.

Kockums were to build both the hull and engines for an inclusive price of 648,000kronor. The dimensions of *Jacob Bagge*'s hull and material specifications were the same as *Örnen*'s. Four fire-tube boilers were to provide the steam for two horizontal, triple-expansion engines, auxiliaries and the steering engine of British manufacture. The contract required Kockums to provide two signalling masts, hooks for 60 hammocks in the crew space, sixteen bunks for stokers and two Tyzack anchors. Regarding the hull plating, the contract required Kockums to make sure that each plate was not thicker at its centre than at its edges. *Örnen*'s builders' contract contained no similar requirements.

Kockums laid down *Bagge* in 1896, and launched the ship in 1898. Acceptance trials were in November 1898 and the new vessel attained the speed of 19.5kts. Strikes at Kockums had delayed completion.

During the First World War *Jacob Bagge* carried out continuous neutrality patrols. Subsequently, it was laid up from 1919 to 1925. In 1925 new boilers were installed. From 1927-1935, after the removal of the 12cm gun aft, the *Bagge* became a seaplane depot ship. In 1941, it became part of a training group attached to the naval col-

lege, and went to the scrapyard in 1947.

The Board placed the contract for the third torpedo cruiser with Lindbergs of Stockholm in September 1896. Lindbergs were to build both the hull and machinery, with exception of the steering engine, which was to be imported from Britain. The vessel's original name was *Eidern* (The Duck). It was changed to *Claes Horn*, after a Swedish Admiral who defeated the Danish fleet off Bornholm in 1564, and again near Öland in 1566.

The dimensions of hull, particulars of machinery and armament were the same as for *Örnen*. *Claes Horn*'s launch took place on 9 February 1898, and delivery in June 1899. The contract had called for completion in eleven months from its execution. The Board investigated the delays. It found that the yard had given priority to more lucrative commercial orders, and consequently, delayed *Claes Horn*'s completion.

Claes Horn served with the coastal fleet until 1912. In that year, owing to the Balkan wars and disturbances in Russia, she became a guard ship at Rattan on the northernmost Swedish/Finnish border. During 1914–1918, *Claes Horn* carried out neutrality patrols and merchant ship escort duties. Early in 1920, *Claes Horn* and a torpedo boat squadron visited Riga. On the return voyage heavy seas closed down two boats. The torpedo cruiser had to take both in tow until reaching Gotland. A 1921 survey revealed the *Claes Horn*'s poor condition. It was stricken in 1923 and sold for scrap.

The last two of the torpedo cruiser 1895 construction programme differed from the earlier vessels. In March 1898, the naval board ordered two vessels from Motala Verkstad. It arranged for the two hulls to be built by its associate Bergsund of Stockholm. The price for each vessel was 719,000kronor.

The first vessel, *Psilander*, bore the name of the commander of the 60-gun ship *Öland*, built in 1681. In 1704, close to Orfordness, eight English ships, commanded by G Whetstone, demanded *Öland* lower the topsails to acknowledge English superiority. *Öland*'s commander, Psilander refused. Consequently, an action began that lasted four and a half hours, during which *Öland* was dismasted and suffered heavy casualties. Moreover, three English vessels were severely damaged. Psilander had no choice but to strike his flag. Following diplomatic negotiations, English dockyards repaired *Öland*. Under Psilander's command, the vessel returned to friendly waters.

The Board decided the second to be called *Claes Uggla* after the admiral who commanded the fleet in successful actions against Denmark off Rugen and Bornholm in 1675. In 1676, he was denied command of the fleet because of his low birth in favour of Creutz, a noble, civil servant, and former commissioner for witchcraft. In a fleet action off Öland with the Danes and the Dutch, Uggla's *Svärdet* (The Sword) blew up, killing him and six hundred members of the crew.

The dimensions of the two vessels were as follows:

Length: 72.9m
Beam: 8.3m
Draft: 3.3m

The increased dimensions were for the accommodation of division chiefs and their staffs. Two triple-expansion 4500ihp horizontal engines driving twin screws gave a maximum speed of 20.5kts. The contract provided penalties for failure to reach 20.5kts during trials. Eight Yarrow coal-fired water-tube boilers 13kg, pressure provided the steam. Both vessels had larger funnels than the earlier ships of the class.

At the time of the order's placing, the navy had been considering using water-tube boilers instead of the fire-tube types. Water-tube boilers had the advantage of raising steam quicker than the fire-tube. The Board had the choice of two water-tube types, either the Thornycroft or the Yarrow design. It decided that the Yarrow boiler, having straight tubes, was both easier to build, and clean.

The contract required the hull's plating be of mild steel, preferably of Swedish manufacture. The thickness of steel for keel, keelson, bulkheads, deck houses, deck and hull were to be similar to *Örnen*'s. A British manufacturer was again to supply the steering engine. The specifications for the rudder and stock were as for *Örnen*. The contracts required the builders to install a capstan that could be driven by steam, or worked by hand. Contracts for the earlier-built vessels make no mention of fitting a steam-driven capstan. The anchor chain was to have 26mm thick links.

The division chief's quarters were to have one sofa, two arm chairs, a writing desk and a bookcase, the latter of teak or walnut. In addition, the builder was to install a zinc bathtub. The commander's accommodation included a bunk with drawers below, desk, bookcase, washbasin and mirror. The wardroom was to have 2 sofas and 8 chairs. The warrant officers' mess was to have nine bunks, one washbasin, one mirror, one table and eight tent chairs. The crew's space was to have 60 hooks for

Psilander in Stockholm 1908. Note the extended mainmast for wireless telegraphy equipment. (Sjöhistoriska Museet)

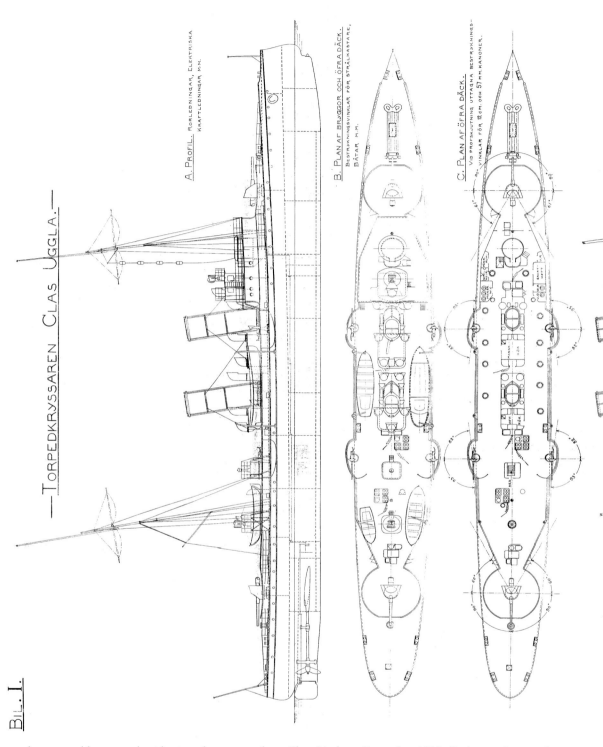

hammocks, one table covered with zinc sheeting and have two benches each for twenty-four men. The sick bay was to accommodate three. Two cells were provided to hold defaulters. The original armament was the same as *Örnen*'s. The underwater torpedo tube was removed in the late 1920s. *Psilander*'s complement was 126, *Claes Uggla*'s 112.

The Bergsund yard launched *Psilander* in November,

Claes Uggla in December 1899. Both vessels carried out two trial runs with forced draft and maintained the contract speed of 20.5kts for four hours. The contract required the builder to buy Welsh coal from the Ocean Coal Company for the trials. The Navy took delivery of *Psilander* in July and *Claes Uggla* in October 1900. Both vessels were fitted with wireless telegraphy equipment in 1904. Its range was 300 miles.

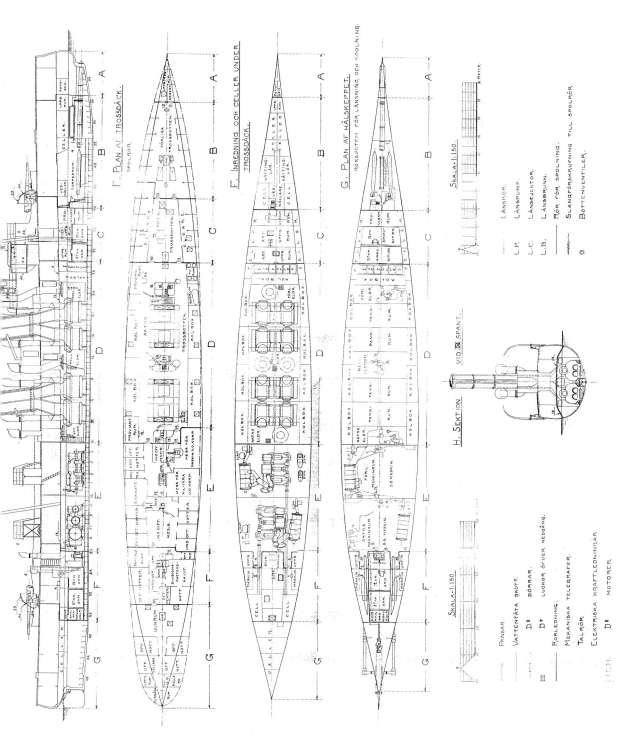

Plan and sections of Clas Uggla. (Krigsarkivet, Stockholm)

In 1905, both vessels were stationed on the west coast during the critical period of the Norwegian/Swedish Union's dissolution, to act as leaders of torpedo boat flotillas. During the November 1905 strikes and disorders in St. Petersburg, the Swedish government recalled its Minister for consultations. In December, it ordered *Psilander* to return the Minister to his post in St.

Petersburg, and to be available for the evacuation of Swedish citizens. On 12 December, after a voyage of 290 nautical miles. *Psilander* anchored off Kronstadt and fired a salute of 21 guns, which after some delay, was answered by the fort. *Psilander* fired a second salute of 17 guns for the Russian Admiral commanding the base. It was not answered. *Psilander*'s commander learnt, on making his

Claes Uggla underway in the Stockholm skerries during 1916. Astern is a Hugin *class torpedo boat.* (Sjöhistoriska Museet)

official call on the Admiral, that owing to the troubles all remaining ammunition and breech-blocks of vessels guns stationed in the port had been removed elsewhere. *Psilander* continued to St. Petersburg and landed the envoy. As there seemed to be no immediate danger to Swedish citizens, the Minister ordered *Psilander* to return to home waters.

Both *Psilander* and *Claes Uggla* took part in neutrality patrols and escort duties during the First World War. In June 1917, *Claes Uggla* grounded while exercising with torpedo boats off Sundsvall in the Gulf of Bothnia. Attempts by the torpedo boats and salvage tugs failed to move her. Divers found that rocks had penetrated the hull. The salvors proposed to blast the rocks holding the vessel after the salvage of guns, and other moveable equipment. Unfortunately in early September, a south-easterly gale lifted *Claes Uggla* and broke the hull in two.

In 1919, *Psilander* took part in the demolition of Russian fortifications on the Åland islands. In 1923, *Psilander* and two torpedo boats visited Stralsund, Germany. From 1933 to 1935, *Psilander* was attached to the naval academy's training squadron to teach cadets seamanship and pilotage in confined waters. The cadets were also to gain experience of the engine room and stoke hold. In 1935, *Psilander* visited Estonia's Pernau, however, although the cadets and officers were well received by the city fathers and invited to an excellent dinner, at its conclusion, the guests were surprised to learn that they had to pay the dinner bill! *Psilander* was laid up in 1936 and stricken in 1937. Used as a target, it was sunk by a 45cm torpedo in 1939.

The low speed of the *Örnen* class made them already obsolete by 1910. Two proved useful for neutrality patrols and escort duties during the Second World War. The two retained, being coal burners and thus useful for training schools and miscellaneous duties, enabled valuable oil stocks to be reserved for front line vessels.

Sources
Naval Defence Policies
Amiralitets Kollegiets Historia Vol. IV, (Stockholm: 1980)
Kryssarer-Borgenstam et al, (Värnamo: 1993)
Svenska Flottans Vol. 3, (Malmö: 1943)
Tidskrift Sjovasendet, (Karlskrona: 1896)

Construction Machinery & Armament
Contract Amiralitets Kollegiet Motala/Lindholm 1896 re *Örnen* K.A.
Contract Amiralitets Kollegiet Kockums Varv 1896 re *J. Bagge* K.A.
Contract Amiralitets Kollegiet Motala/Bergsund 1896 re *Psilander* & *Uggla* K.A.
Contract Amiralitets Kollegiet Lindberg 1896 re *Claes Horn* K.A.
G Halldin, *Skepps Byggmastare*, (Malmö: 1948)
SvenskaÖrlogs Fartygs 1855-1905 Westerlund et al 1992

General Trials – Service Lives, etc.

Kryssarer, Borgenstam et al   (Värnamo: 1993)
Tidskrift i Sjovasendet   (Karkskrona: 1897)
Tidskrift i Sjovasendet   (Karkskrona: 1898)
Tidskrift i Sjovasendet   (Karkskrona: 1899)

SOME THOUGHTS ON BRITISH MINES OF THE FIRST WORLD WAR

In this article **Eur Ing David K Brown, RCNC** will explore the reasons why British mines were ineffective at the outbreak of the war and shows how they became a major cause of U-boat losses by 1918, with an even brighter future.[1]

Fisher

Sir John Fisher's criticism of British mines in the early years of the war must be contrasted with his personal involvement in their development and problems. His keen interest in technology was shown early in his career when in 1868 he published *A Short Treatise on Electricity and the Management of Electric Torpedoes*.[2] (Note that at that date mines were referred to as torpedoes; electric torpedoes were mines controlled from a shore station). In 1869 he visited German mine warfare establishments and does not seem to have been impressed, particularly opposing their 'free' mines (as opposed to controlled).

Later (ca1873) he was a strong supporter of the plan to separate *Vernon* as a Torpedo school from the Gunnery school, *Excellent*. A Committee on Torpedoes was set up in 1874 and though Fisher was not a fulltime member he was directed to give as much assistance as his other duties permitted. In 1874 Dr Albert Hertz visited *Vernon* and offered the RN the use of his 'Horn' firing device. This offer was turned down by the Torpedo Committee and there is no evidence that Fisher dissented either then or later when he re-visited Germany. As Director of Naval Ordnance (DNO), Fisher directed an attempt by *Vernon* to design an independent mine in 1877 which was not successful.

British pre war mines

In 1932 Admiral Sir Reginald Bacon provided a sympathetic account of the problems with pre-war British designs of mine.[3] Some twenty years before the war there was an 'electric' mine which contained a wet battery, a detonator and a circuit closer. The closer depended on a gap which would be closed by mercury splashed up when the mine was struck. There were many problems: the mercury oxidised, the battery ran down quickly in the damp atmosphere and the contents corroded, so it was decided that 'electricity' had no place in a mine. This is an all too common problem in technical decision mak-

ing. Failures which, though serious, may be quite easily cured, are generalised and a high-level decision is made to avoid a whole area of technology, such as 'electricity'.

A new mine, known as the naval spherical mine, had been designed in 1905 and 1000 were ordered.[4] A number of problems were soon recognised and slow progress was made in curing them. An improved method of depth-keeping was introduced in which mine and sinker sank together until they reached a pre-set depth, at which a pressure sensor would release the mine while the sinker continued to sink to the bottom. This still restricted the speed of laying and, later, it would be found that it was not very reliable.

The original firing gear was found to be too sensitive and liable to fire prematurely in a seaway. In 1913 a new design was approved in which the movement of an external firing lever released a cocked spring, so firing a percussion detonator. This implied that the firing mechanism was ready to function when it was inserted into the mine prior to laying and may have contributed to the numerous prematures.[5] These mines remained unsatisfactory and there were numerous cases in which German submarines reported hitting a mine which failed to explode. Depth-keeping was unsatisfactory and the sinkers were too light, allowing the mine to move in a strong current such as that in the Straits of Dover. Despite these defects a large order for mines was placed in October 1914. About half of these were of the 'British Elia' type based on an Italian design but with a different firing pistol.[6] This was said to function satisfactorily but was expensive and difficult to make.

A mechanical mine was devised which worked well in trials against surface ships where the fairly large beam gave a solid thump to the mine when struck. The narrower submarine gave a lighter blow and the mine often failed to detonate. No trials had been held against submarines.

The Royal Navy noted the successes due to mines in the Russo-Japanese War and set to work to design an effective means of sweeping.[7] In 1906 Captain Ogilvy proposed the use of a sweep wire between two ships spread by otters. This was soon proved to be viable and twelve torpedo gunboats were converted to sweepers. In 1908 Fisher felt confident in telling the Committee for Imperial Defence that mines could easily be swept. Later, a trawler reserve was established. The belief that mines could easily be swept contributed to neglect of British mine design and production.

In considering the lack of development of British mines before the war it is essential to remember that the early operational submarines of the 'A', 'B' and 'C' class were seen as 'mobile mines' for the defence of harbours and anchorages largely eliminating the need for moored mines. Offensive mining in enemy waters was thought to be impracticable, which it was with the slow old cruisers converted for mine laying.

The British H II Mine

This was designed at *Vernon* in 1916, produced in 1917, and was very closely based on the German design. It was a contact mine using the Herz horn, invented by Dr Hertz of the German Mine Defence Committee in 1869. The Hertz horn contained the components of an electric battery, separated from each other until contact was made.

The horn itself contained a glass bottle of a bichromate solution which would break when hit by a ship. The cell was then completed with a carbon plate and a zinc plate and would generate about 1.8 volts. This current would fuse a thin platinum wire embedded in mercury fulminate, which would detonate a dry gunpowder primer and hence the main charge; 320lbs of TNT. The Herz horn was dry until struck and the circuit was continuous, overcoming all the old electrical problems. Almost certainly

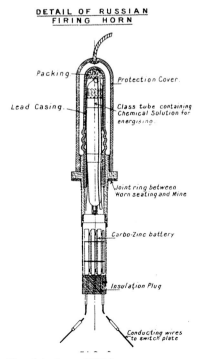

Detail of a Herz firing horn. (CPL)

the reason for the delay in production was the national shortage of TNT. Toluene was used before the war in the dye industry but was not made in the UK and imported from Germany. It took time to set up the necessary plant and TNT was scarce even in 1917. It seems that mines (and depth-charges) were given high priority second only to shells for the army.

Effectiveness of Mines

Mines were one of the best ways of sinking U-boats and fear of mines limited the freedom of action of submarines considerably. Only in the last year of the war did the depth charge overtake the mine as the principal weapon.

Sinking of U Boats

Year	By Mines	All causes
1914-16	10	46
1917	20	63
1918	18	69
Total	48	178

Note: 'All causes' includes 10 UC-boats sunk by accidental explosion of own mines.

The Acoustic Mine[8]

In 1917, A B Wood, a brilliant young physicist who would dominate British underwater acoustics for about 40 years, was investigating the performance of hydrophones at the Admiralty Experiment Station, Parkeston Quay (Harwich). He identified a number of applications for hydrophones, one of which was as the firing mechanism for an acoustic mine. A hydrophone was laid in the entrance gate to Harwich which worked two relays, one a very sensitive one which would warn of an approaching ship and one with a coarser setting which indicated that the ship was overhead by ringing a bell. Destroyers and surfaced submarines rang the bell at 200-300 yards, the current rising to several hundred micro-amps.

By May 1917 is was clear that an acoustic mine was indeed practicable and a formal proposal was submitted to the Board of Invention and Research, chaired by Fisher. The proposal was greeted with enthusiasm and given high priority though development trials were not able to start until October 1917. The 'A' attachment, as it was known, was intended to be fitted to the standard H II moored mine, just entering service. The magnetic mine with a code name of 'M Sinker' (usually known to its designers as M destructor) was being developed at the same time and there was useful cross-fertilisation. The magnetic firing gear could not be used in a moored mine as the swaying in a current would activate it.

Early trials involved measuring the sound distribution round various types of ship to identify the sensitivity required. The early trials went very well but a test of its liability to counter-mining was an unpleasant shock. The

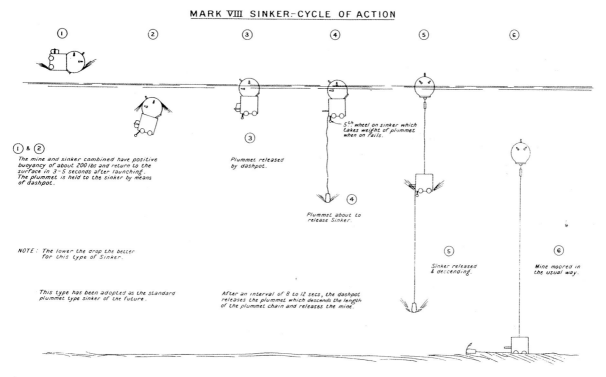

The method of laying a British moored mine on a Mk VII sinker. (CPL)

explosion of a nearby charge dished the diaphragm and broke the carbon granule microphone, while more distant explosions activated the firing mechanism. These problems were overcome; a thicker diaphragm, a vibrating contact in place of the fragile microphone and a delay mechanism which would cut out the firing circuit for a minute after the shock wave from an explosion reached the mine.[9]

The 'A' attachment went into production and by the end of the war several thousand were ready for laying. By this time Wood had designed an improved acoustic firing unit, the shunt relay, which was simpler and had a longer life; it was to form the basis of the British Second World War acoustic mine.

The Antenna Mine (US Mk 6)[10]

The final plan for the Northern Barrage envisaged a total length of 244 miles of which the middle section, to be laid by the US Navy was 134 miles, in deep water. It was hoped to mine this to a depth of 300 feet and it soon became clear that the number of contact mines needed would be astronomic. However, the Bureau of Ordnance suggested the use of the novel antenna mine. This worked on the principle that a current would be generated when two dissimilar metal plates (electrodes) were immersed in salt water (the electrolyte) and connected. In the case of the Mk 6 a copper plate on the mine served as one electrode, the sea was the electrolyte, whilst the steel hull of a ship (U-boat) formed the other electrode. A copper wire, supported by a float, ran up from the mine

and a similar wire ran down towards the sinker; it seems that the original length of each wire was 50ft. If a steel hull touched either wire, the circuit would be completed and the mine, with a charge of 300lbs of TNT, would explode.[11] Thus a single mine would cover a depth of 100ft reducing the number of mines required by a factor of at least three.

In view of the urgency, the mines were put into production with little full-scale testing and, when laying commenced, many problems came to light. During the first lay a number of mines exploded, often detonating a number of neighbours.[12] A number of safety devices were fitted which reduced the problem, though it was never eradicated. Even before laying started, it was decided to limit the lower antenna and it was soon found that swaying of the top buoy would break the upper wire, which had to be reduced in length to 35ft.

At the end of the war the US Navy agreed to sweep these mines and further problems were revealed.[13] The new US Navy minesweepers of the 'Bird' class had steel hulls, which could actuate the mine. It was thought that it might be necessary to use wooden-hulled vessels but a trial showed that they were unlikely to be strong enough. Finally, an 'Electric Protection Device' was devised in which the positive terminal of the ship's dynamo was earthed and the negative terminal to an insulated cable several hundred feet long with a few feet bare at the far end. This raised the electro-potential of the hull to that of copper and prevented the mine from activating.[14] It was also found during trials that a very good contact with a steel hull was necessary. It must be assumed that had the war continued a similar protective device would have been developed for submarines. The full story of the difficult and dangerous clearance operation cannot be told here but when it was completed in September 1919 21,352 US mines had been cleared, leaving 30,685 unaccounted for![15] One trawler was sunk and twenty vessels damaged during the operation with a considerable number of casualties.

The Magnetic Mine (M Sinker)[16]

The magnetic mine 'Sinker Mk I (M)', or M Destructor as it was known informally, was developed at Dovercourt during 1917.[17] The firing mechanism involved two bar magnets, one with a large moment of inertia and the other small. There was a time delay after laying to allow the magnets to settle in the North-South direction after which a steel hull passing overhead would deflect the small magnet relative to the larger one and cause the mine to explode. The mine itself was a simple truncated cone of concrete containing 1000lbs of TNT. It was carried on a concrete trolley running on non-magnetic wheels which separated on laying. There was a safety pin to hold the battery switch on 'Off' before laying and another safety switch worked off a soluble sal ammoniac plug, which should have ensured that it could not explode for forty minutes after laying.

Wood tells how he was teased by the magnetic team that their mine did not need elaborate counter mining devices as did his acoustic mine. However, a countermining trial was arranged with the firing unit on the bottom wired to a bell in the trials ship, which would ring if the unit was activated. Half a ton of TNT was exploded on the bottom and, to the designers' chagrin the bell rang on for a full minute. Wood's anti countermining unit was hurriedly adapted for the magnetic mine, but, it was at best a partial remedy.

The world's first magnetic mines were laid by six destroyers on 8 April 1918 some 8 miles north of Dunkirk. There were 234 mines laid 300ft apart and at least two exploded prematurely. The next lay was on 22 August, when five destroyers laid 198 mines 17 miles north of Zeebruge. This time most exploded prematurely, accounts vary from 98 to 131. A test lay of forty mines was carried out by a single destroyer on 6 September 21 miles north-west of Ostend, with thirteen prematures. No more were laid before the Armistice. Some were laid in Soviet waters during 1919.

Reports differ on their effectiveness and on the German reaction. Grant[18] says that the Germans came out three days after the April lay with magnets. Burton says the Germans did not know till long after the war that we had used magnetic mines. Neither suggest any kills. The 1939 German mine still used a dip needle measuring the magnitude of the vertical field; the Royal Navy had gone to the variation of the horizontal field, much more difficult to counter.

Notes

1 This article is drawn from an early draft of a book on Anti-Submarine Warfare in World War I.

2 R F Mackay, *Fisher of Kilverstone*, (Oxford: OUP, 1973), p.44 points out that this book was based almost entirely on Professor Abel's lectures at Woolwich.

3 Admiral Sir R Bacon, *The Concise Story of the Dover Patrol*, (London: Hutchinson 1932), p.65.

4 J S Cowie, *Mines, Minelayers and Minelaying*, (Oxford: OUP, 1949), p.36.

5 This could have contributed to the accidental loss of *Princess Victoria*.

6 Cowie, *op cit.*, p.47.

7 D K Brown, *The Grand Fleet, Warship Design and Development 1906-1922*, (London: Chatham, 1999), pp.27, 136.

8 This note is based on The A B Wood Memorial Number, *Journal of Naval Science* July 1965, (mostly an autobiography).

9 This delay circuit was later fitted to the magnetic mine.

10 This section is largely based on Cowie, *op cit.*, and H C Armstrong, 'The Removal of the North Sea Mine Barrage', *Warship International*, 2/1988, Toledo

11 Several writers refer to this mine as a 'magnetic' which, of course, it was not.

12 Armstrong, *op cit.*, says 4392 mines exploded prematurely.

13 *Ibid.*

14 The steel sweep wire frequently caused the mine to detonate.

15 Reports from U-boats crossing the barrier frequently mention hearing explosions and it is likely that most of the missing mines self detonated. Some were washed up in Norway.

16 T Burton, 'The Origins of the Magnetic Mine', *Warship 5*, (London: 1978).

17 Wood refers to F E Smith as the designer with Prof McLennon and R W Paul.

18 R Grant, (London: Putnam, 1964), *U-Boats Destroyed*.

THE FRENCH CRUISER *ALGÉRIE*

The last of the seven 10,000tW Washington Treaty cruisers built for the *Marine Nationale* between the wars, *Algérie* was seen by many as marking the apogee of Treaty cruiser construction. Here **John Jordan** examines the developments of a ship which, with her single funnel, distinctive 'tower' superstructure and 110mm hull armour, hade a considerable impact abroad.

*A*lgérie was radically different in design and appearance from her predecessors. The first of the *Marine Nationale*'s Treaty cruisers, *Duquesne* and *Tourville* (1924 Programme), were arguably the world's most extreme examples of the imbalance between speed, gunpower and protection inherent in the type. Armed with the standard four twin 203mm (8in) turrets, and with a designed speed of 34.2kts (more than 36kts was achieved on trials), they were given minimal protection: a 30mm 'box' around the main magazines and steering gear, and plating of similar thickness on the conning tower and turrets, the overall weight of protection being a mere 460 tonnes. The machinery spaces, which accounted for much of the ships' length, were virtually unprotected.

Finding sufficient weight for protection within the 10,000-ton straightjacket imposed by the Washington Treaty was to challenge the constructors of the major navies throughout the 1920s. The first ships built for the US Navy, the British Royal Navy, the Imperial Japanese Navy, and the French and Italian Navies were all markedly similar in their general characteristics. All were seen as essentially 'eggshells armed with hammers', fast ships with heavy firepower which would nevertheless be unable to sustain an engagement with their own kind because of their flimsy construction and light protection.

Algérie as completed on 18 October 1934, with her original funnel cap. She entered service the following day, subsequently becoming flagship of the 1ʳᵉ Escadre at Toulon. (Marius Bar)

As long as it was possible to sustain the illusion that these ships were 'scouts' for the heavy ships of the battle-fleets, with an ancillary rôle of protecting sea lines of communication, the lack of armour protection was acceptable. It could be justified by the argument that their most likely opponents would be the small 'fleet' cruisers armed with a handful of 6in/150mm and 4in/105mm guns which proliferated prior to and during the First World War, or war-built fleet destroyers and torpedo boats, armed with 4in/105mm guns. Against even these smaller-calibre weapons the 20-30mm plating of *Duquesne* and *Tourville* would have provided little more than splinter protection.

By the late 1920s, however, the naval situation had evolved in ways which few had anticipated. In the absence of new capital ship construction the naval 'arms race' - such as it was in a time of great financial stringency - was becoming increasingly focused on 10,000-ton cruiser construction. The ageing battlefleets of the major powers, for the most part capable of barely 20kts, were being fast left behind by technology, and some navies now envisaged that their cruiser squadrons would be the first major forces engaged in any large-scale naval action, with the battlefleet pottering along some distance in the rear. This was certainly true of the two Pacific powers, the United States and Japan, and these ideas were gaining currency in the Mediterranean, where the French *Marine Nationale* would be opposed by the fast, powerful cruisers being built for the Italian Navy. Indeed, when in the late 1920s the Italian and French navies contemplated using the limited battleship tonnage made available to them in the wake of the Washington Treaty, both drew up designs for fast, battlecruiser type ships intended to hunt down and destroy Treaty cruisers (see 'The origins of *Dunkerque* and *Strasbourg*', *Warship 1999-2000*, pp.99-114).

Moreover, the destroyers of the postwar generation were no longer the feebly-armed 800-ton ships of the First World War. The standard postwar destroyer guns were 120mm (4.7in), 127mm (5in) or even 130mm (5.1in), firing shells nearly twice as heavy as their predecessors (25-32kg as compared with 15kg for the 100/105mm gun). The latest ships of the French *contre-torpilleur* type were armed with 138.6mm guns firing a 40kg shell, and these ships would soon be opposed by the small Italian cruisers of the 'Condottieri' type, armed with eight 152mm (6in) guns each firing a 55kg shell. The 6in-gun cruiser was also soon to be adopted enthusiastically by the Royal Navy, which saw the type as the answer to its trade protection problem (the 8in Treaty cruiser was simply too costly to build in the numbers required).

Thus the choice was no longer between building ships which could be protected against 8in shells (an impossibility on the displacement), and ships with splinter protection against small-calibre gunfire. The Treaty cruisers could now be opposed by a whole plethora of intermediate weapons mounted in nominally inferior vessels, all of which were capable of disabling a lightly-armoured warship.

The pace of these developments was so rapid that they were incorporated into Treaty cruiser construction as it was developing. The third French Treaty cruiser, *Suffren*, had 50mm (2in) side armour over all her vital spaces (in compensation power was reduced from 120,000shp on four shafts to 90,000shp on three shafts, for a maximum designed speed of 31.6kts). The next ship, *Colbert*, had a similar level of protection, while in *Foch* and *Dupleix*

Algérie at Brest on 10 August 1934 just prior to entering service in October of the same year. (CPL)

there was an internal armoured caisson covering the magazines, shell rooms and machinery spaces, with side thicknesses of 54mm and 60mm respectively and an armoured deck of 18-20mm in the former increasing 30mm in the latter. In *Dupleix* the total weight of protection reached 1553 tonnes (almost four times that of *Duquesne*).

The next cruiser design, officially designated C4, was originally to have been a development of the *Dupleix* (C3). Although the 60mm armour of the latter was considered more than adequate against the 120mm (4.7in) guns of the latest Italian fleet destroyers and 'scouts' (the twelve *esploratori* of the *Navigatori* class), the Italians had laid down their first four 6in cruisers of the *Alberto di Giussano* class in 1928, and more would surely follow. The French Naval Staff therefore demanded an 'immune zone' against 155mm shellfire between 15,000m and 20,000m, the probable range of engagement for their Treaty cruisers in the relatively clear conditions of visibility prevailing in the Mediterranean theatre. It was subsequently calculated that this would require an additional 400 tonnes of armour over *Dupleix*, which could be bought only by further reducing installed horsepower to 84,000shp (a two-shaft installation was proposed giving a maximum speed of 31kts).

However, the internal 'box citadel' adopted for the protection of magazines and machinery in the *Dupleix* and her immediate predecessors was criticised as providing insufficient protection against underwater explosions. It also contributed little to hull strength, which was to prove a problem when the earlier ships entered service; the light scantlings resulted in abnormal working of the hulls amidships, leading to leaks from oil-fuel bunkers and reserve feed tanks. France's seventh Treaty cruiser, which would later be named *Algérie*, was therefore a totally new design from the keel up, incorporating the latest thinking and taking advantage of the latest developments in technology.

The earlier ships were elegant ships with a raised forecastle (for good sea keeping), tripod masts and twin, raked widely-spaced funnels. *Algérie* marked a complete break with this layout. The forecastle deck was deleted saving 80 tonnes; this would be at the cost of inferior sea keeping. The heavy tripod foremast of the earlier ships was replaced by a tower structure, atop which were located the main and secondary fire control directors. Developments in superheated steam propulsion technology permitted a reduction from eight boilers in four boiler rooms to six boilers in three boiler rooms. The three boiler rooms were adjacent, permitting the exhaust uptakes to be led up into a single, broad raked funnel. The adoption of superheated steam propulsion brought a weight saving of 275 tonnes (1335t vs 1610t) over the initial C4 design, and reduced the length of the ship which would need to be protected.

There was considerable debate over whether the ship should have three propeller shafts, as in her immediate predecessors, or revert to the four shafts of *Duquesne* and *Tourville*. The three-shaft arrangement had its attractions, as it permitted a finer hull with less resistance. However, four shafts were eventually adopted in order to reduce the power loading on each shaft, to optimise power transmission, and to reduce cavitation.

The internal *caisson* of *Dupleix* was expensive in terms of weight of armour, as the vertical sides had to extend down virtually to the keel of the ship. By reverting to an external belt the height of vertical armour could be reduced from 6-6.5 metres to 3.75-4.5 metres, for a saving of 370 tonnes. All these savings could then be invested in the substantially thicker armour required if the new ship were to resist 6in shellfire. The result was a main belt 110mm (4in) thick, topped by an armoured deck with a thickness of 80mm (3in) over the magazines, shell rooms and machinery spaces. Moreover it was possible to provide 70-100mm armour plating for the conning tower and the main turrets. In *Algérie* the total weight devoted to protection attained 2035 tonnes, or 20 per cent of standard displacement; moreover, the disposition of the armour was far superior to that of the ship's predecessors, in which incremental improvements had been made in a purely *ad hoc* fashion, as and when additional weight became available.

These achievements are all the more impressive in that the French, like the British and the Americans, succeeded in keeping the standard displacement of all their cruisers, including *Algérie*, within the 10,000-ton Treaty limit. By contrast, the Italian and Imperial Japanese Navies, which attempted to produce well-armoured cruisers with similar capabilities, largely exceeded the limits. The Italian *Zara* class weighed in at 11,300 tons, and the Japanese *Atago* class was also found postwar to have had a standard displacement as built of 11,350 tons. The German Navy, which subsequently modelled its three permitted 'treaty' cruisers of the *Admiral Hipper* class on the *Algérie*, produced a ship with a standard displacement of 14,050 tons!

Armament

The main armament of *Algérie* was identical to that of the earlier Treaty cruisers: 8-203mm/50 cal Model 1924 guns mounted in twin turrets fore and aft, firing the standard range of armour piercing (OPf) and high explosive (OEA) shells. The earlier model shells weighed 123.1kg and 123.82kg respectively, and were fired using two half-charges with a combined weight of 53kg. Muzzle velocity was 850m/s, giving a range of 31,400 metres at the maximum elevation of 45°, and 28,000 metres at 30°. The shells of the next series, which had longer bases, were lighter and weighed 119.07kg and 119.72kg respectively. The last AP shell developed was the Model 1936, which weighed 134kg; it used a 47kg charge giving a lower muzzle velocity of 820m/s. The firing cycle was theoretically 12-15 seconds; four rounds per minute was generally attained in service.

The gun mounting and hoist arrangements were also essentially unchanged. The guns were in separate cradles with individual toothed elevating arcs. There was a 22.5hp electric training motor with hydraulic drive, and a 30hp motor with hydraulic drive for elevation. The guns could be elevated to +45° and depressed to -5°, with loading carried out between +10° and -5°, employing catapult rammers. The magazines and shell rooms fed three-tier dredger hoists (each holding one shell and two half-charges) serving an upper working chamber, where shells and charges were transferred to the two upper cage hoists. These came up outside each gun, and the shells were transferred to swinging arms which locked to the guns for loading.

The secondary armament of twelve 100mm guns in twin mountings was a marked improvement on the HA installation of earlier French Treaty cruisers. The early ships had been armed with 8-75mm single guns, while *Colbert*, *Foch*, and *Dupleix* had 90mm (single in the first two, but twin mountings in *Dupleix*). The adoption of the 100mm calibre served to bring the *Marine Nationale* into line with the other major European navies, which from the outset had favoured a secondary armament with a genuine dual-purpose capability.

The 100mm/45 Model 1930 was developed specifically for *Algérie*. In the low-angle rôle it fired the OPf Model 1928, a fixed round weighing 24kg. The corresponding HE shell was the OEA Model 1928, which weighed 22.7kg. Starshell Model 1921/31 could also be fired to illuminate a potential surface target.

The guns were in a common cradle which allowed an elevation of +80° to -10°. Maximum range in the anti-surface rôle was 15,600-15,800 metres at an elevation of 45°, with a ceiling in the anti-aircraft rôle of 10,000 metres, and the firing cycle was around 6 seconds. The twin mounting Model 1931 had a 5mm shield and was equipped with an optical sight, and aiming and correction systems designed to follow aircraft with a maximum speed of 250km/h, a figure considered adequate at the time. It weighed 13.5 tonnes.

Algérie was to have been equipped with the new automatic 37mm Model 1935, but this weapon was subject to numerous development problems and its introduction into service was delayed (it was eventually cancelled). Four single 37mm Model 1925 guns were therefore fitted as a temporary measure, two being installed on the forecastle and two on the quarterdeck. They were complemented by Hotchkiss 13.2mm/76 machine guns Model 1929, in the quadruple mounting Model 1929 first installed in the *Dupleix*. There were four mountings, disposed at the four corners of the shelter deck fore and aft of the secondary 100mm mountings. Like the machine guns of other navies they were to prove too lightweight to be effective against modern aircraft.

The armament was completed by two triple TT mountings Model 1929T mounted at upper-deck level amidships, firing the now-standard 550mm torpedo Model 1923D. A total of nine torpedoes was carried: six in the tubes and a further three reserve torpedoes in a steel-plated locker adjacent to the torpedo workshop. In wartime the torpedo warheads were fitted but not fuzed; in peacetime they were stowed in deck-edge lockers, to facilitate rapid disposal in the event of an on-board fire. The torpedoes were handled by the aircraft crane, and manoeuvred for loading in the tubes using trolleys on a system of deck rails.

A starboard quarter view of Algérie *taken in February 1935. Note the Gourdou-Leseurre GL 812 floatplane in its 'parking' position forward of the twin 100mm AA mountings. This led a number of reference sources to state that there was a second catapult to starboard, but the official drawings make it clear that this was not the case. (Marius Bar)*

Table 1: ALGÉRIE

Name	Builder	Laid down	Launched	In service
1930 Programme				
Algérie	Arsenal de Brest	19.03.31	21.05.32	19.10.34

Characteristics (as completed)

Displacement:	10,000 tons standard
	10,950 tonnes normal
	13,677 tonnes full load
Length:	180 metres (pp), 186.2 metres (oa)
Beam:	20 metres
Draught:	6.15 metres
Machinery:	Six Indret small-tube boilers, 27kg/cm^2 (325°);
	four-shaft Rateau-Bretagne geared steam turbines for 84,000shp
Speed:	31kts (designed)
Oil fuel:	2935 tonnes; radius 8000nm at 15kts, 4000nm at 27kts
Armament:	8-203mm/50 Model 1924 in twin mountings Model 1929;
	12-100mm/45 Model 1930 HA in twin mountings Model 1931;
	4-37mm/50 Model 1925 AA in single mountings;
	16-13.2mm/76 Model 1929 Hotchkiss MG in quad mountings Model 1929;
	6-TT for 550mm torpedoes Model 1923D in triple mountings Model 1929T (nine torpedoes)
Aircraft:	2-GL 812 HY seaplanes
Protection:	belt: 110mm
	deck: 30-80mm
	CT: 100mm sides, 70mm roof
	turrets: 100mm face, 70mm sides, 50-85mm rear, 70mm roof
Complement:	746 as flagship

Fire control

The adoption of a tower superstructure in place of the sturdy tripod foremast of the earlier ships allowed the three principal fire control directors (main armament plus two secondary) to be carried high above the waterline, permitting accurate ranging at the maximum distance. The upper platform of the tower was 25 metres above the waterline, with the main Director Control Tower (DCT) at its summit, topped by a short topmast for the riding lights and the long radio aerial, and the secondary DCTs on platforms extending directly beneath it to port and starboard. The main DCT was initially equipped with a coincidence range-finder with a 5-metre base and a stereoscopic RF with a 3-metre base, the secondary DCTs with a single stereoscopic RF with a 3-metre base. Access to the directors was via ladders in a central tube, which divided into three at its upper end and which also contained the fire control cabling.

The principal drawback to this arrangement was the concentration of weights high in the ship. The main DCT weighed 10.5 tonnes (including personnel), and each of the secondary directors 5.5 tonnes. This was presumably deemed acceptable because of the improvement in stability due to the heavy armouring of the hull and the reduced freeboard resulting from the suppression of the forecastle deck. Nevertheless every effort was made to ensure that the tower structure was as light as possible. Its outer structure was of light steel plating on a framework of T-bars, and all access ladders were constructed of lightweight duralumin alloy.

Besides the main DCT there were RFs with a 5-metre base on three of the four 203mm turrets (SOM coincidence RF on turrets II and IV and an OPL stereoscopic model on III), all of which could be trained independently up to a maximum of 13°. There was also a 3-metre RF on the roof of the conning tower. Data from these instruments was coordinated by a calculator located in the main transmitting station low in the hull, with fire control being exercised from the conning tower.

The calculator positions for the secondary directors were located beneath the conning tower, where there was also a transmitting station with remote power control (RPC) for the 100mm mountings. Fire control for the small AA weapons was limited to four 1-metre range-finders, two of which were located fore and aft at upper-deck level in close proximity to the 37mm guns, the other two being located on the shelter deck to port and starboard of the searchlight tower.

Three 1.2 metre 'combat' searchlight projectors for night firing were installed on a tower which effectively took the place of the second funnel. The centreline projector was located on the top platform, the remaining two being located directly beneath on platforms projecting to port and starboard, permitting two projectors to be trained on either beam. The outer projectors were controlled via remote power control (RPC) from the secondary directors, the centreline projector being directed

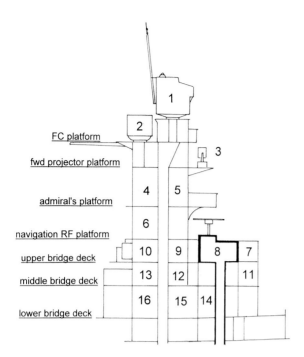

FC platform

fwd projector platform

admiral's platform

navigation RF platform

upper bridge deck

middle bridge deck

lower bridge deck

Layout of the Command Spaces
The tower structure adopted for Algérie enabled the command spaces to be arranged in a more logical and effective way than in previous ships. A similar arrangement was subsequently adopted for the fast battleships Dunkerque and Strasbourg, and all three ships were to serve as force flagships at some stage of their respective careers. (John Jordan)

Key to Command Spaces:

1. main DCT	9. chart room
2. secondary DCT	10. CO's day cabin
3. 0.75m searchlight projector	11. Admiral's compass bridge
4. operations room	12. W/T office (reception)
5. Admiral's bridge	13. Admiral's day cabin
6. optical control station	14. HA transmitting station
7. CO's compass bridge	15. HA RPC station
8. conning tower	16. officers' day cabin

from special sights located at the after corners of the lower platform of the tower.

There was also a fourth 0.75-metre 'manoeuvre' projector mounted on a platform projecting from the forward side of the tower mast. This projector was trained and elevated mechanically from a sight-equipped position immediately beneath it, at the forward end of the admiral's bridge.

Command spaces

The *Algérie* was designed to perform the rôle of force flagship, and was equipped with extensive command spaces. The navigation bridge for the CO was above the Admiral's navigation bridge at the forward end of the superstructure. Directly behind it was the armoured conning tower, to which access was gained via a heavy, gas-tight door. Behind the conning tower was the chartroom and beneath was the main radio office, with the AA fire control position and RPC room below (see drawing). The base of the tower housed the day cabins for the CO, the Admiral and the latter's staff.

At the forward end of the tower itself, directly beneath the 0.75-metre projector, was the admiral's bridge, with a sheltered position giving access to an open platform which would give a commanding view of the accompanying ships of the force. Directly behind it was located a fully-equipped operations centre.

On arrival at Toulon in October 1934 *Algérie* became flagship not only of the *1re Division Légère*, comprising the latest of France's 10,000-ton cruisers, but also of the *1re Escadre*, France's main operational fleet in the Mediterranean, the ageing dreadnought battleships being despatched to Brest. Flying the flag first of Vice-Amiral Mouget, then of Vice-Admirals Abrial and Duplat,

Algérie would remain flagship of the First Squadron and its successor, the Mediterranean Squadron, until July 1939, when a major operational reorganisation took place.

Machinery

The boilers adopted for *Algérie* were vertical small-tube boilers with superheating built by Indret, rated at 27kg/cm^2 (325° C). No.1 and No.2 boiler rooms each housed two identical boilers with a surface area of 885m^2; boiler room No.3 had a larger model with a surface area of 1,515m^2 to starboard and a small auxiliary boiler of 300m^2, used to provide power when at anchor, to port.

The propulsion machinery comprised four sets of geared turbines, each powering one of the four shafts. Each of the four turbine sets was constituted by a HP turbine, a MP turbine and a LP turbine working in series via single reduction gearing, and was completely independent in operation, with its own condensers and lubrication. The reverse turbines were integrated with the LP turbines, which were reaction turbines designed by Brown Boveri. The HP and MP turbines were of the direct-action Rateau-Bretagne type and were built at Indret.

The turbine machinery was distributed between two engine rooms immediately abaft the after boiler room. The forward pair of turbine sets powered the wing shafts and the after pair the inner shafts. The three-bladed propellers were 3.6m in diameter, and the single counterbalanced rudder, powered by an electric motor, had a surface area of 24.76m^2.

Electrical power was provided by four turbo-dynamos each rated at 300kW (400kW overload for one hour). They were grouped in pairs which could be coupled

FRAME 135

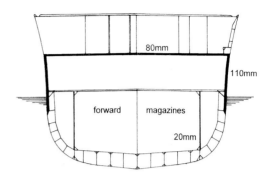

Protection system of Algérie

The cutaways show the protection system in the area of the forward magazines (frame 135), amidships (frame 103) and in the area of the after magazines (frame 52.65). The height of the 110mm armoured belt was reduced abeam the after magazines, the armoured deck being stepped down abaft the machinery spaces to form the ceiling of the magazines. The 40mm torpedo bulkhead covered only the machinery spaces and the control spaces immediately forward of the boiler rooms, so the magazine sides were given 20mm armour plating to compensate. (John Jordan)

FRAME 103

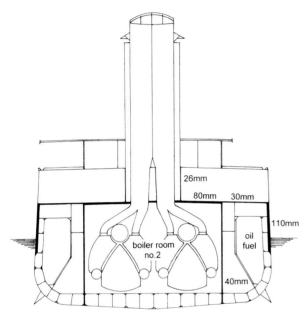

FRAME 52.65

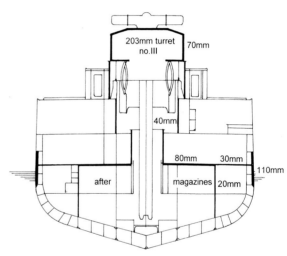

together: one pair was located in the forward engine room, the other in its own compartment forward. Emergency power was provided by two diesel alternators rated at 100kW (120kW max.). These could also be coupled together, and were located in their own compartment forward at upper-deck level between frames 130 and 136. A standard 'cruiser' voltage of 230-235V was employed throughout the ship.

Hull construction and armour

The hull of *Algérie* was of longitudinal construction, using two continuous hull girders 105 metres in length alongside the propulsion machinery and magazines to give the necessary rigidity. The platform decks and those above the magazines were also continuous, not stepped as in the earlier French Treaty cruisers. External armour also contributed to the rigidity of the hull girder, so that despite the much-increased weight of the hull its longitudinal strength was actually increased. The ship thereby

avoided the structural problems which became apparent when the first French Treaty cruisers entered service, and which were to plague the Royal Navy Treaty cruiser *London* after she was rebuilt and re-armoured in 1938-40.

For the first time in a major French warship extensive use of electric welding was made. Welding was employed even for parts of the hull girder, including the inner bottom, the platform decks, the primary and secondary bulkheads and the web-frames. Riveting was however retained for the vertical and horizontal armour, the first platform deck and the main strength elements of the hull girder. Riveting was also employed for the internal partitions, which were of light duralumin alloy. The weight saved by the adoption of modern construction techniques could be put into hull armour (*Algérie*'s Italian counterparts, the *Zara* class, were all-riveted, a factor which contributed to their emerging from the shipyards grossly overweight).

Sixteen primary transverse bulkheads extending from the ship's bottom to the upper deck contributed further to hull strength and divided the hull into seventeen

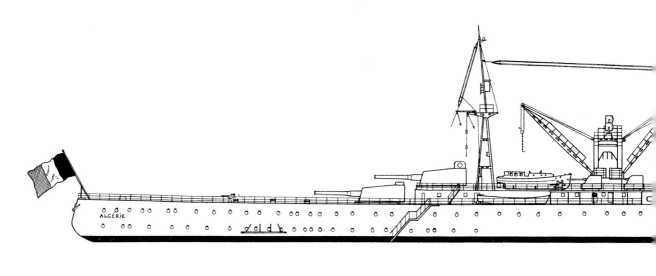

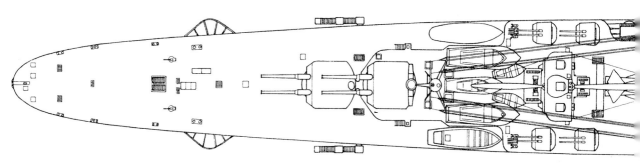

Algérie 1935 profile and plan views

The profile and plan views are based on official plans dated Brest 1 August 1935. They show Algérie with the light AA guns with which she was fitted on completion: single 37mm/50 Model 1925 in pairs on the forecastle and quarterdeck respectively, and 13.2mm/76 Hotchkiss Model 1929 quad mountings mounted at the four corners of the shelter deck. The drawings also show the original funnel cap, replaced in late 1939 with a new model with a prominent curved cowling. (John Jordan)

watertight compartments, with no openings below main deck level. Each compartment had its own pumps, the larger machinery compartments being equipped with pumps of greater capacity than the outer ones. Despite the symmetrical layout of the boilers and propulsion machinery there was no central longitudinal bulkhead as in Japanese cruisers, the French designers rightly fearing that flooding on one side of the ship could lead to a dangerous list and possibly capsizing.

The main armour belt was of uniform 110mm thickness and was constructed of plates of 80kg chrome-nickel steel, each weighing approximately 25 tonnes. It extended from the forward end of the 203mm magazines (frame 144) to the after end of the machinery spaces (frame 60) at a height varying from 3.76 metres to 4.45 metres, the lower edge being one metre below the waterline at normal displacement. It then continued at a reduced height of 2.45 metres alongside the after magazines, terminating at frame 39. The belt was closed by armoured transverse bulkheads of 70mm, also of 80kg steel, at frames 39, 60 and 144. The two outer bulkheads

were reinforced by 20mm steel plate of the same quality.

The longitudinal bulkheads, which formed the outer wall of the machinery compartments, were reinforced by plating of 60kg non-cemented steel 40mm thick, extending from the ship's bottom to the main deck. Thickness was increased to 50/60mm at its outer ends to compensate for the reduction in depth of the underwater protection. This bulkhead served both as splinter protection for shells broken up by the armoured belt or armoured deck, and as a torpedo bulkhead. The magazines and control spaces were outside the area protected by this bulkhead, and were therefore given side splinter protection of 80kg steel with a thickness of 20mm.

The vertical protection was completed by 26mm plating for the uptakes between the main deck and the upper deck, and by 20mm plating on the access tubes for the machinery spaces, all in standard 50kg construction steel.

The armoured deck was of 80kg chrome-nickel steel; between frames 60 and 144 it rested on the upper edge of the 110mm armoured belt. It had a uniform thickness of 80mm above the machinery spaces and the control

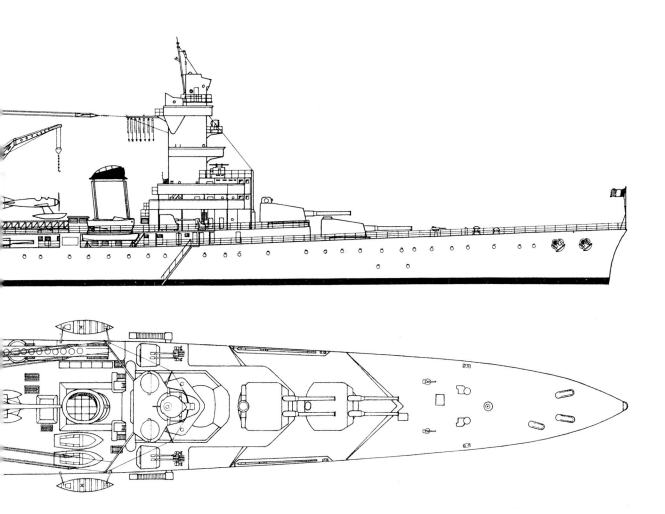

spaces forward, but outboard of the 40mm inner bulkhead thickness was reduced to 30mm. Between frames 130 and 144, over the forward magazines, it extended at 80mm thickness to the full beam of the ship. Aft, between frames 39 and 60, it formed the ceiling of the magazines; thickness was 80mm directly above the magazines reducing to 30mm at the sides. The potential vulnerability of the ship to plunging shells at this point was mitigated by the low level of the armoured deck, the 110mm side armour extending more then one metre above it (see drawings). The steering gear was protected by armour plating of 80kg steel.

The main gun turrets and the conning tower were armoured to a level unprecedented in earlier French Treaty cruiser construction. The 100mm faces of the turrets were angled at 41° to the vertical, the roof and sides had 70mm plating and the turret rears 50-85mm. The floor of the turret was 50mm, and there was a minimum thickness of 40mm on the barbette. There were sighting hoods with 60mm of armour for the end turrets. The total weight of armour allocated to the main armament was 315 tonnes, as compared with only 91 tonnes for the previous ships.

Similar protection was extended to the conning tower, which had 100mm walls, a 70mm roof and a 50mm central tube connecting with the control spaces beneath the armoured deck.

The underwater protection system was based on the customary combination of free-flooding spaces and fuel bunkers. In order to minimise flooding in the event of armour plating being displaced by shell hits, the inner bottom was extended up to main deck level, giving a free-flooding space 1 metre across. Inside this was a fuel bunker 2.2 metres wide at its upper end, the containing bulkhead being angled out towards the bilge keel at its lower end. There was then a free-flooding space just over one metre in width at its upper end between the inner wall of the fuel bunker and the engine room bulkhead (see drawings). This gave a maximum depth of 4.35 metres at the widest point amidships, the best which could be done with a ship of these dimensions, but which would almost certainly have proved inadequate in the event of the ship being struck by a torpedo or mine.

In order to prevent the simultaneous flooding of both engine rooms, which would have serious consequences for the ship's survival, there was a secondary watertight longitudinal bulkhead of 50kg steel located 1.3 metres inside the main bulkhead at the junction of the two spaces. It extended 3 metres either side of the dividing transverse bulkhead at frame 76.

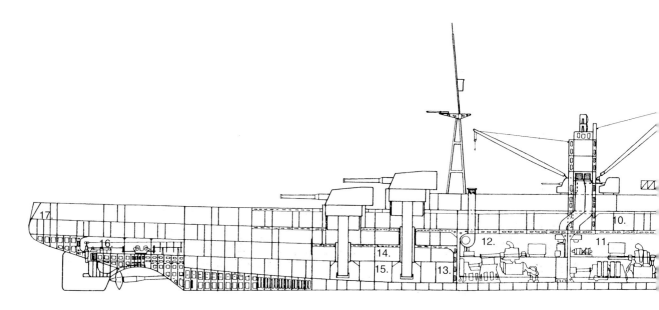

Algérie: *Inboard Profile*
The three boiler rooms, each housing two vertical small-tube boilers, were grouped together in order to combine the uptakes into a single funnel. Weight was also saved because the wing shafts were shorter than would have been the case with a 'unit' layout. The drawback of this arrangement was that the engine rooms were adjacent, leaving the ship vulnerable to having both flooded in the event of a torpedo hit amidships. The ship's designers endeavoured to compensate for this by doubling the torpedo bulkhead at this point. (John Jordan)

A Gourdou-Leseurre 810 Hy float-plane, similar to the two embarked on Algérie from 1934 until 1938. The standard embarked spotter/reconnaissance aircraft of it day, the GL 810/812 was to be superseded by the larger Loire 130. With a top speed of 200km/h, it could remain airborne for 4-5 hours. (Marius Bar)

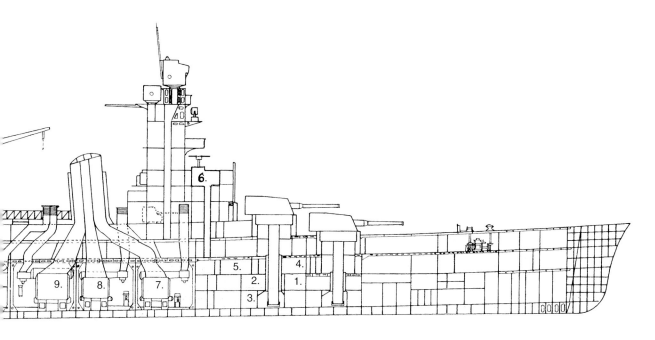

Key to Inboard Profile

1. fwd 203mm magazine
2. fwd 100mm magazine
3. fwd 203mm shellroom
4. diesel generators
5. transmitting station

6. conning tower
7. no.1 boiler room
8. no.2 boiler room
9. no.3 boiler room
10. W/T office (transmission)

11. fwd engine room
12. aft engine room
13. aft 100mm magazine
14. aft 203mm magazine
15. aft 203mm shellroom

16. steering gear compartment
17. aviation fuel tank

Note: *See drawing 'Layout of the Command Spaces' on p.108 for forward superstructure*

Aviation facilities and boats

There was a single trainable catapult to port, its broad cylindrical pedestal being located between the funnel and the searchlight tower, immediately forward of the port-side TT. Because it was seated on the upper deck, the beam of the catapult barely protruded above the shelter deck. As in earlier French Treaty cruisers there was no hangar to protect the aircraft from the elements, so the second spotter-plane carried was parked on a cradle to starboard, leading many writers to conclude that there were catapults port *and* starboard. The ship's plans, together with a close observation of the existing photographs, make it clear that this was not the case.

The catapult, ordered in May 1933, was a compressed-air model designed to launch seaplanes weighing up to 3,000kg at 98km/h. It had an overall length of 22.3 metres, the launch beam itself being 21 metres long. The aircraft were handled by an articulated crane with a reach of 19.7 metres, also with a capacity of 3000kg, the machinery for which was located at the base of the searchlight tower.

When *Algérie* entered service she operated two of the then-standard Gourdou-Leseurre 812 Hy monoplanes, which were specifically designed for spotting and for reconnaissance. The 812 model had folding wings, and a span of 16 metres. It had a maximum speed of 200km/h, and a range of 560km.

They were soon replaced by the Loire 130, which began development in 1933 as a replacement for the Gourdou-Leseurre 810-812 series. The Loire 130, which had an identical wingspan to the GL 812, was nevertheless a heavier, more substantial aircraft, similar to the British Walrus. It had a higher maximum speed of 225km/h, and a substantially improved range of 800km. The original catapult had to be strengthened and lengthened, the work being undertaken during a refit between August 1936 and February 1937. Capacity after modification was a 3300kg aircraft with a launch speed of 103km/h. The first Loire 130 was embarked in *Algérie* during October 1938, and a second was embarked following modifications to the aviation facilities in January 1939.

Since *Algérie* was designed as a force flagship a full complement of boats was carried, ranging from two 5 metre dinghies to an 11.5 metre rowing boat. Most were on cradles on the shelter deck between the searchlight tower and the tripod mainmast, although those outboard had to be stowed at upper-deck level, as the shelter deck was cut away at this point in order to secure good arcs astern for the after 100mm and 13.2mm AA guns. These boats were handled by a boat crane which, like the aircraft crane, had its machinery located at the base of the searchlight tower, a neat, practical solution which economised on deck space.

The remaining boats were carried on either side of the single funnel. There were two 8.5 metre whalers on

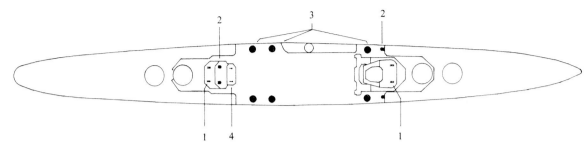

AA armament 1 August 1942

Key
1. 37mm/50 Mod. 1933 CAD
2. 13.2mm/50 Hotchkiss Mod.1929 CAQ
3. 100mm/45 Mod. 1930 CAD
4. 13.2mm Browning CAS

davits, and two 7 metre motor boats on rails to starboard, the latter being handled by the aircraft crane.

Subsequent modifications

The major modifications made to *Algérie* following completion concerned the fire control arrangements for the main artillery, improvements to the flag command facilities, and the light AA provision.

During a 1936-37 refit the 5-metre coincidence RF in the main DCT was replaced by an 8-metre stereoscopic model. This modification was extended to the RF in turret No. III in late 1938. During the same refit the admi-

ral's bridge at the forward edge of the tower was given a glass windscreen, and a roof was added the following year. The bridge wings on the forward superstructure were also extended. In December 1939 a new, more prominent funnel cap was fitted, with the aim of keeping funnel gases clear of the tower structure.

The most significant modifications concerned the AA armament. During a refit in 1937-38 the 37mm guns originally installed on the forecastle were moved to a less exposed position on the quarterdeck, where they were grouped with the other two 37mm. In compensation one of the after 13.2mm quads was moved to the roof of the conning tower, the other being relocated to starboard above the stern. In late 1938 the HA directors were cov-

Algérie on 16 October 1941. Her external appearance had changed little by this time, save for the modified funnel cowling, designed to take the funnel gases clear of the rangefinders atop the forward tower. Note the tricolor identification markings on no.II and no.III turrets. (Marius Bar)

Bow and stern quarter views of Algérie taken on 24 August 1942, shortly after the major refit in which her AA armament was substantially upgraded. Note the distinctive 'pergola', with its stepped structure for the after light AA weapons, located in the position of the original tripod foremast. The latter was replaced by a simple pole mast fixed to the forward side of the searchlight tower. (Marius Bar)

ered over to give the crew greater protection from the elements.

In December 1939 the long-promised 37mm Model 1933 twin mounting finally became available, and was fitted in place of the single mountings. And in May 1941 the close-range AA armament was reinforced by the installation of four single 13.2mm Browning MG: one on the DCT, one on the quarterdeck, and two in the positions formerly occupied by the after 13.2mm quads.

These *ad hoc* installations were clearly less than satisfactory. The AA positions forward were badly exposed to the elements, while those amidships had poor arcs obstructed by boats, cranes, the catapult and the secondary gun mountings, hence the preference for the quarterdeck. A more permanent solution was proposed, involving the construction of a new deckhouse with tiered platforms (designated the *pergola*) in place of the tripod mainmast, which was replaced by a simple pole mast seated at the forward edge of the searchlight tower. In order to cover forward arcs the admiral's bridge was to be replaced with an AA platform. Most of the existing AA weapons were relocated to one or other of these two positions.

The necessary modifications were made during a refit from May to August 1942. The four 37mm Model 1933 were redistributed fore and aft, two mountings being relocated to the AA platform which replaced the former admiral's bridge, the other two occupying the after (lower) platform of the *pergola*. The forward 13.2mm Hotchkiss quad mountings were retained in their original position at the forward end of the shelter deck, while the other pair was relocated to the upper platform of the *pergola*. Two of the four 13.2mm Browning MGs were installed immediately abaft the Hotchkiss quads at the top of the *pergola*, and it was envisaged that the remaining two would be fitted forward atop the DCT.

The new arrangement of the light AA was symmetrical, and was clearly superior to the previous layout. However, the AA weapons themselves were of three different types, were markedly inferior in capabilities to the 20mm Oerlikons and 40mm Bofors being installed in Allied cruisers during the same period, and fire control was virtually non-existent. It was the best the French could do in very difficult circumstances, with the bulk of their military-industrial complex in occupied territory and political constraints imposed by the crippling conditions of the Armistice, but had the *Algérie* come under attack from modern aircraft in late 1942 there can be little doubt regarding the probable outcome.

Conclusion

In the event the undoubted military qualities of the *Algérie* were untested. Following service with 'Force X' in the South Atlantic in the Autumn of 1939, there was only a brief bombardment sortie against the northern Italian ports of Vado and Genoa before hostilities ceased with the Armistice of 25 June 1940. From that time *Algérie* served with the *Forces de Haute Mer* as flagship of the *1re Division de Croiseurs*. She was scuttled with the remainder of the French Fleet at Toulon on 27 November 1942.

Sources
J Moulin and Patrick Maurand, *Le croiseur Algérie*, (Nantes: Marines Editions, 1999)
R Dumas, *Genèse des croiseurs de 10 000 t*, 'Marines' no.41, (Bourg-en-Bresse: Marines Editions, 1996)
J Campbell, *Naval Weapons of World War Two*, (London: Conway Maritime Press, 1988)
Official plans of *Algérie*, Centre d'Archives de l'Armement

PREDREADNOUGHTS VS A DREADNOUGHT

The Action off Cape Sarych, 18 November 1914

The escape of the German battlecruiser *Goeben* and light cruiser *Breslau* from the Royal Navy at the outbreak of the First World War has been described by many writers, but after this dramatic episode the ships disappear from most histories for three years until their brief sortie outside the Dardanelles in January 1918. In between these events the two German ships had active careers in the Black Sea, and on several occasions encountered the Russian Black Sea Fleet. **Stephen McLaughlin** describes one of these actions.

Although relatively little known, the action off Cape Sarych, 18 November 1914, can count a major 'first' amongst its credits; it was the first engagement between capital ships of the First World War.[1] The Battle of the Heligoland Bight on 28 August 1914 saw British battlecruisers in action against German light cruisers, while Coronel, 1 November 1914, was a battle between armoured cruisers. When the Russian Black Sea Fleet encountered *Goeben*, the Battle of the Falklands was still three weeks in the future, while Dogger Bank, the first battle between dreadnoughts, did not take place until 24 January 1915. Although the action off Cape Sarych has many interesting features, the fact that it was inconclusive and fought in a secondary theatre has led to it receiving little attention. Those descriptions that have been published are far from perfect. The German official history is vague, perhaps even disingenuous, while accounts from the Russian side have for many years been mired in personal animosities and ideological debates. However, by comparing the German version with the published Russian accounts, from both Soviet and émigré sources, it is possible to coax out a fairly consistent description of the battle.[2]

The Opposing Forces

The German-Turkish forces were commanded by Rear Admiral Wilhelm Souchon.[3] In the opening days of the war Souchon had proven his boldness by successfully eluding British pursuers and bringing the *Mittelmeerdivision*, his flagship, the battlecruiser *Goeben* and her 'little sister,' the light cruiser *Breslau*, to Constantinople. Soon after their arrival the Turks 'bought' the ships, a transaction even the German official history admits was largely fictitious. *Goeben* was officially

renamed *Yavuz Sultan Selim* and a few Turkish sailors were added to her crew. But the vast majority of the officers and men were German and they continued to refer to their ship by its German name, a practice that will be followed here.

Goeben was practically brand new, having been completed in 1912. Her main battery consisted of 10-28cm (more precisely, 28.3cm, or 11.14in) SKL/50 guns in five twin turrets, one forward, two *en echelon* amidships, and two superimposed aft. These guns could impart a muzzle velocity of 880m/s (2887.3f/s) to the 302kg (665.9lbs) shells. A rate of fire of three rounds per gun per minute could be maintained 'with a strong and well trained crew'.[4] The secondary battery was made up of 12-15cm (5.9in) guns. The ship had a designed speed of 25.5kts, although she made 28kts on trials. She had experienced considerable troubles with her small-tube boilers at the outset of the war, but these were made good after her arrival in Turkish waters and her full service speed was achievable in November 1918.[5] Like all German dreadnoughts, she was well-protected, with a 270mm (10.6in) waterline belt amidships covering her vitals.

The light cruiser *Breslau* also received a Turkish name, officially becoming *Midilli*, but like her 'big sister' her officers and crew remained German. She had a displacement of 4570 tons, was armed with 12-10.5cm (4.1in) guns, and could make 27kts. The remainder of the Turkish fleet was composed of older and less effective units, and took no part in the battle.

In the crucial area of *Goeben's* fire control the available information is unfortunately limited. The ship was equipped with no fewer than nine 3-metre Zeiss stereoscopic RFs, one in each turret, one in each of the secondary battery control positions on the side-decks, and one atop each of the conning towers.[6] Ranges were assessed by the First Gunnery Officer, whose station was located in the after part of the conning tower. Because she had been on a foreign station in the immediate pre-war years, *Goeben*'s fire control equipment does not seem to have been as up-to-date as that of other German cap-ital ships; amongst other things, she lacked the director-pointer system that automatically provided information on target bearing to the turrets. There was a range-clock which could automatically increase or decrease the range at a fixed rate per minute; the changing range was auto-matically transmitted to the guns by follow-the-pointer indicators. German ships used continuous aim for their main batteries, that is, the guns were kept at a constant angle relative to the surface of the sea despite the ship's rolling. Salvos were signalled by the First Gunnery Officer by means of a gong. Upon hearing this, each gun-ner fired his gun. Because the guns were aimed continu-ously, small variations in the moment of firing were not important. It is important to note that, unlike the British director system, the individual German gunlayers (and their Russian counterparts) had to see the target to aim their guns.

It seems almost certain that German pre-war gunnery efforts focused on actions at ranges that would have been considered extremely short by later standards. For exam-ple, pre-war gunnery practices rarely exceeded 8000 metres, while in table-top tactical games just before the war ranges over 10,000 metres were 'ruled out as ineffec-tive'.[7] This would explain the relatively short base-line of the *Goeben*'s RFs, as well as the limited maximum eleva-tion of her main battery guns. Although the 13.5° eleva-tion theoretically permitted ranging out to 17,545 metres

(19,188 yards), in fact the practical elevation limit of the gun would have been somewhat less because of the ship's roll, that is, with the gun kept continuously fixed with respect to the surface of the sea, the elevating mechanism had to allow for both the gun's elevation plus the roll of the ship. Thus in terms of both equipment and doctrine the Germans seem to have anticipated ranges of less than 10,000 metres before the war.

Opposing *Goeben* was the Russian Black Sea Fleet, under the command of Admiral Andrei Avgustovich Ebergard (as it was spelled in Russian; since he was of Swedish ancestry, the name is often given as Eberhard or Eberhardt).[8] Ebergard had commanded the Black Sea Fleet since 1911; he was a competent commander and was well regarded by his staff. Although he eventually came to be seen as overly cautious by the staff at *Stavka* (the Russian GHQ), he manifested a distinctly aggressive attitude after Souchon's arrival in Constantinople, argu-ing that *Goeben* and *Breslau* should be treated as if they were German ships if they entered the Black Sea. In fact Ebergard went so far as to propose a pre-emptive strike:

> upon receiving news of the arrival of *Goeben* and *Breslau* in Constantinople, he had decided that…he would take his best ships and torpedo boats into the Bosphorus Strait on the same basis that the Germans had entered the Dardanelles. If the latter [the Germans] would not leave the Straits, then Admiral Ebergard would destroy them.[9]

Ebergard was overruled by the Ministry of Foreign Affairs, which hoped to maintain peace with Turkey for as long as

The German battlecruiser SMS Goeben, *the most powerful ship in the Black Sea at the outbreak of war, and flagship of Rear Admiral Wilhelm Souchon. (Courtesy U. S. Naval Historical Center)*

Goeben *from her port side.* (Courtesy Alister Greenway)

Goeben's *'Little Sister', SMS* Breslau, *the fastest ship in the Black Sea.* (Courtesy Alister Greenway)

possible, a not unreasonable course of action (or inaction), given the general expectation of a short war.

The same year that Ebergard had taken up his command the Russian government had approved a large building program for the Black Sea, including three powerful dreadnoughts (a fourth ship was subsequently added to the programme), but none of these ships was complete when the war began, so the job of containing *Goeben* fell to the five predreadnought battleships already in service. As can be seen from Table 1, all of these ships were a good 10kts slower than *Goeben*.

Pre-war assessments of the Russian Navy by foreign observers were not flattering, the debacle of Tsushima inevitably coloured the Navy's reputation. Although the Black Sea Fleet had escaped that misadventure due to its geographical isolation, it had suffered a series of violent revolutionary upheavals in 1905-1906, including the famous *Potemkin* mutiny. Another serious revolutionary plot had been uncovered in 1912; around 200 sailors were arrested, of whom eleven were eventually executed. It is therefore easy to understand why both its allies and enemies regarded the Black Sea Fleet as ineffective, in January 1913, the German *Admiralstab*:

> scarcely included the Russian Black Sea Fleet in its calculations. The military value of this force was very small because of the poor discipline of its crews and its obsolete ships.[10]

But while the Russian fleet certainly suffered from political turmoil below decks, great strides had been made in gunnery since the war with Japan.[11] Russian shells had proven defective during that war, often failing to explode or exploding before penetrating armour. These problems

had been solved by the introduction of the Model 1907 and Model 1911 shells, which featured a TNT bursting charge and improved fuzes. At the time of the action off Cape Sarych the Russian predreadnoughts were apparently still using the 331.7kg (731.4lb) M.1907 12in AP shell, rather than the heavier M.1911.[12] This M.1907 shell had a 6kg (13.23lb) bursting charge.

The slow rate of fire of Russian big guns, a crucial handicap in the Russo-Japanese War, had been addressed by installing new turret machinery and the fast-opening Welin breech-block. By 1914 the 12in/40 guns of the predreadnoughts could sustain a rate of fire of one round every 40 seconds, as opposed to the 90-second firing interval that had been the best speed during the late war. Similar improvements had been made to medium-calibre guns.

But the most important improvements to Russian gunnery came in the area of fire control. Here the Black Sea Fleet led the way, serving as a laboratory for new methods of long-range fire control in the years immediately after the Russo-Japanese War.[13] The need for accurate data at long ranges was recognised, compared to *Goeben*'s 3-metre rangefinders and the 9ft instruments that were standard equipment on British dreadnoughts, the Russian predreadnoughts seem to have carried 12ft instruments.[14] To reach longer ranges, the new-model 12in turrets of the *Evstafii* and *Ioann Zlatoust* could elevate their guns to 35°, while older ships had their elevation limits increased, *Tri Sviatitelia* was modified to allow 25°. As for *Panteleimon*,

Table 1: THE RUSSIAN BLACK SEA FLEET

	Completed	Displacement	Armament	Speed
Evstafii	1911	12,850 tons	4x12in, 4x8in, 12x6in	16kts
Ioann Zlatoust	1911	12,850 tons	4x12in, 4x8in, 12x6in	16kts
*Panteleimon**	1905	12,900 tons	4x12in, 16x6in	16kts
Tri Sviatitelia	1897	13,000 tons	4x12in, 14x6in	16kts
Rostislav	1900	10,500 tons	4x10in, 8x6in	15kts

***Note:** ex-Kniaz' Potemkin Tavricheskii*

Admiral Andrei Avgustovich Ebergard, commander of the Russian Black Sea Fleet; a portrait taken in 1908. (Courtesy A Plotto, via George Nekrasov)

there is conflicting information; she was modified to allow either a 25° or 35° maximum.[15]

But there was more to long-range fire control than good rangefinders and high elevations. The Russians realised that salvo firing was essential, at long ranges hits were often invisible, especially with AP shells designed to explode deep inside the enemy ship. At the same time, it was generally impossible to see shells falling beyond the target because their splashes were obscured by the target ship itself, not to mention the great clouds of funnel-smoke coal-burning ships belched out at high speeds. So fire control boiled down to counting how many shells out of a salvo fell short of the target, if there were fewer splashes than the number of guns fired, it was safe to assume that you were straddling the target and, as long as the target remained straddled, there were bound to be some hits.

This was all well and good, but predreadnoughts could only manage two-gun salvos, which made it almost impossible to straddle a target with any degree of certainty. It was clear that Russia's unsettled economy would not permit the building of a dreadnought battlefleet for some years, so there was a distinct possibility that Russian pre-dreadnoughts might find themselves facing German or (British-built) Turkish dreadnoughts. This lent an urgency to the Black Sea Fleet's long-range fire control experiments, which were directed toward finding a way for several predreadnoughts to concentrate their fire on a single target, a difficult business, since the salvos of the different ships were apt to become confused, making effective spotting impossible. It is to the great credit of

The Russian predreadnought Evstafii, *flagship of the Black Sea Fleet. This picture was taken in 1913; note the long-base rangefinder atop her conning tower. Her sister* Ioann Zlatoust *was almost identical in appearance. (Courtesy Sergei Vinogradov)*

the Russian artillerists that an effective system of fire-concentration was developed. The method was based on gunnery control by a 'master ship', ideally, the centre ship in a three-ship group; with more than three ships the system would become confused. The middle ship was chosen as the control ship because it was anticipated that the enemy would concentrate fire on the leading ship, thus leaving the fire control officer in the second ship relatively undisturbed as he worked out his sight-settings. In the Black Sea Fleet the three newest ships, *Evstafii*, *Zlatoust* and *Panteleimon*, formed the core of the fire-concentration group; as for *Tri Sviatitelia*, she

> was not considered a unit in the nucleus of the battleship brigade, but was kept nearby as a reserve ship, joining in centralised firing only if one of the other three ships went out of action.[16]

The differing ballistics of *Rostislav*'s 10in/45 guns meant that she could not combine her fire with the other ships, so she was often assigned to shore bombardment duty, thereby preserving the guns and ammunition of the other ships for battle at sea.

Before fire was opened, the gunnery officer in the master ship would track the enemy's course by manual plotting based on a succession of rangefinder readings. This would allow him to estimate the rate-of-change-of-range, which was then set on the range-clock. Like its German counterpart, the Russian range-clock could only handle fixed rates of change, any manoeuvres by the firing ship or the target could quickly throw off the fire-control solution. Again like the German range-clock, the Russian one was linked directly to follow-the-pointer indicators at the guns.

At the same time that the master ship was sending the sight-settings to its own guns, it also transmitted these by wireless to the two subordinate ships.[17] In each ship there was a 'brigade post' manned by a gunnery officer and a wireless operator. Fire control transmissions were handled by a wireless system completely independent of normal inter-ship communications, with its own dedicated antennas rigged amidships on either side on bamboo spreaders. Bamboo was apparently used because it was cheap, readily available and easy to replace if damaged. The actual sight-settings and fire-control orders:

> were issued by the master ship in a special code, which contained abbreviated commands....for example, 'P-575, P-575' meant a sight setting [*pritsel*] of 57.5 cables [11,500 yards], 'Ts-60, Ts-60' a deflection setting [*tselik*] of 60; 'ZLP' meant salvo firing [*zalp*], 'PRI' meant ranging fire [*pristrelka*], 'REV' mean siren [*revun*]. Thus all the ships received an identical command corresponding to the sight-settings on the ship that was controlling the firing.

Corrections were handled in much the same way. The master ship's spotters might call for a correction of 'up 4 cables,' but to make use of these the subordinate ships would have had to set the initial data for range and rate-of-change on their own range-clocks, then apply the spotting corrections as they were received from the mas-

ter ship. In time, the ships could easily get out of synchronisation, and then they would be firing with different sight settings, undermining the entire point of the system, which was to fire enough guns with the same sight settings to produce useful salvo patterns around the target. So the brigade post in the master ship recalculated the sight settings, based on its own range clock and incorporating the spotting corrections, then transmitted these to the other ships in the same form as the initial settings.

The only calculations performed by the subordinate ships was a 'formation correction' in the range setting; this took account of the relative position of the subordinate ship to the master ship, the distance between ships in the squadron being measured with short-base rangefinders. The new sight settings were received by the subordinate ships, corrected for place in formation, then passed directly to the guns. What happened next was described by another Black Sea Fleet gunnery officer, N N Kharin of the *Panteleimon*, in an account of a shore bombardment mission:

> In accordance with a wireless signal from *Ioann Zlatoust* we prepared to open fire. The signal gave the needed range and deflection sight settings [*pritsel* and *tselik*] for firing at an 8-inch battery located on a headland to the left of the entrance to the bay. Upon the signal 'Tovs' ['ready'] the 12-inch guns of the three battleships were laid on the indicated point ashore. At the signal 'Zalp' [salvo] the three ships fired as one.
>
> The fire of all the ships was controlled by wireless and they fired at one and the same target so simultaneously that the impression was created that the guns of these ships were controlled by one gun-layer.[18]

Presumably there was a salvo-siren in the brigade post of each battleship, so that the moment the *zalp* signal was received, the officer in the post could signal it to the guns. The 'ready' signal mentioned above, at which the gun-layers laid their guns on the target, may indicate that the Russian predreadnoughts used continuous aim, which would have been necessary for a truly simultaneous salvo, since each ship would be at a different point in the roll when the signal to fire was received. One gun from each turret was fired, producing a six-gun salvo, making the three predreadnoughts into a species of decentralised 'dreadnought' with the respectable armament of twelve 12in guns.

The Russians believed that the combination of long-range gunnery and concentration of fire would give the predreadnoughts a fighting chance against the super-dreadnoughts being built in British yards for Turkey. Immediately after the outbreak of war the threat of those ships vanished, only to be replaced by the *Goeben*. But the appearance of the German ship did not lead to any fundamental change in the Russian tactics. Indeed, the Russians were well aware of the German short-range doctrine, and planned to take advantage of it.[19] The Black Sea Fleet Staff contemplated fighting at ranges on the order of 80-100 cables (circa 16,000-20,000 yards), noting that the best course of action for the Russian squadron

Panteleimon, *formerly Kniaz' Potemkin Tavricheskii, the third ship in the Russian battleline. This picture, taken in 1918 when the ship was laid up at Sevastopol, shows her wartime appearance. Note the German ensign flying from her gaff, Sevastopol fell to the Germans in May 1918. The ship behind her is* Tri Sviatitelia. *(U.S. Naval Historical Center)*

would be 'to knock the *Goeben* out at long ranges, where the Germans do not know how to shoot at all'.[20]

Preliminary Movements

After his arrival in Constantinople in August 1914, Souchon applied himself to the task of bringing Turkey into the war on the side of the Central Powers. It was not an easy job; the government was deeply divided over the question of entering the war. The pro-German party was headed by the Minister of War, Enver Pasha, who proved to be Souchon's closest ally. On 21 September *Goeben* cruised briefly in the Black Sea, apparently in the hopes of provoking the Russians to attack her.[21] As noted above, Ebergard would have been only too happy to oblige, but was prevented from doing so by direct orders from the Russian Government.

After impatiently waiting two and a half months for the hesitant Turkish government to make up its mind, Souchon, conniving with Enver Pasha, managed to pre-cipitate hostilities. In his sealed orders to the fleet on the eve of war, Enver wrote:

> The Turkish Fleet shall win naval mastery of the Black Sea. Seek out the Russian Fleet and attack it wherever you find it without a declaration of war.[22]

On 29 October 1914 *Breslau* and the more modern units of the Turkish fleet (commanded by German officers) attacked Novorossiisk and Odessa, while the prize target, the main Russian naval base at Sevastopol, was reserved for *Goeben*. However, her bombardment accomplished little and she was driven off after receiving three hits from the shore batteries, the first hint that Russian gun-nery might not be as inept as some pre-war estimates had assumed.[23] Had the Russians been more alert, *Goeben* might have suffered a far worse fate; the German ship steamed through a field of controlled mines during her bombardment, but these had not yet been activated, despite the fact that Sevastopol had known for several hours of the German-Turkish night attack on Odessa. Naval Minister I K Grigorovich, as well as others in the nation's political and military leadership, eventually came to see this as the first of several failures on the part of Ebergard and his staff.[24]

The Ottoman Government refused to disown Souchon's attacks, and on 2 November 1914 Russia declared war on Turkey. The first encounter at sea between the two fleets of the two enemies came just over two weeks later. Events were set in motion on 15 November when Admiral Ebergard led the Black Sea Fleet out of Sevastopol, bound for the south-eastern cor-ner of the Black Sea. The fleet's objective was a bom-bardment of Trebizond, the main Turkish disembarkation point for men and supplies destined for the Caucasian front. The Russian force included all five battleships, as well as three cruisers and thirteen destroyers. The order of battle was as follows:

First Battleship Brigade:
Evstafii, (Captain 1st Rank V I Galanin), flagship of the Fleet Commander, Vice Admiral A A Ebergard.
Ioann Zlatoust (Captain 1st Rank F A Vinter).
Panteleimon (Captain 1st Rank M I Kas'kov), flagship of Vice Admiral P I Novitskii, Commander, Battleship Brigade.

Second Battleship Brigade
Tri Sviatitelia (Captain 1st Rank V K Lukin), flagship of Rear Admiral N S Putiatin, Commander, Second Battleship Brigade.
Rostislav (Captain 1st Rank K A Porembskii).

Cruiser Brigade
Pamiat' Merkuriia (Captain 1st Rank M M Ostrogradskii), flag of Rear Admiral A E Pokrovskii, Commander, Cruiser Brigade (7070 ton, 23kts, 12-6in).
Kagul (Captain 1st Rank S S Poguliaev) (7070 tons, 23kts, 12-6in).
Almaz (Captain 2nd Rank Zarin) (3285 tons, 19kts, 7-120mm).

Torpedo Brigade (Minnaia brigada)
First Division: *Gnevnyi*, flying the broad pennant of Captain 1st Rank M P Sablin, Commander Torpedo Brigade and Commander of the First Torpedo Division. The First Division also included two more ships of the *Derzkii* class, (1190 tons, oil-burning, 35kts, 3-4in, 10-TT; the other ships of this division were *Bespokoinyi*, *Derzkii* and *Pronzitel'nyi*, but it is not known which two of these were present during this action).[25]
Third Division (Captain 1st Rank Prince V V Trubetskoi): *Leitenant Shestakov, Kapitan Saken, Kapitan-Leitenant Baranov* and *Leitenant Zatsarennyi* (*Leitenant Shestakov* class, 635 tons, coal-fired, 24kts, 2-120mm, 3-TT).
Fourth Division (Captain 1st Rank Gezekhus): *Zhutkii, Zhivoi, Zharkii* and *Zhivuchii* (*Leitenant Pushchin* class, 450 tons, coal-burning, 24kts, 2-75mm, 2-TT).
Fifth Division: *Zvonkii* and *Zorkii* (also *Leitenant Pushchin* class).

The three new destroyers of the First Torpedo Division were the only Russian ships faster than *Goeben* or *Breslau*. Thus Ebergard had to keep all his ships close enough to the main body to prevent an isolated vessel from being overtaken and overwhelmed by the German ships.
On the morning of 17 November *Rostislav, Pamiat' Merkuriia* and a division of destroyers moved inshore to bombard Trebizond while the rest of the fleet remained to seaward as a covering force.[26] As part of the operation, the minelayers *Konstantin* and *Kseniia*, operating out of Batum with their own escort of torpedo boats, laid a series of minefields the following night, 123 mines near Trebizond, 77 off Platana, 100 off Unye and 100 near

Samsun.[27] The bombardment completed, the fleet then cruised westward along the Turkish coast as far as Giresun (sometimes spelt Kerasun), searching for enemy shipping. Finding none, at about 13:45 on 17 November the fleet shaped course for Sevastopol.

News of the Russian bombardment was soon received in Constantinople, and at 08:50 on 17 November *Goeben* (*Kapitän zur See* Richard Ackermann) and *Breslau* (*Korvetten-Kapitän* Kettner) were ordered to raise steam.[28] Reports of the Russian strength were relatively accurate, five predreadnought battleships, two cruisers and twelve torpedo boats, so Admiral Souchon had a pretty fair notion of what he was up against. The German ships raised anchor at 13:00. Initially Souchon expected to find the Russians somewhere along the northern coast of Anatolia, in the vicinity of Sinop. But at 15:50, while the two ships were still negotiating the Bosphorus channel, word was received that seven large Russian warships (the five battleships and two larger cruisers) had been seen heading on a northerly course from Giresun, so Souchon changed his plans, now intending to intercept the Russians on their return path to Sevastopol. The two ships cleared the Bosphorus at about 16:00 and set course for the Crimea. *Goeben* proceeded at 15kts, while *Breslau* was sent ahead at 18kts to scout; wireless silence was to be maintained unless the enemy was sighted.

Encounter

On the afternoon of 17 November, as the Black Sea Fleet steamed toward Sevastopol, Ebergard was informed by a wireless message from the Naval General Staff in Petrograd that *Goeben* was at sea. Given its promptness, it is likely that this information came from Russian intercepts of German wireless communications (possibly decoded using materials from the cruiser *Magdeburg*, whose code book and cypher tables were captured when she ran aground in the Baltic in August).

Ebergard decided against searching for the enemy ship since this would have involved turning toward the Bosphorus. Most of his ships were running short of fuel. The wartime cruising speed of the battleships was generally 12kts, as opposed to their pre-war 'economical' speed of 10kts, so they were probably burning more fuel than in normal cruising, while the small coal-burning destroyers had consumed as much as three-quarters of their fuel after three days at sea. So Ebergard held his course for Sevastopol, but ordered 'increased vigilence'.

During the night the German ships steamed through a rainstorm, but the morning of 18 November found the sea calm. The weather was misty; visibility was variable, with scudding streaks of thick fog. During the course of the morning the weather cleared somewhat, but visibility remained patchy. The wind was blowing from the WNW, and very light, 1-2 on the Beaufort scale ('light airs' to 'light breeze,' wind speed 1-3 or 4-6kts).[29] *Breslau* sighted the coast near Balaklava before noon in 'very misty weather'. There was as yet no sign of the Russians.

In fact, the Russians were very close indeed. At noon *Goeben* recorded a position of 44° 0' N, 33° 47' E, while

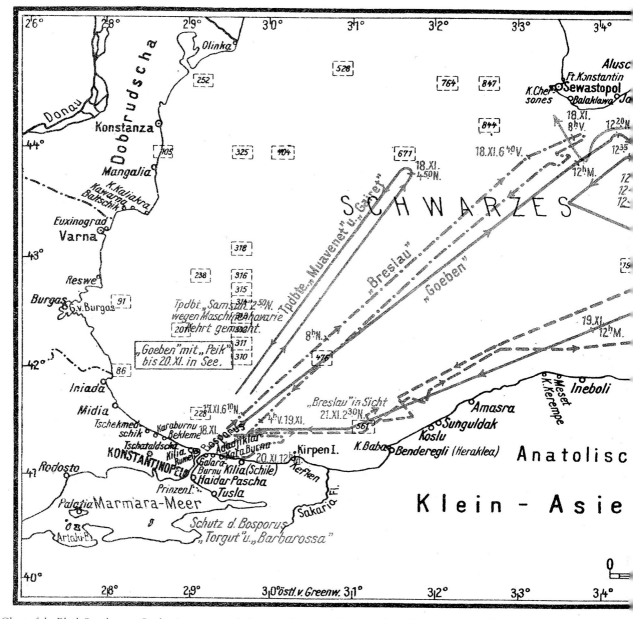

Chart of the Black Sea showing Goeben's movements before and after the battle, taken from the German official history. Although the area of the battle is not to scale, the chart otherwise accurately reflects the rough track chart in Goeben's war-diary.

at that time *Almaz* calculated her position as 44° 03' N, 33° 32' E; this places the Russians somewhat to the west of the Germans, which cannot be correct, one or both of the positions is incorrect. Nevertheless, the fixes agree tolerably well and give a fair notion of the site of the action, more or less directly south of Cape Sarych, the southernmost point on the Crimean peninsula. The Black Sea Fleet had been steaming in its low-visibility formation on course 292°. Under normal conditions, the three cruisers would have been scouting ten miles ahead of the main body, but due to the poor visibility the cruisers stayed within three and a half miles of the battleships, sometimes falling back to about a mile in advance when the fog grew thicker. *Almaz* was directly ahead of the bat-

tleships, while *Kagul* and *Pamiat' Merkuriia* bore 45° from the flagship to port and starboard respectively.[30] The five battleships were in a column led by the flagship, *Evstafii*, followed by *Ioann Zlatoust*, *Panteleimon*, *Tri Sviatitelia* and *Rostislav*; the interval between ships was 4 cables (800 yards). The destroyers and torpedo boats were in two columns behind the battleships, with *Gnevnyi* leading the starboard column.

Goeben caught up with *Breslau* not long before noon. Since there was as yet no sign of the Russians, Souchon decided to search in an easterly direction, and sent a wireless signal to *Breslau* to that effect. The course adopted was 71°, roughly ENE. The Russians intercepted these signals, but they did not cause any particular alarm, wire-

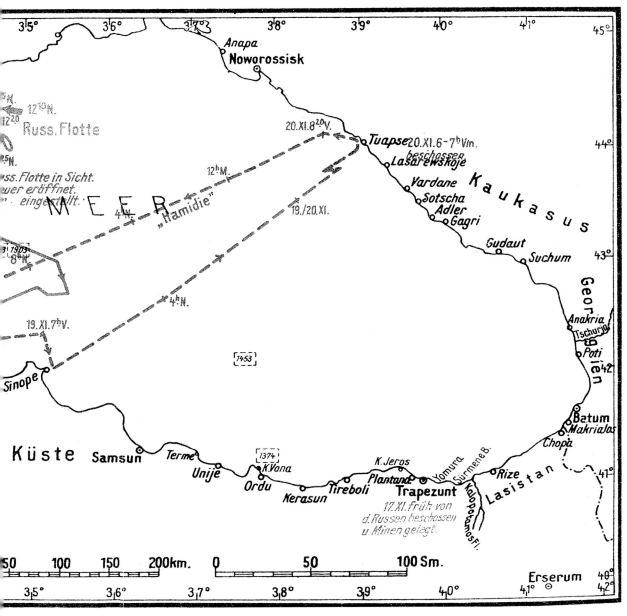

less transmissions did not necessarily mean that the enemy was close at hand. At 11:40, however, *Almaz* signalled by lamp to the flagship that she could see 'a lot of smoke'. Course was altered slightly to investigate, and Admiral Ebergard ordered his battleships to close up the intervals between ships to 2.5 cables (500 yards). The lower speed of the trailing battleships, *Tri Sviatitelia* and *Rostislav*, meant that they could only close the distance slowly and in fact the action was over before they had reached position. Ebergard also ordered the cruisers to begin falling back on the main body, afraid that in the poor visibility they might run into *Goeben* before the Black Sea Fleet's battleships could support them.

The scouting cruisers on both sides sighted each other at about the same time. According to the German official history, *Breslau* sighted a cruiser to starboard at 12:05 (German time) while at 12:10 (Russian time) *Almaz*

'sighted two indistinct, large silhouettes in the mist 7° on the port bow'. It seems likely that the sightings were nearly simultaneous, and that the German clocks were a few minutes behind the Russian.[31] According to some Russian accounts, when sighted the German ships were proceeding at a very low speed and making almost no smoke, which contradicts the report that *Almaz* saw 'a lot of smoke' before sighting the enemy ships. *Breslau* was on *Goeben*'s port beam, and somewhat ahead of her big sister.[32] *Almaz* signalled the code letter 'G' by lamp, 'I see the enemy in the forward sector'. Upon receiving *Breslau*'s sighting report *Goeben* had turned toward *Almaz* and began working up to full speed. Soon afterwards *Goeben* sighted a second ship in the mist to starboard, presumably *Kagul*, on the left wing of the Russian scouting line. By this time *Almaz* was turning to starboard, away from the enemy to join the main body; as she sheered off, her 9ft Barr & Stroud rangefinder indicated that the enemy force was 32 cables (6400 yards) distant. It is likely that this was actually the range to *Breslau* only, and that *Goeben* was still considerably farther away but on almost the same bearing from *Almaz*'s point of view. Like *Almaz*, *Breslau* fell back, thus clearing the ring for the main event.

Up to this point there was some uncertainty as to just what *Almaz* had seen; some of Ebergard's staff thought it might simply be the old battleship *Sinop*, which usually provided cover for the minesweepers operating outside Sevastopol. Lieutenant A M Nevinskii, *Evstafii*'s senior gunnery officer, who was in the flagship's conning tower, provides the following description of the next few minutes:

> Suddenly one of the signalmen reported: 'I see smoke ahead to starboard'. In fact smoke of a very considerable thickness had appeared in the indicated direction. Those on the bridge decided that this was undoubtedly the smoke of *Goeben* or *Breslau*. Then everything was once again obscured by fog and haze, and the smoke disappeared. The [fleet] commander ordered speed increased to 14 knots, so that the ships could even-up the formation. *Kagul* was ordered to take station at the head of the brigade, [and] *Pamiat' Merkuriia* [was ordered to take station] at the tail end of the column. In closing up all the ships made a lot of smoke, since all the boilers were brought on line.[33]

Almaz joined *Pamiat' Merkuriia* at the rear. Meanwhile the destroyers of the Fourth and Fifth Torpedo Divisions moved forward to a position abreast *Evstafii* on her port side.[34] Nevinskii reports that the range to the smoke was 'on the order of 80-90 cables' (16,000-18,000 yards); he

says that he proposed to Captain Galinin, the ship's commander, that the battleships move into a line-abreast formation, so that they could instantly turn to port or starboard and so greet *Goeben* with full broadsides the moment she appeared. This seems a somewhat presumptuous suggestion coming from a mere lieutenant, and it was probably also impractical, with *Goeben* liable to appear out of the mist at any moment, changing formation would have been a risky business. Whether on his own account, or because of Nevinskii's prompting, *Evstafii*'s commander, Captain Galanin, reportedly urged Admiral Ebergard to turn the column immediately to cross *Goeben*'s 'T'. But Ebergard said that it was too soon; he very probably had in mind the example of the opening stages of the Battle of Tsushima, where Admiral Rozhestvenskii had ordered a change in formation soon after sighting the Japanese, an unnecessary manoeuvre that led to confusion and delay in his deployment. Ebergard's situation also bears a striking resemblance to that faced by Jellicoe at Jutland just before he deployed from cruising formation to a single line of battle. Without knowing the exact position or course of the *Hochseeflotte*, Jellicoe had to decide whether to deploy on the port or starboard wing, knowing that if he chose incorrectly, he would be at a disadvantage when the enemy appeared. Ebergard had as little information to go on as Jellicoe, although *Goeben*'s smoke had been briefly sighted from the flagship, the enemy's course and exact bearing were still unknown. If he turned the wrong way now, *Goeben* might appear well ahead or well abaft his beam; given the close range and the battlecruiser's greatly superior speed, *Goeben* would be able to work around ahead or behind the Russian line, crossing Ebergard's 'T'. The Russian line would be forced to make a second turn under enemy fire

A fuzzy but interesting photograph of Tri Sviatitelia, *fourth ship in the Russian line, taken circa 1914 in Sevastopol harbor. The ship on the right is auxiliary cruiser* Almaz, *the ship that first spotted the Germans.* (U.S. Naval Historical Center)

to meet this threat, and during the turn the Russians would not be able to return fire effectively, since their fire control equipment and methods essentially limited them to straight-line courses while shooting.

So like Jellicoe at Jutland, Ebergard hesitated. Some accounts state that he waited until *Goeben* came into sight before turning to bring his broadsides to bear, but this is contradicted by Nevinskii, who says that Ebergard ordered an eight-point (90°) turn in succession to port before the enemy was sighted.[35] This is confirmed by the German official history; soon after sighting *Almaz* and the second ship, again, almost certainly *Kagul*, as *Goeben* continued on an easterly course, 'five battleships appeared on a southwesterly course between the first two ships sighted and numerous torpedo-boats were observed on other bearings'. So it would seem that the Russian squadron was well along in its deployment by the time it was sighted by *Goeben*, with at least some of the battleships already having made their 8-point turn to port, which would have put them on a course roughly SSW, a good match for what the Germans observed. The German official history describes the feeling aboard the German ships as the Russians came into sight: 'At last the long desired opportunity to measure strength with the enemy seemed to have arrived'.[36]

Aboard *Evstafii*, Nevinskii estimated the range as 45 cables (9000 yards), thanks to the misty conditions, the range was already half that prescribed by the fleet staff for engaging the enemy, and well within the range limits considered effective by the Germans before the war. The Russians had lost their first advantage, but worse was soon to follow. The range-taker on *Evstafii* was unable to obtain a reliable reading because of the mist, while the after turret reported that it was having trouble seeing the target, the wind was light, so the smoke from the ship's own funnels, quickly cooling in the chilly and damp November air, was hanging low on the water.[37] Ebergard's staff passed the order for 'less smoke' to the boiler rooms.

But aboard the next ship in line, *Ioann Zlatoust*, visibility was even worse. Having followed in *Evstafii*'s wake, her gunnery officer, Lieutenant V M Smirnov, was having a hard time making out the enemy due to the combination of mist and smoke from the flagship. *Ioann Zlatoust* was the 'master' ship for brigade firing, so although Ebergard had already hoisted the flag signal to open fire, *Evstafii* waited for several agonising minutes before shooting, expecting to receive the data for centralised firing from *Zlatoust*. Finally a signal was received, 'P-600,' that is, set the sights for 60 cables (circa 12,000 yards). This was greeted with incredulity aboard *Evstafii*, where the range was known to be far less. Apparently *Zlatoust*'s rangetakers had obtained an inaccurate reading due to the poor visibility.

The situation was growing urgent. Aboard the flagship, *Goeben* could be seen starting to turn to starboard. This would bring her onto a parallel course and unmask her full ten-gun broadside. The staff aboard *Evstafii* had already tried to transmit the correct range to *Zlatoust*, but the latter's constant repetition of the 'P-600' sight-setting was jamming the flagship's transmissions; the flag gunnery officer, Senior Lieutenant D B Kolechitskii,

next tried to semaphore *Zlatoust* to pass control to *Evstafii*, but again the there was no response, only the repeated signal 'P-600'. The flagship was at last getting good ranges, and these showed that the distance to the enemy was down to 40 cables (8000 yards) and closing. Nevinskii reported that he was ready to open fire on local data. Finally, Admiral Ebergard reportedly muttered: 'We cannot wait any longer....This is not a training exercise. Open fire at once!'[38]

Evstafii opened fire at about 12:24 using a range of 38.5 cables (7700 yards); instead of the normal single ranging shots prescribed by the gunnery instructions in force, Nevinskii ordered a two-gun salvo, perhaps because the range was so short. One gun from each turret fired, and at least one hit was observed amidships on *Goeben*.[39]

Russian accounts say that it was about a minute before *Goeben* replied, while *Goeben*'s own war-diary puts the delay at about two minutes. She may not have completed her turn yet.[40] In addition, the war diary indicates that she was having a great deal of trouble making out the Russians, since the fog was thicker in their direction. The official history reports that fire was opened at a range of 7000-7200 metres (7656-7874 yards), which agrees remarkably well with the Russian range estimates.

The first German salvo was 'over,' falling between *Evstafii* and the destroyer *Zharkii* some 300 yards to port. The Russians judged that the salvo had a wide scattering in deflection, which may indicate that *Goeben* had fired it before her turn was completed.[41] Nevertheless, it was a lucky salvo for the Germans; one shell passed through *Evstafii*'s middle funnel and burst over the port side; its splinters wrecked a motor-launch and damaged two davits. Far more importantly, the splinters swept away the antennas for the flagship's gunnery control wireless, making it impossible for the flagship to correct the inaccurate ranging data being transmitted by *Ioann Zlatoust*. The antennas were repaired within a quarter of an hour, but by that time the battle had ended.

Soon after *Evstafii*'s first salvo, the Torpedo Brigade commander, Captain M P Sablin, 'on his own initiative,' led the destroyers forward in an attempt to launch a torpedo attack.[42] However, they were not able to close, the older, slower destroyers probably held the group back, and toward the end of the action Ebergard ordered the attack cancelled. In any case, the torpedo craft had trouble even seeing the enemy.

By this time *Zlatoust* had opened fire using the incorrect 60-cable range; she never came near the target, and in fact only her forward turret could even see the enemy. It may well be that she continued transmitting the 60-cable range because she assumed *Evstafii*'s clearly visible hit had been scored with that sight setting, which had been transmitted just before fire was opened. Indeed, if *Zlatoust* saw that *Evstafii*'s shells were falling near the target, and believed that the flagship was using the transmitted range (but for some reason otherwise ignoring the centralised firing commands), she might well have thought hits were being scored. In any event, she continued to transmit the 60-cable range throughout the course of the action. *Panteleimon* never even opened fire, because of the mist and the funnel smoke of the two lead-

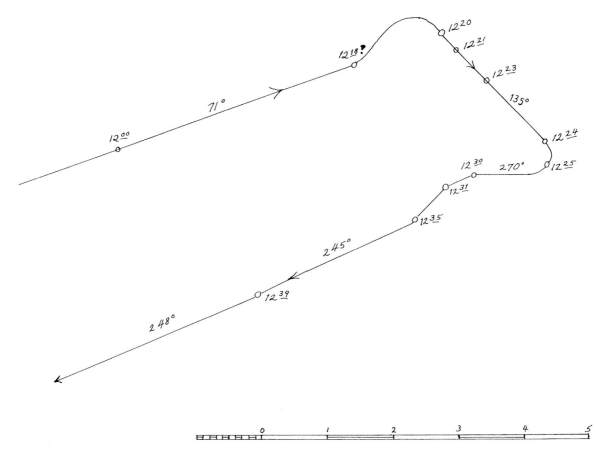

Goeben's track chart for the battle, traced from her war-diary. Note that the time/distance relationships in the chart are not reliable, despite the scale (unlabelled, but presumably in nautical miles) at the bottom, for example, Goeben's speed between 12:20 and 12:24 works out to more than 33kts!

ing ships, 'her turrets did not see the enemy at all', which may indicate that the elevated fire control positions could see the enemy.[43] Nevinskii reports that, since *Tri Sviatitelia* was lagging behind the other ships, she turned later and 'saw the entire battle much better than *Panteleimon*'. However, she was using *Zlatoust's* incorrect range data, so she also was wide of the mark. *Rostislav*, which was not part of the centralised fire system because her 10in/45 guns had such different ballistic qualities from the 12in/40 guns of the other battleships, fired a few rounds at *Breslau*, which was trailing *Goeben*; the cruiser sought shelter by moving toward the battlecruiser's disengaged side. *Tri Sviatitelia* fired on *Breslau* with her secondary battery, although she apparently also fired a few 6in salvos at *Goeben* using a range obtained by the junior gunnery officer, Lieutenant Milashevich, who measured the height of *Goeben's* funnels through his binoculars.[44] To all intents and purposes, however, the brief engagement was essentially a duel between *Evstafii* and *Goeben*.

Under the circumstances, it is hardly surprising that the Russian flagship began to suffer. Since the first salvo was clearly an 'over', *Goeben's* fire control officer, *Korvetten-Kapitän* Knispel, ordered the range reduced by 200 metres; the second salvo fell short, but *Evstafii* had been bracketed within very narrow limits and the third

salvo was dead-on, scoring at least two hits. The fourth salvo was also on target. But *Goeben* was by no means having things all her own way. Although the Russian flagship suffered heavy casualties from these hits, she was not critically damaged, and, having hit her enemy once, *Evstafii* was now firing with all the guns that would bear. *Goeben's* war-diary reports that the '*Die russischen Salven liegen gut*', 'The Russian salvos fell well', so well, in fact, that the German official history believed that 'The *Goeben* then lay under the concentrated fire of five battleships', despite the fact that *Evstafii* was in fact the only ship firing on the German battlecruiser with an accurate range. It may be that the numerous splashes from *Evstafii's* 8in and 6in guns mislead the Germans into thinking they were being subjected to the combined fire of the entire Russian squadron.

The Russians in fact were convinced that they were hitting *Goeben* repeatedly. The two sides were on almost parallel courses, so the rate of change of range was low, while the range was so short that the 'danger space' of the big guns, the error in range estimate that would still allow a hit, was large. Nevinskii wrote:

with the third salvo I saw a hit on the after part of *Goeben*. I consider this hit quite certain, since it was confirmed by observers standing on the bridge. In the subsequent salvos hits were clearly seen amidships, abaft the after funnel, as well as in the area of *Goeben's* second turret. It is difficult to judge the hits with complete confidence, although fire and black smoke were seen.[45]

In fact it was even more difficult to judge the hits than Nevinskii realised, *Evstafii's* opening salvo scored the only hit for the Russians, and after that it would seem that the Russian flagship was firing long until the very end of the action. It is very likely that Nevinskii thought he was hitting, misinterpreting the flashes of *Goeben's* own guns for hits. Thus he may never have regained the range after his second salvo, which was definitely an 'over'. In any event, only one hit was scored, but that hit probably decided the outcome of the action.

Breaking Off

At the opening of the action, according to the official history, Souchon 'attempted to draw round ahead of the enemy at high speed', when that was accomplished, he would presumably have tried to cripple the leading Russian ships one by one, concentrating his full broadsides on them in turn, while the rest of the Russian squadron was unable to reply effectively. The official history goes on to say that this move was frustrated 'by a change in course on the part of the Russians'. There is, however, no evidence in *Goeben's* track-chart of the action or her war diary that any such manoeuvre was actually started or that the Russians altered course at any time during the action. But it is likely enough that Souchon harboured some such intention at the outset of the battle. The question of why he did not make more use of *Goeben's* vastly superior speed is one of the more puzzling riddles of the battle.

In any event, instead of overtaking the Russians, *Goeben* maintained a course that was almost parallel to the Russian line-of-battle, the two forces converging slightly. Then, after only a few minutes of gunfire, when the range had closed to about 34 cables (circa 6800 yards) and *Evstafii* had been heavily hit, *Goeben* turned sharply away from the Russians. The German official history tries to put a good face on this abrupt retreat, stating that 'the Russian line disappeared like a phantom in the fog', as a result of a course change.[46] But here again, *Goeben's* own war diary and trackchart of the action show that it was *Goeben* that turned away from the Russians at 12:24 German time, probably about 12:28-12:29 Russian time.

Why the sudden withdrawal? Before the action Souchon seems to have shown no qualms about engaging the entire Russian force; there is a very good chance that he, like most foreign observers, thought the Russians would be inept and so fall easy prey to his ship despite their superior numbers. But at about 12:22 (German time; circa 12:26-12:27 Russian time) word reached the bridge that there was a fire in casemate no. III. *Evstafii's* opening two-gun salvo had scored one hit, and as it turned out serious damage had been caused.

No. III 15cm casemate was amidships on the port side; an after-action report described the hit in the following terms:

> The projectile, probably a 30.5cm shell of older construction, appears to have penetrated the 150mm thick casemate armour just barely despite the short distance of only 65 hectometers; at any rate a large part of the projectile fragments remained outboard and were deflected downward, where the torpedo net and the net supports were heavily [damaged] and the barrels of the nos. 4 and 5 15cm guns were slightly damaged, and where the only pieces of the enemy shell were found. Furthermore, shell fragments damaged the left barrel of 'E' 28cm turret.[47]

But the shell's effects were by no means limited to the ship's exterior. A large hole was torn open in the armour and shell splinters and armour fragments penetrated into the casemate, detonating three high-explosive 15cm ready-use shells and breaking up two armour-piercing shells; sixteen propellant charges were set on fire.[48] The fire and its effects were soon visible:

> The commander of "B" turret, overlooking the upper deck and no. 3 casemate, felt the hit and saw flames and later smoke over the [deck edge] railing and [the flames and smoke] probably also appeared through two coal [scuttle] hatches that were blown open above the upper deck.[49]

Thanks to the armoured screening bulkheads between the 15cm guns, the fire did not spread to the neighbouring casemates; but the effects were nevertheless very serious, 'Flames entered the magazine which supplied both the above casemate and the one adjoining, but did not ignite any charges'.[50] Georg Kopp, a wireless operator aboard *Goeben*, provides a more dramatic description of events in his post-war memoirs:

> In a moment an appalling shoot of flame swept through the ammunition hoist below and endangered the magazine in the bottom of the ship....It was only through the presence of mind of a petty officer that this catastrophe was averted. Below, in the ammunition compartment, he heard the explosion in the casemate through the hoist. Hazily guessing what had happened above, he quickly opened the flooding-valves. The ammunition compartment therefore lay under water at the moment when the flames shot below.[51]

If Souchon had entertained hopes of an easy victory over the Russians, they were shattered by that first Russian salvo. His ship had been severely, perhaps almost fatally damaged and he believed himself to be 'under the concentrated fire of five battleships'. So it seems likely that Souchon decided the game wasn't worth the candle. The Russians saw *Goeben* suddenly turn away, she fired several salvos from her after turrets then disappeared into the mist. That it was *Goeben* and not the Russians who sheered off is also noted by Kopp:

> Time dragged on in tormenting uncertainty [in the wireless room]. The echoes of the fight resounded dully

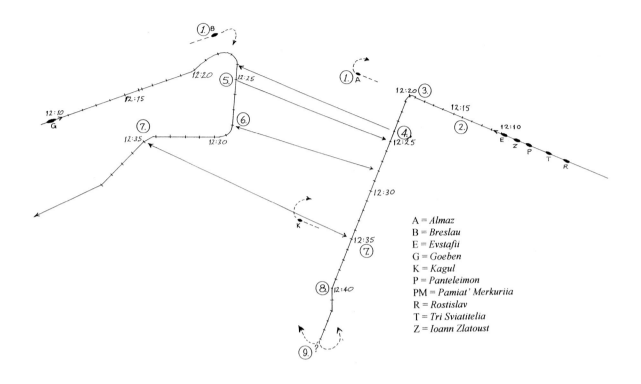

The author's reconstruction of the battle. German times have been advanced by four minutes to bring them into agreement with Russian times; Goeben's course has been adjusted from the 135° given in her war-diary to 185°, which accords better with other accounts of the battle (see note 40). Note that, despite the apparent precision of the times and ranges given, the contradictions between the various accounts of the battle make it impossible to be certain of the movements of the opposing sides.

Key: 1) ca. 12:10 Breslau and Almaz sight one another, range approximately 32 cables (6400 yards). 2) ca. 12:14 Goeben's smoke is briefly sighted from Evstafii's bridge at approximately 80-90 cables (16,000-18,000 yards). 3) ca. 12:19 the Russian fleet begins an 8-point turn to port. 4) ca. 12:24 Evstafii opens fire at a range of 38.5 cables (7700 yards). 5) ca. 12:25 Goeben opens fire at a range of 7656-7874 yards. 6) ca. 12:28 Goeben turns away from the Russians; the closest range during the action is about 34 cables (6800 yards). 7) ca. 12:35 both sides cease fire. 8) ca. 12:40 Russian squadron turns approximately 20° to port to avoid a suspicious floating object; the fleet resumes its previous course after a few minutes. 9) ca. 12:45 The Russian fleet reverses course and steers for Sevastopol. According to Soviet-era sources, the fleet turned to port; émigré publications state that it turned to starboard.

through space. Then the *Goeben*'s hull began to tremble; a rhythmic quiver. So we were at full speed again. Then we heard only the two after-turrets firing. In the forepart the ship was silent. After, the silence became complete.[52]

Kopp's memory was accurate, *Goeben* increased speed and turned away from the Russians, so she was able to fire at them with only her aft turrets, just as the Russians observed and in direct contradiction to the German official history. According to *Goeben*'s war diary, firing ceased at 12:32, which, recalling that the German time was probably about 4-5 minutes behind Russian time, synchronises fairly well with the figure of 12:35 for the end of firing given in Russian publications.

In his after-action report, Admiral Ebergard described what happened in the first minutes after *Goeben* pulled her disappearing act:

> Firing ceased. The fleet continued to remain on its previous course, in readiness to continue the battle should *Goeben* reappear....At about 12:40, not having seen *Goeben* and having the intention of closing with her, I gave an order for a turn to starboard. The rudder had been laid over to starboard, when straight ahead on the bow a floating object was seen. Wary of the possibility of running onto floating mines, I changed direction and made a turn to port.[53]

This was not an unreasonable fear, given that the action

had been fought close to the extensive minefields guarding the approaches to Sevastopol, and the fact that moored mines often broke free from their anchors in rough weather. Lieutenant N S Chirikov, the senior navigating officer aboard *Almaz*, recorded in his notebook that the fleet made a 20-25° turn to port at 12:37, then, once the floating object had been avoided, resumed its former south-westerly course for a few minutes. Then, at 12:45, Ebergard reversed course; according to émigré publications, he turned to starboard (toward *Goeben*'s last known position), while most Soviet-era descriptions say that the turn was to port (away from *Goeben*). Ebergard soon realised that *Goeben* had successfully slipped away from him. Lacking the fuel and speed to intercept her, he ordered the fleet back to Sevastopol, where it arrived later that afternoon.

As for *Goeben*, the German official account of her post-battle manoeuvres is vague and misleading:

> In the prevailing fog it was unfortunately impossible to pick up the enemy battleships or torpedo-boats and cruisers to renew the engagement. The *Goeben* had been unable to take advantage of her superior armament and speed at the short range which obtained during the action.
>
> On the assumption that the enemy would return to Sebastopol [sic]….The *Goeben* remained at sea together with the *Peik* [a Turkish torpedo boat] until November 20 without, however, sighting the enemy again.[54]

If we accept this account, we must believe that, despite *Goeben*'s greatly superior speed, a correct estimate of the enemy's intentions and full knowledge of that enemy's recent location, Souchon was unable to intercept the Russians before they returned to Sevastopol. This is quite simply unbelievable. It is far more likely that Souchon had no wish to resume the action, and therefore avoided the presumed course of the Russian squadron. This is confirmed by the track chart appended to *Goeben*'s war-diary and accurately reproduced as *Karte 4* in the official history, which shows that after the action *Goeben* steered away from Sevastopol, first travelling south-west, then south-east and finally returning to Constantinople along the northern coast of Anatolia. So, despite the impression conveyed in the official account that *Goeben* went hunting for the enemy and only failed to find them due to the fog, she had actually avoided the likely path of the enemy squadron.

Damages and Casualties

Both *Evstafii* and *Goeben* had suffered fairly serious damage due to fires started in the secondary batteries. This type of damage proved all too common during the war, and in the densely-packed and densely-manned secondary batteries could lead to horrific casualties. HMS *Malaya* was almost destroyed by a fire in her secondary battery at Jutland, and suffered 102 casualties from this alone.[55] In comparison, both *Evstafii* and *Goeben* got off lightly. The entire twelve-man crew of *Goeben*'s No. III

casemate was killed, one of them a Turkish sailor, and one man in the handling room died after the battle from smoke inhalation.[56] The fumes from the fire, and the need for immediate damage control work, probably put the entire portside 15cm battery out of action. This would explain why *Goeben*'s secondary battery never joined in the firing, despite the fact that it was German practice to fire 15cm salvos between big-gun salvos.[57] It is even possible, as Kopp suggests, that the ship may have been in danger of a catastrophic explosion in the secondary magazines, although here Kopp may have been 'spicing up' his story a bit, since there seem to have been a lot of ships saved in the nick of time by a heroic petty officer in the magazines during the First World War.

Russian sources have claimed much heavier German casualties. These credit *Evstafii* with no less than fourteen hits: three 12in and the rest 8in or 6in shells, with 115 men killed and 59 wounded. These figures are of the same order as the number of casualties suffered by *Malaya*, and so are not inherently improbable. However, they were based on reports from Russian agents in Turkey (probably including the 'numerous Armenian and Greek residents scattered about the port' who, Ebergard suggested in his after-action report, would be a useful source of information regarding *Goeben*'s damage).[58] They are not corroborated by any of the German accounts of the battle, and so must be considered grossly inflated. *Goeben* remained at sea for two days after the action, an unlikely activity had her casualties been as great as the Russians believed. In typical fashion, the German official history downplays the damage, saying that 'Since the ammunition at the guns did not explode but simply burned, the material damage was slight' but this is no doubt substantially correct. *Goeben* was next at sea on 6 December, which indicates that no very great damage was done to the ship.

As for *Evstafii*, she sustained a hit on her middle funnel in *Goeben*'s first salvo, which destroyed the fire control wireless antennas and a motor launch and damaged the davits. One shell, very probably from the third salvo, struck the foremost 6in casemate on the starboard side; the shell hit at the joint between two 5in plates, breaking off the top of one plate and the corner of the other; the 6in gun was damaged and its 10-man crew wiped out, as well as the battery commander. The shell or its splinters ignited some of the ready-use ammunition and a serious fire erupted, which was only brought under control by the efforts of the 6in gun crews from the disengaged side.[59]

Another shell, probably from the third salvo also, hit a 6in casemate amidships. It made an almost perfectly circular hole in the 5in armour, then travelled clear across the ship before exploding near the port side, scattering splinters over a wide area and causing numerous casualties. Another shell struck one of the casemates (one account saying that it struck an 8in casemate, another that it hit the foremost 6in casemate), but it broke up after passing through the armour and failed to explode. It was found lying on the deck, its cap and base torn off. Finally, one shell, usually attributed to one of *Goeben*'s last salvos, struck the water close alongside and caused splinter damage to the hull forward in the region of frame 22. Total casualties were five officers and 29 men killed and another 24 men wounded. Repairs to *Evstafii* were complicated by the fact that some of the damaged armour plates were of complex shape; they were replaced by plates of similar shape taken from the old battleship *Dvenadtsat' Apostolov*. The ship was repaired and back in service 29 November, and was next at sea on 11 December.

In the gunnery duel that developed between *Goeben* and *Evstafii*, the German ship had several important advantages. To begin with, there was the simple fact that she was a dreadnought, and could therefore fire salvos with enough shells to allow meaningful spotting. This, after all, was the *raison d'être* of the dreadnought battleship. With five-gun salvos, *Goeben* could see if her entire salvo was short (five splashes visible), over (no splashes visible), or straddling (fewer than five splashes visible). *Evstafii*, on the other had, could fire two-gun salvos at best, and even that proved impossible for much of the action. Nevinskii notes that, soon after the second salvo he switched to rapid fire (*beglyi ogon*), meaning that each gun was fired as soon as it was ready.[60] He did this, he explained:

> since the after turret reported on several occasions that it could not see the target due to smoke and mist. The forward turret had good visibility the whole time.[61]

Firing either two-gun salvos or individual shots, Nevinskii could not straddle the target in any meaningful way; one or two 'shorts' were not enough to keep the enemy in the pattern of straddling splashes, while 'overs' were lost behind the target's hull and smoke. Thus it is likely that Nevinskii was relying on observing hits on the target to correct his shooting. But the 'hits' he thought he saw were probably the flashes of *Goeben*'s own guns, or were perhaps caused by the fire and secondary explosions that followed *Evstafii*'s one *bona fide* hit on No. III casemate. In fact the fire and explosions triggered by this hit may well explain Russian claims that two shell hits were observed in the first salvo, rather than one. Nevinskii reports that *Evstafii*'s second salvo was long, and it is likely that her subsequent shots also fell beyond the target.

Another significant advantage for *Goeben* was the higher muzzle velocity of her 28cm/50 guns compared to that of *Evstafii*'s 12in/40 guns. This fact, combined with the somewhat more aerodynamically efficient shape of the German shells, gave *Goeben*'s guns a much flatter trajectory at the ranges of the battle, as Table 2 clearly shows.

As can be seen, at the battle ranges of the Cape Sarych action the danger space of *Evstafii*'s guns was only 70 per cent as large as that of *Goeben*'s guns. Given the

Rostislav, the last ship in the Russian line; a photograph taken in 1913 when the ship was part of an international squadron dispatched to Constantinople to maintain order in the wake of the Balkan wars. (U.S. Naval Historical Center)

inherent variations in the performance of any group of guns, this means that *Goeben* could expect to score 30 per cent more hits, all else being equal. Thus between her denser salvos and the flatter trajectory of her shells, *Goeben* had a significant advantage over the Russian predreadnought, a fact reflected in the greater number of hits she scored.

The ammunition expenditure of both sides is interesting. According to her war-diary, *Goeben* had fired only nineteen 28cm shells, twelve while abeam the enemy and seven 'when the enemy was astern'. This seems a rather low figure for a ten-minute exchange of fire, but it is likely that poor visibility reduced the rate of fire and also caused some turrets to miss firing in a salvo. This would go a long way toward explaining Russian reports that *Goeben* had fired 'not less than six salvos'.[62] Given her known expenditure of shells, *Goeben* probably fired three four-gun salvos while on an almost-parallel course with the Russians and another three salvos from her aft turrets after turning away. The supposition that *Goeben* fired while turning away may also explain the two 'stray' shells that splashed 10-16m from *Rostislav*'s starboard side toward the end of the action. Like the Russian fire control system, the German system could not handle rapid manoeuvres of its own ship, so the ship's sudden turn probably threw off the gunners.[63]

Reports on *Evstafii*'s ammunition expenditure vary, most accounts say she fired twelve 12in shells, while Nevinskii says sixteen rounds were fired, of which 'eleven or twelve' were from the forward turret. She also fired fourteen 8in and nineteen 6in rounds.[64] As for *Ioann Zlatoust*, she had fired six 12in shells, while *Tri Sviatitelia* fired twelve 12in. However, since these ships were firing at the incorrect range of 60 cables (12,000 yards), their

shells fell into the empty sea and had no effect on the action. *Rostislav* fired two 10in and six 6in rounds at *Breslau*, since she was forbidden to join in the 'brigade firing' at the main target. According to one source, the entire squadron fired no less than 162 6in shells, which seems rather high, given *Evstafii*'s modest expenditure of medium-calibre shells.[65]

Consequences and Controversy

The brief action off Cape Sarych had a number of interesting consequences. In the first place, *Goeben* never again sought action with the combined Black Sea Fleet; during another short engagement off the Bosphorus on 10 May 1915 Captain Ackermann (Souchon was not aboard during this action) was willing to engage *Evstafii*, *Ioann Zlatoust* and *Rostislav*, but when *Panteleimon* and *Tri Sviatitelia* joined in *Goeben* again used her superior speed to escape, having suffered two hits from *Panteleimon* without scoring any on the Russian ships.

For the Russians, the action underscored the fact that any isolated detachment of ships would be easy prey for the faster and more powerful *Goeben*; only the combined firepower of the predreadnoughts could counter the German ship. Even the 23kt cruisers were too slow for independent activities. As Admiral Ebergard noted:

> The complete absence of fast cruisers in the Black Sea Fleet places us in an extremely unfavourable position for patrolling and the maintenance of a blockade [of the Bosphorus], since with the exception of the four destroyers that have just entered service, there is not a single vessel that can be detached from the fleet.[66]

Table 2: COMPARISON OF EVSTAFII'S AND GOEBEN'S GUN TRAJECTORIES

Evstafii's 12in/40 guns:

Angle of Elevation	Range (metres)	Angle of Descent	Danger space against *Goeben* (metres)
3.0°	5178.7	4.226°	167
3.25°	5482	4.64°	154.7
3.5°	5774.3	5.066°	144.1
3.75°	6056.1	5.502°	135
4.0°	6328.2	5.949°	127
4.25°	6591.1	6.405°	120
4.5°	6845.4	6.87°	113.8
4.75°	7091.4	7.343°	108.3
5.0°	7329.8	7.824°	103.4
5.25°	7561	8.312°	99
5.5°	7785.4	8.806°	95.1
5.75°	8003.4	9.305°	91.5

Goeben's 11in/50 guns:

Angle of Elevation	Range (metres)	Angle of Descent	Danger space against *Evstafii* (metres)
2.25°	5334	2.93°	220.9
2.5°	5788.8	3.28°	199.7
2.75°	6229.2	3.643°	182
3.0°	6655.6	4.017°	167.1
3.25°	7068.5	4.403°	154.4
3.5°	7468.3	4.798°	143.5
3.75°	7855.8	5.204°	134

I am indebted to Kent Crawford for this data, which was developed using the ballistic computer program developed by William J Jurens. Although it is impossible to be absolutely certain of the accuracy of this extrapolated data, it is certainly of the right order. There are several formulae for calculating danger space; I have used this one:

Danger space = Target width + Target height/Tangent of Angle of Descent. For both ships I have used the maximum beam as the width (*Goeben* 29.5 metres, *Evstafii* 22.55 metres), while for the height I have used the distance from the waterline to the tops of the highest turrets (*Goeben* 10.16 metres, *Evstafii* 10.15 metres, as measured from scale drawings).

Evstafii's hit on Goeben's *no. III 15cm casemate.* (Courtesy Bundesarchiv, Koblenz)

Ebergard's point was well taken. Fortunately, the fast new *Novik* type destroyers were joining the fleet in increasing numbers, and so it became possible to detach them for anti-shipping sweeps along the Turkish coast. In this they proved very effective, since Turkey's railway transport system was so underdeveloped, coal for Constantinople had to be moved by sea, and the destroyers soon swept up most of the larger colliers and many of the smaller ones. By the summer of 1915 the Turkish capital was suffering a severe fuel shortage, which greatly hindered the operations of *Goeben* and *Breslau*. This situation persisted throughout the latter part of 1915 and all of 1916.

Like all inconclusive battles, the action off Cape Sarych has generated a good deal of controversy and second-guessing over the years. Soon after the battle Naval Minister Admiral I K Grigorovich personally bestowed upon Ebergard the Order of the White Eagle with Crossed Swords for his performance in the battle, but this may have been a back-handed compliment. The Order of White Eagle was originally a Polish decoration subsumed into the Russian system of awards when Poland was incorporated into the empire; certainly by the 1870s 'the Order of the White Eagle was not held in very high regard'.[67] There was only one class, and the fact that it was issued with crossed swords merely means that it was awarded for meritorious military, rather than civilian, service. As noted previously, from the very outset of war in the Black Sea there was dissatisfaction with Ebergard at the Russian high command, and his rela-

tionship with Grigorovich had been strained even in the pre-war years. His relations with the Grand Duke Nikolai Nikolaevich, supreme commander of the Russian armed forces in 1914-1915, were bad from the start and grew worse after the grand duke was transferred to command the Caucasian Front in late 1915. While much of Nikolaevich's carping was due to his failure to appreciate naval realities, there were also some naval officers who felt that Ebergard's performance was less than adequate. This attitude was especially prevalent amongst some of the naval staff officers at *Stavka*, in particular Captain 2nd Rank A D Bubnov.[68] Bubnov's complaints were directed toward Ebergard's role in larger issues of strategy, such as the blockade of Constantinople, the difficulties the Black Sea Fleet experienced in 1916 in trying to combat the U-boat threat and, in particular, the perceived foot-dragging by Ebergard and his staff over plans for an assault on the Bosphorus. These opinions were bound to colour Stavka's views of Ebergard's performance in the action off Cape Sarych. As a result of these criticisms Ebergard's position with the naval and political hierarchy was gradually undermined, and when *Goeben* escaped from a Russian trap in July 1916, Naval Minister Grigorovich and Admiral A I Rusin, head of the Naval General Staff, agreed that it was time to replace Ebergard. Vice Admiral A V Kolchak was appointed in his place.

After the war Ebergard's decisions before and during the action off Cape Sarych came in for severe criticism by

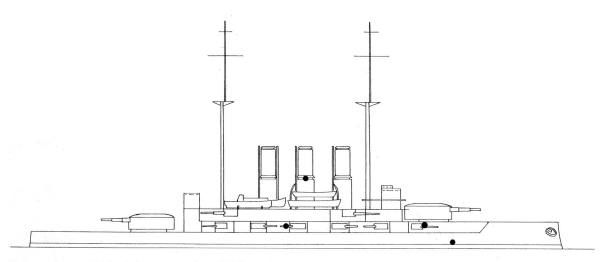

Diagram showing Goeben's *hits on* Evstafii; *a fifth hit, a dud, apparently struck one of the 8in casemate guns on the upper deck.*

the Soviet naval theorist M A Petrov, a former officer of the Imperial Navy. In his book *Two Battles*, Petrov took Ebergard to task for a number of alleged failures at Cape Sarych, and many of his charges have been repeated by Soviet and post-*glastnost'* Russian writers. By the time Petrov had penned his critique, Ebergard was no longer able to defend himself; he had died in 1919, probably as a result of the terrible privations of the civil war years. Another crucial witness, Captain Galanin of the *Evstafii*, had died in the spring of 1915 of a brain haemorrhage.[69] Ebergard's defence was therefore taken up by a former officer living in emigration, Captain 1st Rank Ia. Podgornyi, who made use of material compiled by former officers of Ebergard's command. Unfortunately, both Podgornyi and his informants were frequently working from memory, without access to official reports, and their accounts of the action have sometimes confused rather than clarified matters. Podgornyi also seems to have had a very hazy understanding of the Black Sea Fleet's combined-firing technique. Petrov's criticisms, Podgornyi's responses and further observations on Ebergard's conduct of the battle are summarised below.

Petrov's fundamental criticism was that the Black Sea Fleet's leadership had a 'purely artillery-based understanding' of naval tactics.[70] In Petrov's view this was the root source of the other faults manifested during the battle. The first of these was that the centralised system of fire control was 'artificial' and 'poorly suited to combat conditions'. He believed it was unnecessary because:

> The losses and damage to *Goeben* exceeded those of the Russian fleet. This once again shows that individual ships fired well and the failure [to win a victory over *Goeben*] can be entirely attributed to combat organization and tactics.[71]

Petrov's assessment was based on the inaccurate wartime intelligence reports to the effect that *Evstafii* had scored no less than fourteen hits on *Goeben*. Proceeding from this false information, Petrov concluded that the battleships could have scored enough hits firing independently to cripple *Goeben*. We now know, as Petrov did not, that in fact only a single hit had been scored, and that *Evstafii*'s small salvos greatly limited her ability to judge her hitting by spotting. Thus, even if Petrov's judgement that the centralised fire method was 'artificial' and 'ill-suited to combat conditions' is true to some degree, some such system was clearly a matter of necessity given that the predreadnoughts would have to fight dreadnoughts. In fact, the battle had proven not that the fleet's centralised fire control techniques were fundamentally flawed, but rather that they were simply too rigid in the face of an unforeseen set of circumstances, a fact which the next (1915) edition of the spotting rules sought to address. The following passage was clearly derived from the experiences of 18 November 1914:

> The control of the fire by the second ship…cannot be taken as a general rule, because if an unexpected encounter occurs when weather is rainy or foggy, the enemy will surely be observed by the first ship before the second can see it, and a substantial delay in orders would surely follow.[72]

Petrov also overlooked the problem of spotting confusion likely to occur if several ships were firing independently on a single target. This is a curious lapse on his part, because in the Tsarist Navy he had been a gunnery officer, and so must have understood the problems of concentrating fire. But there are several other places where Petrov either deliberately ignores or displays ignorance of basic gunnery matters.

A case in point is his very next argument, that the demands for rigid station-keeping implicit in the centralised fire control method imposed an 'inflexible' single-column cruising formation on the fleet, whereas Petrov argued that a two-column formation (three battleships in one column, two in the other) would have permitted the fleet to deploy into battle formation twice as fast. This overlooks several important factors. First, as Podgornyi noted, this argument ignores the fact that, thanks to her superior speed, *Goeben* might have approached from any point of the compass, not merely from dead ahead.[73] Had *Goeben* emerged from the mist on the squadron's beam, the Russians would have already been in battle order, while under these circumstances Petrov's two-column formation would have meant that one column would have been masked by the other. But both Podgornyi and Petrov missed an even more fundamental point, since 'brigade shooting' was limited to three ships due to the confusion in splashes and spotting that could result with too many ships firing, Petrov's two-column formation would not have led to a more rapid deployment of the three leading ships. These were, the very ships that would be engaging the main enemy. Again, as a gunnery officer, Petrov must surely have been aware of the three-ship limit.

It may also be noted that, depending on which wing the two-column formation deployed on, the fleet flagship might wind up in the middle, rather than at the head of the formation. This would be inconvenient, since in battle the simplest and surest method of co-ordinated manoeuvring was the follow-the-leader system.

Petrov's next point was that Ebergard, knowing that *Goeben* was at sea, should have disposed his torpedo craft at the head of the formation, so that they could launch an immediate torpedo attack on the German ship. Such an attack might have led to damage that would slow the enemy down, thus 'forcing the elusive *Goeben* to battle'.[74] But Nevinskii notes that the destroyers and torpedo boats were astern of the battleships 'in order not to hinder the shooting of the battleships in case an enemy suddenly

appeared'.[75] In the first place, in poor visibility it was considered unwise to station the torpedo boats where they might be mistaken for enemy ships; perhaps more importantly, the smoke from the funnels of the older, coal-fired torpedo boats could have interfered with the gunnery of the battleships, especially in the light winds and cool air. Certainly *Evstafii*'s funnel smoke had had an effect on the ships astern of her and may even have affected her own after turret's ability to see the target.

After noting that only the First Torpedo Division was made up of modern destroyers that were faster than *Goeben*, Petrov states that the four torpedo divisions could have launched attacks aimed at 'enveloping [the enemy] in a circle of four divisions, or striking from two sides'.[76] Just how the older torpedo boats, good for only a little more than 20kts by 1914, were going to 'envelop' the far faster *Goeben* is left unexplained. Furthermore, the German battlecruiser had already shown herself well able to beat off daylight torpedo attacks. On the opening day of the war, *Goeben* had encountered three Russian destroyers off Sevastopol and had seriously damaged *Leitenant Pushchin* with 15cm shellfire at ranges in excess of 50 cables (10,000 yards), that is, at a range about 2000 yards greater than that of the entire action at Cape Sarych.[77] It seems fair to conclude that even in the misty conditions on 18 November the chances of the destroyers being able to get close enough to *Goeben* to launch an effective torpedo attack were not great.

Petrov also claimed that Ebergard's scouting cruisers were not far enough in advance of the battle fleet to pro-

Post war view of the Turkish navy's battlecruiser Yavuz Sultan Selim (*ex-*Goeben). (CPL)

vide adequate warning of the enemy's presence. This overlooks *Goeben*'s superiority in speed over any of the Russian cruisers. *Pamiat' Merkuriia* and *Kagul* were good for about 21kts in 1914, while *Almaz* had a best speed of 18-19kts. Had Ebergard pushed his scouting line beyond the limits of visual contact in the patchy visibility, he would have risked the destruction of one or more of his cruisers by *Goeben* before the main body of the fleet could come up in support. In fact it was the slowest ship, *Almaz*, that first came into contact with the German force. Had she been ten miles ahead of the squadron, as the Black Sea Fleet's orders specified in clear weather, instead of three and a half miles, she surely would have been caught and overwhelmed by the faster German ships. Petrov also argued that Ebergard could have used his three new destroyers as scouts, a role for which they were certainly well suited, but by dispersing them in a scouting line, he would have lost all chance for launching an immediate and concentrated torpedo attack of the sort Petrov himself had recommended. Clearly, the lack of suitable scouts was a critical handicap for the Black Sea Fleet when faced with a fast and powerful opponent such as *Goeben*.

Podgornyi believed that Petrov's arguments were the result of a Bolshevik-inspired desire to denigrate the achievements of the imperial navy. But while Petrov was certainly not above using ideologically-based arguments, it seems likely that he had another and more personally compelling reason for judging Ebergard so severely. Petrov was one of the leading thinkers of the so-called 'Old School' of Soviet naval strategy, and one of the central tenets of this strategy was that a combination of heavy ships and light forces, including torpedo-armed destroyers, could successfully oppose an enemy fleet of superior numbers.[78] In particular, Petrov held that torpedo attacks could whittle down the enemy's battleline sufficiently for the weaker Soviet battleships to have a realistic chance of victory. By arguing that a more aggressive use of the destroyers on the part of the Black Sea Fleet would have 'evened the odds' against *Goeben*, Petrov was clearly using the action off Cape Sarych to support his own contention that a similarly aggressive use of light forces in the Baltic would give the Soviet navy a fighting chance against a more powerful western enemy. In making this case, however, Petrov seems to have either ignored, deliberately or unintentionally, many of the factors operating at Cape Sarych.

Despite Petrov's criticisms, which have often been repeated in subsequent Russian-language versions of the battle, it seems fair to say that Ebergard had performed well, if not brilliantly, in the trying circumstances encountered on 18 November 1914. As for *Evstafii*, a predreadnought engaged in a gunnery duel with a far more powerful dreadnought, it seems fitting to close with Ebergard's own assessment of her performance:

> Due to the weather conditions on 5 (18) November, the battle with this powerful ship [*Goeben*] came down to an individual struggle with the lone battleship *Evstafii*, since the other ships, travelling in column formation, either did not see the enemy at all or [saw him] intermittently, and the entire weight of the battle fell to the lot of my flagship.[79]

Notes

I would like to express my thanks to the people who provided materials or otherwise helped in the research and writing of this article: Byron Angel, *Kapitän zur See* Baer, Kent Crawford, Alister Greenway, Professor Paul G Halpern, John Harland, J Dane Hartgrove, Tim Lanzendörfer, Dr. Timothy Mulligan, George Nekrasov, Nathan Okun, A Plotto, Bill Schleihauf, Jan Torbet and Dr. med. Norbert Weismann. Of course, none of these generous individuals can be held responsible for the opinions or errors in the article.

1   This important but overlooked point was noted by Commander G M Nekrasov, RAN in a letter to *Journal of the Royal United Services Institute*, April 1993, p.85.

2   The basic German account is H Lorey, *Der Krieg in den türkischen Gewässern*, 2 vols., (Berlin: E S Mittler, 1928-1938), vol. 1, pp.64-66. I have used an English translation prepared by the US Navy, *The War at Sea 1914-1918: The War in Turkish Waters*, vol. 1: *The Mediterranean Division* (translated by H S Babbitt; typescript held at the Naval War College, Newport, RI). The corresponding material appears on pp.92-94. This will be cited as the 'Lorey translation'. However, Lorey must be used with some caution, as becomes clear when his description of the battle is compared with *Goeben*'s war diary (*Kriegstagebuch*, or KTB), available on microfilm from the US Naval Archives and Records Administration (Records of the German Navy, 1850-1945: KTB, 2 August 1914-31 December 1915: file PG 63187, T1022, roll 311). For the Russian side, there are three eyewitness accounts, the most important of which is A M Nevinskii, 'Boi s lineinym kreiserom "Geben" 5 Noiabria 1914 g. u Mysa Sarych', [The Battle with the Battlecruiser *Goeben* on 5 [18] November 1914 Off Cape Sarych], in *Russkoe voenno-morskoe iskusstvo: sbornik statei* [The Russian Naval Art: A Collection of Articles] (Moscow: Voenno-Morskoe Izdatel'stvo, 1951), pp.407-415. Nevinskii was senior gunnery officer aboard the battleship *Evstafii*; his account seems to be supported in all its major points by other sources, although his Soviet editors noted that the article 'was written by the author from memory and contains a number of questionable statements'. Next comes N S Chirikov, 'Admiral A A Ebergard. Doklad, sostavlennyi i prochitannyi kap. 2. p. N.S. Chirikovym v Morskom Sobranii v Parizhe 28 maia 1961 g', [Admiral A A Ebergard. A report composed and read by Captain 2nd Rank N.S. Chirikov at the Naval Gathering in Paris on 28 May 1961], *Morskiia zapiski*, vol. XIX, nos. 3-4, 1961, pp.3-35. Chirikov was senior navigating officer of the cruiser *Almaz* at the time of the action with *Goeben*. The last eyewitness is Nestor Monasterev, *Dans la Mer Noire (1912-1924)* (Paris: Payot, 1928), who was serving as a junior officer aboard the torpedo boat *Zharkii* during the action. His account is brief but provides a number of useful details. Secondary accounts include Ia. Podgornyi, 'K 15-letiiu boia Chernomorskogo flota c germanskim lineinym kreiserom "Geben" 5/18 noiabria 1914 g', [To the 15th Anniversary of the Black Sea Fleet's Battle with the German Battlecruiser *Goeben* on 5/18 November 1914], *Zarubezhnyi Morskoi Sbornik*, nos. 7-8, 1929, pp.3-35. V Iu. Gribovskii, 'Chernomorskii flot v boiakh s "Gebenom" (1914-1915) gody)', [The Black Sea Fleet in Battles with the *Goeben*, 1914-1918], *Gangut*, no. 10

[1996], pp.21-34. N B Pavlovich (ed), *The Fleet in the First World War*, vol. 1: *Operations of the Russian Fleet* (Originally published by the Ministry of Defense, USSR, Moscow, 1964; English translation: New Delhi: Amerind Publishing Co. Pvt. Ltd., 1979; Published for the Smithsonian Institution), pp.296-300. G Nekrasov, *North of Gallipoli: The Black Sea Fleet at War 1914-1917* (Boulder, CO: East European Monographs, no. CCCXLIII; distributed by Columbia University Press, New York, 1992), pp.29-34. The latter work is especially useful for its references to émigré literature.

3   There is a brief but useful biography of Souchon in H H Herwig and N M Heyman, *Biographical Dictionary of World War I* (Westport, Conn.: Greenwood Press, 1982), pp.323-324.

4   J Campbell, *Naval Weapons of World War Two* (Annapolis: Naval Institute Press, 1985), p.394.

5   N J M Campbell, '*Battle Cruisers: The Design and Development of British and German Battlecruisers of the First World War Era*' *Warship Special 1*, (London: Conway Maritime Press Ltd, 1978), pp.22-26.

6   For German fire control I have relied heavily on G von Hase, *Kiel and Jutland* (London: Skeffington & Son, Ltd., [n.d.]), especially pp.45-51. Additional information was supplied by K Crawford (e-mail to author, 15 February 2001) and W Schleihauf, who loaned me a copy of the Royal Navy's Intelligence Department's 'Reports on Interned German Vessels. Gunnery Information' (PRO, ADM 186/240, dated February 1919). However, the Germans had stripped most of the moveable gear from the ships before the British could inspect them.

7   Von Hase, *op cit*, p. 86; W Schleihauf, 'A Concentrated Effort: Royal Navy Gunnery Exercises at the End of the Great War', *Warship International*, vol. XXXV, no. 2 [1998], p.122. See also J T Sumida, *In Defence of Naval Supremacy: Finance, Technology, and British Naval Policy 1889-1914*, (London: Routledge, 1989), pp.252-253.

8   Herwig and Heyman, *Biographical Dictionary of World War I*, pp. 136-137 has a brief biography.

9   Chirikov, *op cit*, p.12.

10   P G Halpern, *The Mediterranean Naval Situation 1908-1914* (Cambridge, Mass.: Harvard University Press, 1971), pp.230-231; see also pp. 301-302 of similar pre-war foreign assessments of the Russian navy.

11   In general, see S I Titushkin, 'Russkaia korabel'naia artilleriia v 1904-1917 gg.' [Russian Shipboard Artillery in 1904-1917], *Sudostroenie*, no. 5, 1992, pp. 50-55 and A B Shirokorad, *Entsiklopediia otechestvennoi artillerii*, [Encyclopaedia of Domestic Artillery] (Minsk: Kharvest, 2000), p.433.

12   Russian accounts agree that the shells used at Cape Sarych were 331.7kg, rather than the much heavier 470.9kg M1911 shell weight. The lone dissenter is Gribovskii, 'Chernomorskii flot v boiakh s "Gebenom",' p. 25, who quotes a 380kg AP shell.

13   The following discussion is based on R M Mel'nikov, *Bronenosets 'Potemkin'* (Leningrad: Sudostroenie, 1980), pp.208-216; A V Platonov, 'Otechestvennye pribory upravleniia artilleriiskoi strel'boi' [Domestic Gear for Controlling Artillery Fire], *Tsitadel'*, no. 6 [no. 1, 1998], 92-115; Office of Naval Intelligence, 'Fire Control, Russian Navy' (Report filed by Rear Admiral J H Glennon, USN,

dated 20 August 1917; National Archives and Records Administration (NARA), Record Group 38, Reports of Naval Attachés, 1886-1940, U-2-E, Register No. 9121); and Nevinskii, *passim*.

14   This estimate is based on measurements from drawings and photographs.

15   V Iu. Usov, 'Tri Sviatitelia', *Gangut*, no. 6 [1993], p.60. For *Panteleimon*, Gribovskii, 'Chernomorskii flot v boiakh s "Gebenom",' p.26, and Shirokorad, *Entsiklopediia otechestvennoi artillerii*, p.436, both say 35°, but Nevinskii, *op cit*, p.407, says 25°.

16   Nevinskii, *op cit*, p.407, n.2.

17   For what follows, see Nevinskii, *op cit*, p.409.

18   N N Kharin, 'Pokhod s angliiskim admiralom Fillimorom na lin. kor. "Panteleimon" v 1916 g.' [A Trip With the English Admiral Phillimore on the Battleship *Panteleimon* in 1916], *Morskiia zapiski*, vol. XXI, no. 1, [1963], p.103.

19   See the letter from a Russian officer, probably the naval attaché in London (Captain 1st Rank N A Volkov), to Arthur Pollen quoted in Sumida, *op cit.*, p.253.

20   Gribovskii, 'Chernomorskii flot v boiakh s "Gebenom",' p.26.

21   B Langensiepen and A Güleryüz, *The Ottoman Steam Navy 1828-1923* (London: Conway Maritime Press, 1995), p.28; Lorey translation, p.59.

22   Lorey translation, p.62. I have altered the somewhat clumsy translation slightly.

23   Given that a great deal of the uncertainty over the action at Cape Sarych revolves around the number of hits obtained by the Russians, it is worth noting that these hits are confirmed by the Lorey translation, pp.68-69.

24   I K Grigorovich, *Vospominaniia byvshego morskogo ministra* [Memoirs of a Former Naval Minister], (St. Petersburg: Deva, 1993), p.145.

25   Chirikov, *op cit.*, p. 24; R M Mel'nikov, *Eskadrennye minonostsy klassa 'Dobrovolets'* (St. Petersburg: Naucho-populiarnoe izdanie, 1999), pp.128-129. Note that there is some uncertainty regarding the commanding officers of the Third and Fourth Torpedo Divisions; these are the names given by Podgornyi, *op cit.*, p. 35.

26   Mel'nikov, *Bronenosets 'Potemkin,'* pp.236-237; N Monasterev, *Sur Trois Mers (La marine russe dans la guerre mondiale d'après les documents officiels et les récits des combattants)* (Tunis: E. Saliba & Cie., 1932), p.125.

27   R Greger, *The Russian Fleet 1914-1917* (Translated by Jill Gearing; London: Ian Allan, 1972), p.46.

28   All movements of the German ships are taken from *Goeben's* war-diary.

29   Monasterev, *Sur Trois Mers*, p. 127-128, says it was blowing from the NW at 10:00 but had veered to the SW by the time of the battle.

30   There is some disagreement in Russian accounts regarding both the course being steered by the fleet and the position of the cruisers relative to the main body. Podgornyi, *op cit.*, p.3, says the fleet was steering north-by-west, that is, about 350°. But his main source is Chirikov's notebook, and in his own article Chirikov says the fleet was steering course 292° (p. 23). Nevinskii, *op cit.*, p.410, agrees, saying the fleet was on a course of 'about 300°'. As for the location of the cruisers, accounts differ as to whether they were one mile or 3.5 miles ahead of the fleet; Monasterev, *Sur Trois Mers*, p. 127, says

they were 1,000 metres to 3,000 metres ahead, 'depending on the visibility', and this variation may explain the different figures reported by other authors. Finally, Nevinskii, *op cit.*, p.410, says the cruisers bore 30° from the flagship rather than 45°.

31 Chirikov, *op cit.*, p.24. Coordinating the German and Russian times is made difficult by the fact that the one event that might be used to synchronise the clocks of the two sides, the moment when *Evstafii* opened fire, is variously given by Russian accounts: 12:18, 12:21 and 12:24. Two numbers, however, are universally accepted by Russian writers, the battle was 14 minutes long and ended at 12:35, and it is likely that some writers have subtracted the one from the other to arrive at 12:21 as the moment when *Evstafii* opened fire. However, Nevinskii, *op cit.*, p.412, says that 'fire was exchanged for about *ten minutes*, although *Goeben* was visible for about *fourteen minutes*' (emphasis added). Assuming he is correct, then fire was actually opened at about 12:24. *Goeben*'s war diary says that the Russians opened fire at 12:20, and so it would seem that the German clocks were about four minutes behind those of the Russians. This accords quite well with the moment of sighting, *Breslau* saw *Almaz* at 12:05 German time, while *Almaz* sighted *Breslau* at 12:10 Russian time. If the German clocks did indeed lag by about four minutes, then the two ships sighted each other almost simultaneously, which seems likely under the circumstances.

32 The German movements immediately before the battle, and in particular the relative positions of *Goeben* and *Breslau*, are not stated clearly in any available sources. The description given here is based on Monasterev, *Sur Trois Mers*, p.127 and B Langensiepen, D Nottelmann and J Krüsmann, *Halbmond und Kaiseradler: Goeben und Breslau am Bosporus 1914-1918* (Hamberg: Verlag E.S. Mittler & Sohn GmbH, 1999), p.29.

33 Nevinskii, *op cit.*, p.411.

34 Monasterev, *Dans la Mer Noire*, pp. 88-90; Chirikov, *op cit.*, p.24. Podgornyi, *op cit.*, p.4, says that *Kagul* joined the tail-end of the column rather than the head, but this is unlikely, since it would have meant crossing between the Russians battleships and *Goeben*, or making a very long detour around the disengaged side of the Russian squadron. Furthermore, Podgornyi's main source is Chirikov's notebook, and Chirikov himself says that Kagul took station at the head of the formation (Chirikov, *op cit.*, p.24).

35 Nevinskii, *op cit.*, p.411.

36 Lorey translation, p.93.

37 I am grateful to Byron Angel for pointing out the probable effect of the cool, damp air on the funnel smoke.

38 Chirikov, *op cit.*, p.25.

39 Several descriptions (e.g., Chirikov, *op cit.*, p.25, Pavlovich, *op cit.*, p.299) say that it was both guns from the forward turret that fired the opening salvo, but this is contradicted by Nevinskii, *op cit.*, p.412, and Monasterev, *Sur Trois Mers*, p. 128, both of whom were present at the action. Nevinskii later notes, however, that the forward turret did most of the subsequent shooting because the after turret was hindered by the fog and smoke, and this may be the origin of the forward-turret salvo reported by some writers.

40 There is an irreconcilable contradiction regarding *Goeben*'s new course after turning to parallel the Russians; the war-diary and the track chart annexed to it shows the ship turn-ing to course 135°, that is, SE, whereas the Russians by their own accounts (as confirmed by the German official history), were steering a course of about 200° SSW. If this were correct, the two fleets would have been on rapidly converging courses, which we know from all the accounts was not the case. The only explanation for this that is even remotely plausible is that an error was made in converting the handwritten ship's logs into the neatly typed war-diary, perhaps 185° was misread as 135°. This is far from satisfactory, but with the material at hand I can think of no other explanation.

41 Various writers have given different figures for just how far 'over' *Goeben*'s first salvo was. Chirikov, *op cit.*, p.25, says that it was 15-20 *sazhen*' (fathoms), that is, 30-40 yards, 'over', while Gribovskii, 'Chernomorskii flot v boiakh s "Gebenom",' p.27, says it was 2-3 cables (400-600 yards) long. Monasterev, who was aboard *Zharkii*, says that it fell between his ship and *Evstafii* (*Sur Trois Mers*, p.128), and further states that *Zharkii* was 300 metres to port of the flagship. The Russian navy did not use metres for distances at sea at this time, and it is likely that a figure in yards was 'metrified' to suit his French audience. At the given range, *Goeben*'s shells would have been falling at an angle very close to 5°, and one shell holed the middle funnel almost exactly 50ft above the load waterline; solving the right triangle so formed indicates that the shell, had it not burst, would have struck the sea about 190 yards off *Evstafii*'s port beam.

42 Nevinskii, *op cit.*, p.412.

43 Podgornyi, *op cit.*, p.23, quoting Petrov.

44 Chirikov, *op cit.*,p.26.

45 Nevinskii, *op cit.*, pp.413.

46 Lorey translation, p.93. This version is repeated in other German-based sources, such as Langensiepen and Güleryüz, *op cit.*, pp.45-46, where it is stated that after fifteen minutes 'the Russians break off the action and retire behind a fog bank'.

47 Appendix to *Goeben*'s war-diary. I am indebted to Tim Lanzendörfer for providing the translation.

48 N J M Campbell, *Jutland: An Analysis of the Fighting* (Annapolis: Naval Institute Press, 1986), p.376.

49 Appendix to *Goeben*'s war-diary.

50 Campbell, *Jutland*, p.376.

51 Georg Kopp, *Two Lone Ships: "Goeben" and "Breslau"* (translated by Arthur Chambers; London: Hutchinson & Co., Ltd., 1931), pp.117-118.

52 *Ibid.*, p.116.

53 Podgornyi *op cit.*, p.25-26, quoting extracts in Petrov's book.

54 Lorey translation, p.94.

55 D K Brown, *The Grand Fleet: Warship Design and Development 1906-1922* (Annapolis: Naval Institute Press, 1999), pp.44-45, discusses the dangers of secondary battery fires at some length.

56 Lorey translation, p.93; Langensiepen and Güleryüz, *op cit.*, p.45; Langensiepen, Nottelmann and Krüsmann, *Halbmond und Kaiseradler*, p.30.

57 Lorey translation, p.94; von Hase *op cit.*, p.83, where it is noted that *Derfflinger* fired two 15cm salvos between main-battery salvos.

58 V D Dotsenko, *Bytvy rossiiskogo flota XVIII-XX vv.* [Battles of the Russian Fleet of the 19th-20th Centuries], (St. Petersburg: Izdatel'stvo 'Petro – RIF,' 1998), p.213.

59 L A Kuznetsov, 'Evstafii' (*Gangut*, no. 10 [1996], pp. 46-71),

p.67; Podgornyi *op cit.*, pp.7-10.

60 Nevinskii, *op cit.*, p.412; letter, Sergei Vinogradov to author, 18 April 2000.

61 Nevinskii, *op cit.*, p.412.

62 Gribovskii, 'Chernomorskii flot v boiakh s "Gebenom",' p.30.

63 *Ibid.*, p.28.

64 Kuznetsov, *op cit.*, p.67; he also states that *Evstafii* fired sixteen 12in, of which twelve were from the forward turret.

65 Chirikov, *op cit.*, p.26.

66 Quoted in Gribovskii, 'Chernomorskii flot v boiakh s "Gebenom",' p.30.

67 For the award, see Nekrasov, *op cit.*, p.34; for the low regard in which this award was held, see R Werlich, *Russian Orders, Decorations and Medals including those of Imperial Russia, the Provisional Government, the Civil War and the Soviet Union* (2nd ed., Washington, D.C.: The Quaker Press, 1981), p.8.

68 A D Bubnov, *V Tsarskoi Stavke: Vospominaniia admirala Bubnova* [At the Tsar's Stavka: The Reminiscences of Admiral Bubnov], (New York: Izdatelstvo imeni Chekhova, 1955), especially pp.128, 225-227.

69 Gribovskii, 'Chernomorskii flot v boiakh s "Gebenom",' p.33 note.

70 Podgornyi, *op cit.*, p.22, quoting M A Petrov, *Dva boia (Chernomorkogo flota c l.kr. "Geben" 5.IX.1914 g. i kreiserov Balt. flota u o. Gotland 19.V.1915 g.)* [Two Battles (The Black Sea Fleet with the battlecruiser *Goeben*, 5.IX.1914, and the Baltic Fleet off the Island of Gotland, 19.V.1915]

(note that these dates are in the Old Style used in Russia until 1918, and are thirteen days behind the western calendar) (Leningrad: RIO MS RKKF, 1926). Unfortunately, this book does not appear to be available in the west, so it is necessary to rely on the substantial extracts from it given by Podgornyi.

71 Cited in Podgornyi, *op cit.*, p.12.

72 National Archives and Records Administration, Record Group 38, Reports of Naval Attachés, 1886-1940, S9121, U-2-e 'Fire control, Russian navy, 1917'. This copy of the Russian spotting rules was almost certainly brought to the United States by a group of Russian naval officers, headed by Admiral A V Kolchak, that visited the Naval War College in 1917. I have smoothed out the somewhat crude translation, which was obviously the work of someone for whom English was not the first language.

73 Podgornyi, *op cit.*, p.19.

74 Cited in *Ibid.*, p.21.

75 Nevinskii, *op cit.*, p.410.

76 Cited in Podgornyi, *op cit.*, p.21.

77 Mel'nikov, *Eskadrennye minonostsy klassa 'Dobrovolets,'* p.127.

78 For Petrov's strategic and tactical thinking, see R W Herrick, *Soviet Naval Strategy: Fifty Years of Theory and Practice* (Annapolis: Naval Institute, 1968), chapter II.

79 VA Zolotarev, I A Kozlov and V S Shlomin, *Istoriia flota gosudarstva rossiiskogo, 1696-1941* (Moscow: Terra, 1996), vol. I, p.299.

THE *BLACKWOOD* CLASS, TYPE 14 SECOND RATE FRIGATES

The *Blackwood* class Type 14 Second Rate Frigates were a product of the Cold War. The ever present possibility that the post-war political situation could degenerate into a military situation vastly more threatening to the Western powers greatly influenced the evolution of their design, as examined here by **George Moore**.

The modern concept of the 2nd class frigate was to evolve in the Second World War where the 1st class role was performed initially by the sloops of the *Black Swan* class and then followed and supplemented by the 'River' class twin screw corvettes. Both classes were ultimately designated frigates. The 2nd class role effectively devolved to the 'Flower' class corvettes, which were the main component of the escort forces in the early years of the war. By 1942, production was switching to the mass-produced frigates of the 'Loch' (20kt) and 'Castle' (16.5kt) classes which were, in effect, 1st and 2nd class escorts respectively. At this point the main constraint on producing the 'Loch' class as the sole anti-submarine frigate design was the size of slipways in the yards and not finance, which was to be the case later when designs became more complex.

The end of 1944 saw new frigate designs beginning to evolve to meet the threat produced by the advent of the

Table 1: *The 1945 Corvette (June 1945)*

Displacement:	About 1000 tons
Armament:	1-4in single
	1-twin Bofors
	4-twin Oerlikon
	5-Depth Charge Pattern,
	(15 depth charges)
	Twin Squid anti-submarine mortar,
	20 salvoes
Speed:	20kts (Six months out of dock in Tropical waters)
Endurance:	4-5000 miles at 15kts

Source: D K Brown RCNC, 'The 1945 Sloops, Designers View', *Warship World*, Vol. 3 No. 3.

German Type XX1 U-Boat and the development of ever more capable aircraft. One response by the Admiralty was proposals for a 25kt sloop. After a very lengthy debate and development period these vessels evolved into the *Whitby* (Type 12) first rate anti-submarine frigate, *Leopard* (Type 41) anti-aircraft frigate and *Salisbury* (Type 61) aircraft direction frigate classes, which emerged from the shipyards in the mid-1950s. By April 1945, when the designs were very much in their formative stage, the new anti-aircraft and anti-submarine frigates were expected to displace some 1600 tons and the Naval Staff was asking if there was 'an additional requirement for a smaller anti-submarine ship of the corvette type'. After discussion it was agreed that this requirement existed even though the war in Europe was clearly drawing to a close.[1] A tentative design was produced by the Director of Naval Construction (DNC) in June 1945, the details of which are set out in Table 1, but with hostilities in Europe now over and no requirement for such a vessel in the war against Japan the proposal for this second-rate design inevitably quietly died. However, development of the 1945 Frigate designs continued.

First Thoughts

In March 1947 there was an immediate requirement for 180 anti-submarine vessels at the outbreak of any future hostilities. It was however apparent that the first class anti-submarine frigate with turbine machinery could not be produced quickly as the propulsion system would be of a new type and endurance requirements in particular could not be guaranteed until this type of machinery had been tested in the *Daring* class destroyers, then under construction. It was to be some three years before the first ships of this class went to sea. There was also some enthu-

The prototype Type 12 First Rate frigate HMS Whitby, *a concept which predated the* Blackwood *class. Shown here with torpedo-tubes removed, modified funnel and single 40mm L/60 Bofors gun aft. (CPL)*

siasm for diesel machinery at this time. The new Admiralty Standard Range diesel (ASR 1) was to be fitted in the anti-aircraft and aircraft-direction frigates of the *Leopard* and *Salisbury* classes, but it did not develop enough power to provide sufficient speed for the new 1st class anti-submarine frigates. The Engineer in Chief (EIC) indicated that it would be five years before he could probably produce a suitable lightweight diesel. It was therefore agreed that a new intermediate anti-submarine frigate was needed. The outline Staff Requirements for this ship, where an Assistant Director of Naval Construction, N G Holt and Constructor M K Purvis were involved in the concept, are set out in Table 2. The framework of the *Blackwood* class can be seen in these requirements but at this stage the theme was not developed.[2]

In October 1948 there was another indication that there could be a requirement for a new second-rate frigate. The DNC now requested a rough shot at an anti-submarine frigate using 'Hunt' machinery. It was assumed that the armament would consist of two Stabilised Tachymetric Anti-Aircraft Gun (STAAG) systems (40mm), a double Limbo Mk 10 anti-submarine mortar with twenty salvoes each and four anti-submarine tubes (eight torpedoes carried). Asdic and anti-torpedo gear (Nightshirt) were to be fitted. The results of this study are set out in Table 3. Holt first looked at a 'Hunt' class hull and machinery, with the ship fitted out as a fast frigate. He then followed up this study with two possibilities, 'A' and 'B' with a new hull but the same machinery. He was not enthusiastic about the results of his studies. It was considered that the use of 'Hunt' machinery would not produce a very satisfactory solution and that Designs 'A' and 'B' were long ships with a shallow draught, with the result that the hull weight was high and the space for oil limited. Design 'A' needed considerable oiling at sea to achieve any worthwhile endurance. Neither design could achieve the indicated Staff Requirement of 27kts when the ship had not been docked for six months in the tropics with 'Nighshirt' fitted. The anti-submarine armament was reasonable but the gun armament was weaker than that fitted in the *Rocket* and *Relentless*, two destroyers which were about to be converted to anti-submarine frigates. These ideas proved to be a blind alley and duly faded away.[3]

Table 2: OUTLINE STAFF REQUIREMENTS FOR INTERMEDIATE ANTI-SUBMARINE FRIGATE, MARCH 1947

Gunnery Role (self defence):	Two STAAGs (40mm) or possibly one STAAG and one twin 4in
Machinery:	Steam driven
Speed:	25kts, deep and dirty six months out of dock
Endurance:	3000 miles at 15kts (endurance of 4500 miles was initially wanted)
Anti Submarine Armament:	Two Limbo's (anti-submarine mortars) 2 x 3 barrels
	Bidders (anti-submarine torpedoes) three fixed tubes a side, six reloads
Provision to be made for propeller silencing	

Source: Ships Cover Destroyers and Frigates General Cover, ADM 138/830 (NMM)

Table 3: *1948 ANTI SUBMARINE FRIGATE WITH 'HUNT' MACHINERY*

	'Hunt' – Weight as designed	Weight as Fast Frigate
Equipment:	115	180
Hull:	595	595
Armament and Radar:	117	145
Machinery:	295	370
Fuel:	279	75 (By difference)
Reserve Feed Water:	21	30
Board Margin:	0	27
	1422 tons	1422 tons

Maximum speed of Fast Frigate 24-25kts. Attention was drawn to oil fuel, 75 tons only.

Possibilities	'A'	'B'
	Water length 360ft	Water length 370ft
	Deep displacement, 2000 tons	Deep displacement, 2250 tons
Equipment:	205	215
Hull:	900	980
Armament and Radar:	145	145
Machinery:	370	370
Fuel:	315	470
Reserve Feed water:	30	30
Board Margin:	35	40
	2000 tons	2250 tons
Maximum speed, six months out of dock with Nightshirt fitted:	26kts	25.5kts
Dimensions:	360ft x 37ft x 10ft	370ft x 38.5ft x 10.5ft

Source: Director of Naval Construction, Correspondence Volume 76 (1) 1948, (NMM)

A Firm Requirement Emerges

The Summer of 1949 was to see the emergence of a far-reaching and invigorating approach to the requirements of the Royal Navy via a study, drafted by Rear Admiral Edwards, the Assistant Chief of Naval Staff, entitled *Ships of the Future Navy*. The Director of Tactical and Staff Duties (DTSD), Admiral Onslow, elaborated when he wrote that 'its aim is to dismiss pre-conceived ideas from our minds, and to argue from first principles but under the over-riding limitation of financial restrictions, what types of ships we must have for war against Russia in ten or more years time'. In his view the most controversial ideas were:-

a. The replacement of the conventional cruiser and destroyer by an all-purpose light cruiser, (the 5in gun armed cruiser/destroyer design which was abandoned in 1954 emerged to meet this requirement).
b. The need in war for a cheap and quickly produced aircraft carrier and the aircraft to fly from the ships. (Little seems to be known about new small carrier designs but the Short Seamew, a basic anti-submarine aircraft, was produced in prototype form. Any thought of producing a small aircraft carrier seems to have died in November 1954 when it was concluded that the smallest worthwhile carrier would displace 30,000 tons).
c. To investigate the value of a completely specialised 2nd rate anti-submarine frigate in order to increase numbers without increasing cost.[4]

The cost of building a frigate was rapidly escalating at this time, due not just to inflation in the currency but also because the cost of producing equipment was rising due to its ever-increasing complexity. An example of this phenomenon was already underway. When the first two frigates were approved by the Cabinet in November 1945 they were each expected to cost £675,500.[5] In less than four years the new 1st rate anti-submarine frigate's estimated cost had escalated to £1,100,000.

Clearly if the new ships were to be produced in numbers something had to be given up. The first estimates indicating the broad outline of a new 2nd rate frigate were produced on 21 June 1949. Details are set out in Table 4. This design would have had a less effective anti-submarine capacity when compared with the first-rate frigate due to a 4kt reduction in speed and the smaller number of anti-submarine torpedo's embarked. The over-riding weakness in the proposal, however, was its cost, which showed only a relatively small and no doubt disappointing reduction.[6]

The design was ruled out by the Sea Lords on 12 July 1949 when refined objectives were formulated after discussion. It was suggested that as the aim was to get increased numbers of anti-submarine frigates; the target should be to build two 2nd rates at the cost of one 1st rate. The discussion was to lead to requirements being put forward for consideration by the DNC which were very close to the specification ultimately adopted when the Type 14 design crystallised. The new Type numbers were incidentally introduced into use in 1950. The requirements are set out in Table 5.

Table 4: COMPARISON OF FIRST RATE AND PROPOSED SECOND RATE ANTI-SUBMARINE FRIGATES, JUNE 1949

	First Rate	Second Rate
Length:	360ft	270ft
Breadth:	40ft	37ft
Draught:	10.5ft	10ft
Displacement (deep):	2260 tons	1550 tons
Machinery:	Steam Y100 type	Diesel ASR 1
Speed (deep and dirty):	27kts	23kts
Endurance at 12kts:	4500 miles	4500 miles
Armament:	Double Limbo	Double Limbo
	12 A/S torpedo's	6 A/S torpedo's
	One twin 4.5in Mark 6	One twin Bofors
	One Staag (40mm)	
Asdics:	162, 170, 172	162, 170, 172
Radar:	M & P, 293Q	M & P (Maneuvering and Pilotage)
	277Q, 262	
Complement:	287	198
Approximate cost:	£1,100,000	£875,000

Note: Figures for Second and for complement and costs of both vessels are estimates only. Diesels for Second Rate are the same as Anti Aircraft Frigate (later *Leopard* Class).

Source: Ships Cover Anti Submarine Frigate Type 14, ADM 138/827, (NMM)

By 1 September 1949 Holt had produced a Preliminary Sketch Design for the new 2nd Rate Anti-submarine Frigate which included a preliminary general arrangement drawing. The following extracts and comments from his report set out the basis for the design. The aim was 'to obtain a long lean ship for maintaining speed into a head sea, together with sufficient draught for seaworthiness and to accommodate the 12ft propeller. This length also helped to achieve a speed of 25 knots deep and dirty, which is a knot in excess of the Staff Requirement'. 'The 1914-18 V & W destroyer was (initially) taken as a type ship but with a long forecastle'. The long forecastle was, however, found to be unacceptable for stability reasons and a short forecastle hull was substituted. It was then found necessary to modify the hull form and a new design based on the 1937 Programme patrol vessel *Guillemot* was adopted. 'The length of the ship [was] greater than really necessary to meet space requirements for habitability, stores etc.,

spaces forward [were] left empty deliberately to keep the fore end light for performance in a seaway and to limit the space allocated for stores to that required for a 45-day endurance, to prevent overloading the ship'. It was envisaged that the hull would be built of mild steel for the main strength structure and aluminium alloy for the lower deck, minor internal divisional bulkheads and superstructure. The bridge front would be steel to permit driving into head seas. It was estimated that if D W steel was used in lieu of mild steel a saving of about 25 tons in hull weight would be made. The accommodation for a total complement of 160 was said to be 'practically that for full modern habitability'. A small laundry was to be provided.

The machinery was essentially half the installation installed in the first rate frigate. The single set of Y.100 steam turbine machinery drove a single shaft running at low rpm (about 220 as envisaged for the 1st rate anti-submarine frigate) for reduction of noise. Provision was also

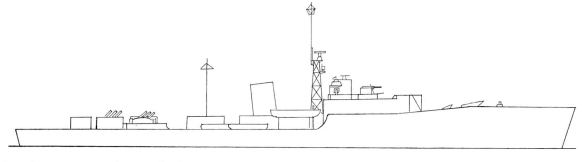

Second Rate Frigate - Preliminary Sketch Design - August 1949. (Drawing by Len Crockford based on original plan in Director of Naval Contstruction papers held by the NMM)

THE BLACKWOOD CLASS, TYPE 14 SECOND RATE FRIGATES

Table 5: Second Rate Anti Submarine Frigate, Suggested Requirements July 1949

Armament:	One Double Limbo
	4-Anti Submarine Torpedoes (4 fixed TT)
	1-twin Bofors with Simple Tachymetric Director (STD)
Asdic:	Types 162, 170, 172
Radar:	M and P. (Manoeuvring and Pilotage sets)
Endurance:	4500 miles at 12kts
Accommodation:	For complement about 160 on a wartime habitability standard
Communications:	M/F – H/F, 3 lines
	V. H/F, 4 lines
	R.W, 1 D/F set
Machinery:	One set Y.100 steam
Displacement:	1300-1400 deep *
Speed:	At least 24kts deep and dirty *

* These figures were quoted as 'may be wide of the mark and DNC is requested to amend as necessary'.

Source: Director of Naval Construction, Correspondence, Volume 77, 1949, (NMM)

made for propeller-silencing equipment. The EIC considered it necessary to fit two boilers to avoid the possibility of the ship being immobilised due to a minor defect. Two boilers, each of 7500shp, were therefore allowed for, although it was a departure from the standard 15,000shp boiler being designed for the 1st rate frigate. Oil stowage consisted of 200 tons in deep tanks and a further emergency supply of 32 tons in double bottom tanks. Using the emergency oil tanks, it was expected that an endurance of 4500 miles would be achieved.

The initial estimated costs were compiled using information supplied by the responsible departments the table produced setting out comparative amounts for the first rate frigate for easy reference:-

Item	Vote	2nd Rate Frigate Cost £	1st Rate Frigate Cost £
Dockyard Labour	8.1	2,000	2,000
Dockyard Material & Stores	8.II	20,000	20,000
Machinery	8.III.A(1) & (3)	261,500	417,000
Hull and Electrical	8.III.A(4)	255,500	430,000
Protection	8.III.A(5)	2,000	2,000
Armament	8.III.A(7)	9,000	214,000
Torpedo Tubes etc	8.III.A(8)	50,000	68,000
Guns, Ordnance Stores Torpedoes etc.	9.	52,000	160,000
TOTAL Votes 8 and 9		652,000	1,315,000

The main difference in costs when compared with the first study lay in the estimated price for machinery. ASR 1 diesels were proposed in the first study, where the total cost was £875,000. In a paper dated 21 July 1949 the EIC estimated in a study comparing diesel and steam turbine installations that the cost of the diesel installation would be £385,000 whilst a single-shaft Y.100 installation would cost £150,000, a difference of £235,000. Given that the two studies were so close in other aspects, the

difference in the cost of the two proposals £875,000/£652,000, i.e. £233,000, virtually equates with the difference in machinery costs. The same paper, however quoted the cost of machinery for a 1st rate frigate as £260,000 which differs wildly from the figure quoted in the comparison made in the latest 2nd rate frigate study! The paper produced by the Chief Engineer did, however, indicate that the figures in his paper were only a guide as neither installation had been built. This episode illustrates the difficulties experienced in producing reliable costings at this time.[7]

The Ship Development Policy Committee considered the preliminary design on 26 October 1949. The points forthcoming in discussion were relatively minor, the principle one relating to the flooding of emergency oil tanks in the double bottom when they were free of fuel. The Committee wanted 4500 miles at 12kts achieved without recourse to this reserve. The only other matters raised were the need for a catwalk and that no noisy machinery should be installed near the wardroom where officers would have to sleep when the ship was on service. The DNC was requested to prepare a sketch design for submission to the Board based on the details before the committee as set out in Table 6. The Committee also decided that an outline design with twin screws using two sets of Deltic diesel engines should be developed once the EIC could provide adequate information. In the event nothing came of this proposal, which seems to have quietly died.[8]

The steam machinery for the new frigates incorporated advances over wartime designs. The steam temperature in the boiler in both the first and second rates was 850°, the same as the *Daring* class but an advance on the 'Weapon' class (750°) and the 'Q' to 'Z' and the 'C' class destroyers (660°). The boiler pressure was also advanced from 300psi in the 'Q' to 'Z' and 'C' classes, 400psi in the 'Weapons' to 550psi in the new frigates. The *Daring* class boilers operated at 600psi. Standards were now equating with those employed in the US Navy 15 years earlier, where wartime experiences had exposed shortcomings in British practices and design.[9]

The Design is Developed

Although designated a 2nd rate frigate there were no compromises in construction which would have resulted in a warship which was structurally weaker than her 1st rate cousins. The one compromise accepted was the provision of a lower standard in accommodation than was normally applicable at that time. Writing in 1957 the DNC, Sir Victor Shepheard, stated in a report that the Type 14 frigates were an austerity version of the Type 12 first rate frigate. The problem put to the DNC (Sir Charles Lillicrap in 1949) was 'can you design a smaller frigate with the same anti-submarine armament at about half the cost of a Type 12. It was well understood that fitting out and accommodation would have to be of an appreciably lower standard. Hard-lying standards were to be accepted if unavoidable. The Type 14 frigates were never envisaged as senior officers' ships and the intention was that they should work in company with a Type 12, all of which are fitted to carry a senior officer'.[10] What was effectively being produced was a 1st rate anti-submarine machine with theoretically a structure having the strength to operate in the worst sea conditions but with second-class accommodation for the crew.

With design work now proceeding, at first events moved fairly rapidly. Staff Requirements were produced before the end of the year (see Appendix 1), one key aim being that the ships should be capable of rapid production. Weight was clearly a critical concern and rather than use mild steel, as originally envisaged, the hull was to be built with DW steel and all-welded. It was estimated that a further 23 tons could be saved by the use of an aluminium alloy in hull construction but this would have resulted in an increase in costs. This use of aluminium does not appear to have been pursued any further than originally anticipated.[11]

One feature introduced in the new frigates was a total change in the design philosophy, implemented in the construction of the hulls. In the *Daring* class there was a small number of relatively large longitudinal cross sections whilst in the new frigates there was a large number of small longitudinals. The change in practice came about as a result of experience in the Ship Target Trials against *Nonsuch*, the ex-German 'Z' class destroyer Z.38. These structures were only 12in apart in the Types 41 and 61, which were the first frigate designs to be developed after the war. In the *Blackwood* class the spacing was changed to 18in apart after the intervention of the DNC,

HMS Palliser *dated 30 December 1957. Note single 40mm L/60 Bofors gun on the quarterdeck and starboard Mk 10 depth-charge launcher trained inboard.* (WSS, J M Maber Collection)

Table 6: *SECOND RATE ANTI SUBMARINE FRIGATE, PRELIMINARY SKETCH DESIGN, OCTOBER 1949*

Dimensions:	Length overall, 310ft, Beam extreme, 33ft.
Armament:	Double Limbo with 20 salvoes
	4-fixed TT with 4 torpedoes (no reloads)
	1-twin Bofors with Simple Tachymetric Director
Asdics:	Types 170 and 172 with Hull Outfit 1, Type 162
Radar:	Manoeuvring and pilotage set
Communications:	M/F – H/F, 3 lines, V.HF, 4 lines, RW, 1 D/F set
Machinery and Speed:	One set of Y.100 steam turbine machinery, with two boilers
	Giving a total of 15,000shp on one shaft
	Screw diameter = 12ft, rpm = 220 approx
	Maximum speeds with Nightshirt fitted but not working:-
	25kts, deep, six months out of dock in tropical waters
	26kts deep, clean bottom, trial conditions
Fuel Stowage and Endurance:	Oil fuel and diesel oil (ex emergency oil) = 200 tons
	Corresponding endurance = 3900 miles at 12kts, six months out of dock in tropical waters under operational conditions.
	Emergency oil stowage = 32 tons, increases above endurance to 4500 miles.
Complement:	160 including 11 officers and supernumeraries.
Stowage of Stores and Provisions:	An endurance of 45 days for Naval Stores, Dry Provisions, Canteen Stores, Refrigerated Stores including fruit and vegetables

Group Weights	Deep Condition	Light Condition
Hull:	585	585
Equipment:	119	58
Armament and Radar:	91	91
Machinery:	231	231
Reserve Feed Water:	10	
Oil Fuel and Diesel Oil:	232	32 (Emergency oil fuel)
Board Margin:	22	22
Water Ballast:		51
	1290 tons	1070 tons

Source: Director of Naval Construction, Correspondence Volume 78, 1949, (NMM)

Sir Victor Shepheard. The shipbuilders nevertheless had to face up to the new and laborious task of building in a great many longitudinals into the ships which involved many joints and patching arrangements where the structures passed through water tight bulkheads. The process and in particular the welding, was difficult, time-consuming and expensive.[12]

The Ship Design Policy Committee considered the design on 31 March 1950 the only matters raised being, firstly, the tightness of the accommodation, which was however considered acceptable, secondly that the machinery should perform in accordance with the Staff Requirements and lastly the practicality of the low bridge layout. The Board of Admiralty considered the design on 11 May 1950. It was reported that ships of this type would be able to cross the Atlantic Ocean without the need to refuel. The Board duly approved the sketch design and legend of particulars. The cost indicated was still £650,000, but this figure was described as a tentative estimate made on the assumption that the prototype would be built under contract. A firm figure was to be submitted to the Board at a later date.[13] By July 1950 it was expected that the machinery for the first pair of ships

would be needed by September 1952, which meant there was no time to go out to tender. By September 1950 the orders for the first two machinery sets had been placed with Thornycroft and White. At this time Yarrow were given a contract for the preparation of specifications and guidance drawings.[14]

The political tension between East and West increased with the outbreak of the Korean War in 1950, and as a result the need for these ships became more urgent. Further orders for three sets of machinery were placed in late 1950 and then anticipating the 1951-52 New Construction Programme orders were placed on 21 March 1951 for twelve ships.[15]

The Board considered the design again on 18 July 1951. They commented that the class was to 'represent the nearest approach at present available to an up-to-date oceangoing anti-submarine vessel which could be produced rapidly in quantity in a future war, as was the corvette in the last war. Its actual building time would be about three months longer than that of the corvette'.[16] The belief expressed by the Board was however some way from what could be expected. Most of the 'Flower' class corvettes built in the Second World War were complet-

The Type 61 aircraft direction frigate HMS Salisbury shows the Type 12 lineage with Type 965 radar fitted. (CPL)

ed in under twelve months, with many vessels of the class being built by Harland and Wolff in under six months.[17] In November 1950 the fastest building time from the date of ordering machinery to the date completed was anticipated to be 27 months, with the first ship delivered in September 1953 and the last of the twelve-ship order completing in March 1955.[18] Even these dates do not tie in with the expectations of the Board and the reality when it came to production was of course infinitely worse. There were, however, already more austere designs under consideration, for studies into such possibilities were underway as early as July 1950. These were to lead to the 3rd Rate Type 17 and Type 42[19] projects, which ran until November 1953 when they were abandoned.[20] One problem envisaged was that 'quantity production would make demands on engine and gear manufacturing capacity which could not at present be met'. However it was anticipated that this limitation should be removed in about 15 months time. The Board clearly understood that if an emergency arose before this capacity became available then 'it looked as if some surrender of an important staff requirement would be necessary in order to arrive at a design which could in practice be mass produced'. Behind this statement lies the reason for the development of the 3rd Rate designs. One shock was the estimated cost, which was now said to be rather more than £1,000,000.[21]

The Statement of General Particulars submitted to the Board set out details of the design, which were mainly in

HMS Russell on 15 June 1972 with 40mm L/60 Bofors gun visible on port side of her foremast. (WSS, J M Maber Collection)

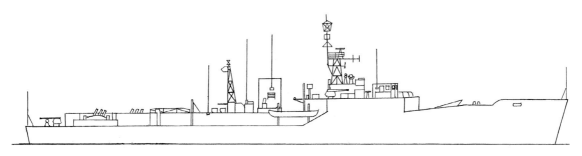

Type 14 - March 1954. (Drawing by Len Crockford based on original plan in the Admiralty Collection held by the NMM)

accordance with the original Staff Requirements. However, tests at the Admiralty Experiment Works, Haslar revealed that the location of the bridge was not satisfactory and that it would have to be higher and placed further aft than planned in order to prevent it being washed down in heavy seas. This resulted in the displacement of the twin Bofors guns that now could only have been mounted on a bandstand located on No.1 deck, a position considered to be too exposed. Sided single Bofors just abaft the bridge were accepted reluctantly by the Director of Gunnery Division in lieu.[22]

The advent of nuclear weapons was also to result in a new policy designed to protect personnel from fallout. The open bridge which had previously been the standard for all destroyers and similar ships, and which was a feature incorporated in the first sketch of the ship, had radar and asdic huts located at the back of the bridge structure. The aim now was to put all the sensor data and control and communications material in one space for the benefit of the command. At this time it was felt that ideally the bridge structure and the operations room should be on the same level but the provision of electrical and cooling equipment meant that this could not be done in the *Blackwood* class. The operations room had to be installed one deck lower than the bridge.[23]

The original plan was for important components such as the Wireless Offices and the Asdic Control Room to be arranged so that they could be erected in the ship as fabricated and completely fitted out units whilst the Board of Admiralty was advised that the hull was designed to facilitate rapid production in war by the use of prefabrication methods. As we have seen however there was now little chance of achieving rapid production due, at this stage in the life of the project, to the complexity of the hull design. The steam turbine and main propulsion machinery was now designated Y.101 type to distinguish it from the units fitted in the 1st class frigates of the *Whitby* Class (Type 12).[24]

The Programme Progresses

Even before the vessels were ordered the Ships Names Committee considered the emotive subject of names. On 26 October 1950 the Committee put forward seven names; *Beaulieu Firth, Cromarty Firth, Dornoch Firth, Moray Firth, Pentland Firth, Solway Firth* and *Westray*

Firth. Their minds were clearly continuing the Second World War theme when geographical places associated with waters such as Lochs, Bays and Rivers were an established and popular choice. This idea was however quashed within the Admiralty and traditional names of loved and honoured heroes were substituted.[25]

The number of vessels planned was the subject of change as the programme progressed. In June 1951, when there were real concerns about defence preparedness, it was proposed that a further twenty 2nd rate frigates should be built in addition to the twelve which were ordered. These additional ships were to be completed by 1958.[26] However, these plans suffered from the vicissitudes effecting the Admiralty's building programme by 'The Radical Review' and subsequent economies. At one stage there seemed to be firm plans to produce a total of twenty-three 2nd rate frigates. Ultimately just the original dozen on order survived. Of the remaining ships three were built for India, seven became 'Tribal' class frigates, whilst one survivor which was authorised in the 1954-55 Programme was cancelled by the Board of Admiralty on 6 January 1955.[27] The programme also suffered delays for in 1952 *Palliser* and *Exmouth* were put back by the Admiralty for a year as an economy measure. Also delayed by this Board edict were the *Tiger* class cruiser programme, where expenditure was to be minimal, and the 1st rate frigates *Blackpool* and *Lincoln* which were also set back for twelve months.[28]

By October 1953 it was clear that the *Blackwood* would not be ready for the first of class trials so it was decided to substitute *Hardy* in this role. She was due to complete in October 1954, but it was to be December 1955 before *Hardy* was ready to complete her trials. She was completed without TT and with Asdic sets 170, 174 and 162 in place of the anticipated final equipment Asdic sets 170B, 176, 177 and 162. The trials were satisfactory, for on the Arran mile *Hardy* achieved 27.85kts at full power, her engines producing 14,830shp with 229rpm on a trial displacement of 1333 tons. Sir Victor Shepheard considered that the ship satisfied the Staff Requirement but he did add that the maintenance of high speeds in heavy weather without damage or washing down the bridge remained to be demonstrated by sea experience.[29]

One salutary feature was the final cost of the ships. The average price was to come out at £1.75 million, which was vastly in excess of the estimates given in 1951 when the Board of Admiralty approved the design. The

Table 7: *Legend of Particulars of Proposed A/S Frigates (FSB) Blackwood Class (Abbreviated)*

Length on waterline:	300ft
overall:	310ft
Breadth, extreme:	33ft
Displacement (deep):	1320 tons
(standard):	1016 tons
Draught, forward:	8ft 10.5in
aft:	10ft 11.5in
Shaft Horse Power:	15,000
Speed in deep condition out of dock for six months in Tropical Waters:	25kts
Endurance at 12kts six months out of dock in Tropical waters:	4500 miles
Complement of Officers and Men:	142
Armament	
Bofors Mark 9 (forward):	2 (1488 rounds per gun)
Bofors Mark 9 (aft):	1 (288 rounds per gun)
Target seeking anti submarine torpedoes:	4 tubes, (4 torpedoes)
Anti-submarine mortar Mk.10:	Double with 20 salvoes
Armour and Protection:	10lbs protective plating to Bridge, Operations Room and Asdic Control Room
Displacement	
General Equipment:	120
Machinery:	236
Armament including radar:	95
Hull:	579
Fuel including Diesel Oil:	259
Reserve Feed Water:	9
Board Margin:	22
Deep Displacement:	1320 tons

cost of a *Whitby* class Type 12 first rate frigate however was £3.5 million, an equally traumatic increase, but one where the rate of escalation was exactly the same as that seen in the 2nd rate *Blackwood* class.[30]

Service

When completed, all ships of the class operated in the waters of the United Kingdom, initially serving at either Portland or Londonderry on anti-submarine duties. The ships based at Portland were largely utilised in the training role. In the fullness of time more exacting duties in a physical sense were to come their way when fishery protection duties became a regular task.[31] The latter role involved patrols in Icelandic waters, which were to expose a weakness in the hull at the break of the forecastle. The cracks in this vicinity were cured by 'careful attention to detailed design at this point'.[32] There were also concerns that damage to the structure could be caused in heavy head or stern seas when slamming and whipping of the stern occurred. In October 1959 the Commanding Officers were instructed to flood all ballast tanks irrespective of the amount of furnace fuel oil on board in order to reduce this phenomenon. Fishery protection duties proved to be quite onerous for the ships' crews for by 1966 50 per cent 'Hard Lying Money' was

being paid when this task was undertaken. There were also some concerns about stability. In 1964 *Pellew* in a moderate wind and sea heeled to 30° and stayed at that angle for sufficient time for the main feed pump to lose suction and break down. It was not thought to be important at the time but twelve years later, when *Dundas* was inclined in January 1976, she did not meet the criteria in use when the ship was designed and fell far short of current standards. The result was that the class members were only permitted to use 60° of the fuel capacity.[33] One ship also suffered a complete blackout in very severe weather whilst on fishery patrol duty when the main switchboard was doused with water. The ship was clearly placed at risk. The lightness of the structure also resulted in corrosion reducing the width of the hull steel plates to very fine tolerances. It was known for the plate to reduce to .2in (8lbs) towards the rear ends.[34]

Some of the class had relatively short lives, with *Murray* scrapped in 1970 surviving for a mere 14 years. *Grafton* and *Pellew* were to follow her to the breakers in 1971. The rest of the class had lifespans more usually associated with that of destroyers and frigates; *Blackwood* went in 1976 after service as a harbour training ship at Gosport between 1967 and 1974, *Malcolm* in 1978 and *Keppel* in 1979. There was then a lull of four years until 1983 when *Dundas* and *Palliser* were scrapped and *Hardy* sunk as a target. She proved very difficult to sink, for it took one Exocet missile, which hit the operations room, one Mk 8 torpedo, one Sea Skua missile and numerous 4.5in and 30mm shells and anti-submarine projectiles to sink the ship. The last two members of the Royal Navy class were *Duncan*, which became a harbour tender to HMS *Caledonia* at Rosyth in 1971 and *Russell* which had replaced *Blackwood* as a harbour training ship in 1974. They were not scrapped until 1985. Of the three Indian Navy ships *Khukri* was torpedoed in December 1971 when war broke out with Pakistan. The two survivors were transferred to the Indian Coast Guard in 1978 and thus completed their role as anti-submarine frigates.[35]

HMS Exmouth

In November 1965 the Board of Admiralty was facing up to 'the demand for higher propulsion power at lower cost in terms of fuel and manpower'. It was stated that the situation 'would oblige us [RN] to turn from steam to gas turbines for the main propulsion plant for future destroyers and frigates'. The Board knew that 'other countries could see this equally clearly' and there were concerns that unless rapid progress was made, the United Kingdom 'would fall behind in the technical race and in tempting export markets'. It was considered that the use of gas turbines alone or in combination with diesels, offered the advantages of the massive research and technical development put into them by the aircraft industry'. The Royal Navy already had gas turbines at sea to provide boost in the 'County' Class guided missile destroyers and the Type 81 'Tribal' Class frigates (Associated Electrical Industries, AEI 06), and as main propulsion in fast patrol boats (Bristol Siddeley Engines, Proteus). The Bristol Siddeley Olympus had already been chosen as the boost engine for the new Type 82 destroyer design, which became HMS *Bristol*; what was needed now was to develop the Olympus engine as a main propulsion unit.

To develop the Olympus satisfactorily meant putting

it to sea in a warship. At that time the first class for which the engine was destined was the new Type 19 Frigate, a project which died in the 1966 Defence Review. The Board was concerned that if the engine first went to sea in the Type 19 frigate then 'we would run the risk of immobilising perhaps the first four of the class'. The recent experience with *Ashanti* and *Devonshire*, the first of class members of the 'Tribal' and 'County' classes, where breakdowns and expensive modifications had been a feature, were emblazoned on the minds of the Board members. The expected cost at £2 million and the use of operational time was regarded as a necessary insurance policy.[36]

HMS *Exmouth* was chosen, and three gas turbines, which were marinised versions of two well-proven aero engines, were installed for propulsion: one Olympus TM1 in a new forward engineroom and two Proteus Type 10M/533 in the after engineroom. The conversion coincided with a planned long refit. The ships' operational capability measured in terms of speed, endurance, manoeuvring performance, noise, weaponry and shock resistance were to be at least equal to a standard *Blackwood* class frigate after a long refit. The need to provide suitable uptakes and downtakes meant a complete redesign of the ships' appearance above the engine room. In place of the existing funnel a squat deckhouse was built, containing the intakes for the Olympus turbine, with the exhaust gases being carried out through a new funnel located further aft. The intakes and exhausts for the Proteus engines were combined in a single structure located above the engine room. The engines drove a single gearbox aligned to a single shaft, maintaining the same shaftline, which was located forward of the two Proteus engines in the after engine room. In order to provide reverse power a standard commercially-designed KaMeWa controllable-pitch propeller was fitted, modified only by the installation of a noise reduction system. At high speed the Olympus engine was used alone, whilst in the lower power ranges, where the fuel consumption of

HMS Exmouth *on 8 August 1969.* Exmouth's *appearance was transformed when she was re-engined, mainly to improve downdraught for the air-hungry gas turbines and provide bigger uptakes for exhaust gas.* (WSS, J M Maber Collection)

A fine shot of HMS Hardy *under way off Portland, showing the weatherliness of the design.* (CPL)

the Olympus turbine was poor, a single Proteus engine was normally employed. The two Proteus engines could be used in combination but they could not be used in conjunction with the Olympus turbine. Particular attention was paid to providing good facilities for the rapid removal and replacement of the gas turbines, with the engines being lifted through their inlet trunks. The aim was to achieve a main engine exchange within 24 hours. The engines could be controlled from the bridge and in order to take full advantage of this facility, bridge steering was also fitted.[37]

HMS *Exmouth* started sea trials on 5 June 1968. The Olympus turbine could produce a maximum power of 24,000hp but only some 15,000hp could be used because of limitations in the shafting and of other material installed in the ship when she was constructed. Nevertheless the trial was valuable, one lesson being learned after only 64 hours running, when an entire row of low-pressure turbine blades in the Olympus turbine were stripped. This was a major setback in the programme. It was discovered that failure was caused by a quite unprecedented level of vibration which was ultimately found to be caused by the design of the air downtake. Various tests led to a solution being found and sea trials were able to start again on 15 October 1968. A valuable lesson had been learned through testing at sea and this was the only major failure to occur during the trials.[38]

The result of the sea trials was the relatively painless introduction of the Olympus power plant in Type 42 destroyers and Type 21 frigates. The ship was broken up in 1979.

Perspective

Judging the success or otherwise of the *Blackwood* class is no easy matter. The ships were built in peacetime but their role was clearly focused on war. Any assessment of their achievements must be judged against these criteria.

The design when approved was meant to be capable of mass-production, with building times close to those achieved for the construction of corvettes a mere ten years earlier. Without question they failed to meet this objective. The shortcomings of the class in gaining this aim were clearly recognised very early on, when 3rd rate designs were developed. Significantly these new designs were to become larger than the *Blackwood* class, thus highlighting a weakness caused by the constraints on the dimensions, which probably unconsciously equated size with cost. In practice the goal of a small size can lead to design complications and increased costs. There is also some evidence that suggests that there were weaknesses in the basic design, particularly the break in the forecastle, which resulted in some fragility appearing in the hull when it was under stress in stormy seas in waters where it would have operated in war. There also seemed to be some question marks raised over stability, which would not have been a good omen for survival if action damage had occurred.

But what of the strengths in the design? Without question the *Blackwood*'s were fine anti-submarine frigates, being virtually the equal of their 1st rate contemporaries the *Whitby* class, and this was gained at half the cost. In relative terms the price paid for the ships turned out to be quite cheap when it is related to the way that costs for all types of warships escalated, a phenomenon which is still with us. One also has to remember that potential enemies were experiencing the same increases in the cost of producing the new submarine designs, which would have been the opponents of the *Blackwood* class. One can criticise the gun armament as being woefully weak but it can be argued that this was a strength. Remember the precise role of the class and ask just when are you going to use a gun when fighting a submarine?

On balance the ships were just a little too small as conceived. Overall, however, they could achieve what was asked of them at the highest standards but their weak-

Appendix 1: STAFF REQUIREMENTS (ABBREVIATED), 22 DECEMBER 1949

Section 'A' General

1. FUNCTIONS
a. To protect convoys of all types against submarines particularly on Ocean routes where threat from air attack is not great.
b. To hunt and destroy submarines.
2. GENERAL REMARKS
a. The ships will supplement (but not replace) the first rate frigate already planned.
b. They should be capable of rapid production and require few men to man them.
c. Ability to operate Asdics at high speed in rough weather is essential.
d. Good seaworthiness is required particularly for steaming at full power into heavy seas without damage and with a minimum washing down of the bridge.
e. Manoeuvrability should be as good as possible consistent with the requirement for good seaworthiness.
f. A single set of steam machinery is to be fitted.
3. SPEED
To be capable of at least 24kts at deep load six months out of dock in tropical waters with propeller silencing fitted. Best possible acceleration from 18kts to full speed is required.
4. ENDURANCE
a. Sufficient oil fuel for 4,500 miles at 12kts in above conditions.
b. Machinery should be designed on the assumption that 80 per cent of time at sea will be spent at 12kts, 15 per cent at 16kts and 5 per cent at 24kts.
5. DEEP DISPLACEMENT AND DIMENSIONS
About 1200 tons x 300ft long
6. SPECIAL FEATURES
a. To be fitted with propeller silencing.
b. To be fitted for service in tropical and cold climates.

Section 'B' Armament

1. ANTI-SUBMARINE ARMAMENT
a. Double Limbo sited aft with a minimum of 12 salvoes.
b. Outfit of four target seeking anti submarine weapons.
2. GUN ARMAMENT
a. One twin Bofors with Simple Tachymetric Director forward.
b. One single Bofors aft (ready use ammunition only).
c. Simple gun direction only (two lookout sights and communications).
Note. Later specified UCSF 2 (interim UCSF 1), 3 single Bofors with visual gun direction.
3. ASDIC SETS
Type 170 – 172 with hull outfit No. 1, Type 162, E/S Type 765
Note. Later specified Type 170B/176 (interim Type 170/174, Type 177, Type 162.
4. ANTI TORPEDO EQUIPMENT
To be fitted with Unifoxer.
Note. Later specified towed and projected Decoys (interim Unifoxer).

COST
Of the order of £650,000.

---

nesses mean they cannot be rated as an excellent design but neither can they be considered a failure. The design was 'focused', to use a current expression, and they deserve to be rated as a 'good' design. They were the right product for their time.

Acknowledgements
My thanks are due to David K Brown RCNC for reading and checking the draft, to Arthur Honnor RCNC for providing such valuable insights into the birth and life of the class, also to Len Crockford for producing the drawings and Richard Osborne of the World Ship Society for providing photographs. I would also like to thank the staff at the Public Record Office, David Ashby at the Naval Historical Branch and Bob Todd and his team at the National Maritime Museum for all their help and kindness.

Notes
[1] Destroyers and Frigates General Cover, ADM 138/830, (NMM).
[2] Arthur Honnor RCNC describes the diesel machinery fitted in the Type 41 and 61 class frigates as 'a very unhandy installation lower in power and very space consuming compared with the steam machinery installed in the Type 12 Frigate. It did have the merit of good endurance but was not particularly good when it came to the matter of reliability'. ADM 138/830, (NMM).
[3] DNC, Correspondence Volume 76(1), 1948, (NMM).

Appendix 2: THE BLACKWOOD CLASS PROGRAMME

Name	Job number	Yard number	Builder	Laid down	Launched	Completed
Royal Navy						
Blackwood	FSB01	4149	Thornycroft	14.9.53	4.10.53	22.8.57
Duncan	FSB02	4150	Thornycroft	17.12.53	30.5.57	21.10.58
Dundas	FSB03	1969	White	17.10.52	25.9.53	9.3.56
Exmouth	FSB04	1970	White	24.3.54	16.11.55	20.12.57
Grafton	FSB05	1971	White	25.2.53	13.9.54	11.1.57
Hardy	FSB06	2012	Yarrow	4.2.53	25.11.53	15.12.55
Keppel	FSB07	2013	Yarrow	27.3.53	31.8. 54	6.7.56
Malcolm	FSB08	2032	Yarrow	1.2.54	18.10.55	12.12.57
Murray	FSB09	638	Stephen	30.11.53	22.2.55	5.6.56
Palliser	FSB10	639	Stephen	15.3.55	10.5.56	13.12.57
Pellew	FSB11	1829	Swan Hunter	5.11.53	29.9.54	26.7.56
Russell	FSB12	1831	Swan Hunter	11.11.53	10.12.54	7.2.57
Indian Navy						
Khukri		1987	White	29.12.55	20.11.56	15.7.58
Kirpan		655	Stephen	5.11.56	19.8.58	7.59
Kuthar		2000	White	19.9.57	14.10.58	11.59

'Nightshirt' cost a lot of power. (D K Brown RCNC)

4 DNC, Correspondence Volume 78, 1949, (NMM). See also Cheaper Carriers, ADM 1/25149 (PRO). A copy of Rear Admiral Edwards paper *Ships of the Future Navy* is held in ADM 205/83, (PRO).

5 New Construction (Revised) Programme 1945, CP (45)291, 22 November 1945, held in CAB 129 (4), (PRO).

6 Anti Submarine Frigate Type 14 General Cover, ADM 138/827, (NMM).

7 DNC, Correspondence Volume 77, 1949 (NMM). D K Brown RCNC comments that 'at that date it was believed that concentrating weights near amidships reduced pitch. Whilst true, the improvement is negligible'. 'It was (also) hoped that low revolutions per minute (rpm) propellers of conventional design would be quiet. They were not, but low rpm contributed much to the success of 'quiet' design propellers'.

8 DNC, Correspondence Volume 78, 1949, (NMM).

9 Naval Construction Department, file 31 (NMM) and letter dated 14.11.2000 from Captain David Garstin RN to D K Brown RCNC.

10 M K Purvis RCNC, 'Post War RN Frigate and Guided Missile Destroyer Design 1944–1969', *RINA*, 1974. The report by Sir Victor Shepheard is held in the Ships Cover, ADM 138/827, (NMM).

11 ADM 138/827, (NMM).

12 Note to the author from Arthur Honnor RCNC, January 2001.

13 Admiralty Board Minutes and Memoranda 1950, ADM 167/135, (PRO).

14 ADM 138/827, (NMM).

15 New Construction Programmes, 1949–1951, ADM 138/827 and ADM 116/5727, (PRO).

16 Admiralty Board Minutes and Memoranda, 1951, ADM 167/136, (PRO).

17 Preston and Raven, *Ensign 3 Flower Class Corvettes* (1973) contains an analysis of the time spent to build each 'Flower' Class corvette.

18 1945 AA and AD Frigates, ADM 138/795, (NMM).

19 Ed. Not the air-defence destroyers designed in the late 1960s.

20 George L Moore 'The 1950s Coastal Frigate Designs for the Royal Navy', *Warship 1995*.

21 Admiralty Board Minutes and Memoranda, 1951, ADM 167/136, (PRO).

22 Admiralty Board Memoranda, 1951, ADM 167/137, (PRO).

23 Note to the author by Arthur Honnor RCNC, January 2001.

24 Admiralty Board Memoranda, 1951, ADM 167/137, (PRO).

25 Minutes of the Ships Names Committee, (Naval Library, MOD).

26 Paper on Defence Preparedness, 1 June 1951, Admiralty Board Memoranda 1951, ADM 167/137, (PRO).

27 E J Grove, *Vanguard to Trident*, admirably sets out the machinations which occurred. The cancellation of the 13th *Blackwood* class frigate is recorded in Admiralty Board Minutes 1955, ADM 167/142, (PRO).

28 Admiralty Board Minutes and Memoranda, 1952 ADM 167/140, (PRO).

29 ADM 138/827, (NMM). D K Brown RCNC comments that the torque reaction gave *Hardy* a list at full power.

30 D Brown and D Andrews *The Design of Cheap Warships* 1980.

31 Warships Supplement No. 41, March 1976, (World Ship Society).

32 M K Purvis, 'Post War RN Frigate and Guided Missile Destroyer Design 1944–1969', *RINA* 1974. Both D K Brown RCNC and A Honnor RCNC strongly criticise the incorporation of discontinuity in the hull structure.

33 ADM138/ 827B, (NMM).

34 Note to the author from A Honnor RCNC, January 2001.

35 *Conways all the Worlds Fighting Ships 1947-1995*; Warships Supplement, No.41, (World Ship Society). The account of the demise of *Hardy* was provided by D K Brown RCNC.

36 Admiralty Board Minutes 1965, ADM 167/165 (PRO). The memorandum relating to this Board Minute (A/P(65)26) was not released at the time of writing.

37 J R Crump B.Sc, RNES 'HMS Exmouth Conversion', *Journal of Naval Engineering*.

38 C E Preston, *Power for the Fleet* (Eton: Eton Publishing, 1982).

ARMSTRONG PORTFOLIO NUMBER FOUR

The National Maritime Museum Ships Plans Division holds two large portfolios of warship designs produced before and during World War One but none of which were built. Portfolio No. Three, covering the period 1909-1914 was described in *Warship 1997-1998*.[1] Here **Peter Brook**, with drawings provided by **Ian Sturton**, examines the contents of Portfolio No. Four.

Armstrong Portfolio Number Four includes colour wash drawings of a protected scout for Turkey, an almost identical design for a light armoured cruiser for Japan, Turkish destroyers, a battleship design for Holland, one stock battleship and four designs for bat-tlecruisers. In addition there are drawings of a crane barge, a salvage ship and a submarine tender. Unfortunately the attractively coloured drawings do not reproduce well and they have been redrawn by Ian Sturton in simplified form.

Torpedo Boat Destroyer, 7 April 1914 (No. 759B)

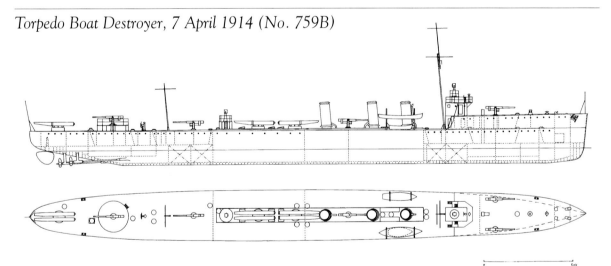

Turkish destroyer, April 1014. Preliminary taken over by Hawthorn Leslie as the Talisman *class.*(Ian Sturton)

Displacement:	1000 tons
Dimensions:	300 pp (312oa) x 28ft 6in x 8
Armament:	5-4in no shields, 6-21in TT (3x2)
Machinery:	3 sets Parsons direct acting turbines, 3 Yarrow, 3 drum small tube boilers, designed speed 32kts
Oil:	90/200 tons

This design for four Turkish destroyers was eventually built by Hawthorn Leslie but, taken over by the Admiralty in November 1914, they became the four *Talisman* class. As completed they were almost identical to the original design but were 3ft shorter oa, displaced 1098 tons, the guns had shields, the quarterdeck pair of TT were removed and 237 tons of oil were carried. The funnels were heightened, the middle funnel moved aft and no three gun placed between the first and second funnels and the boats between the second and third. It seems feasible that Hawthorn's, like Armstrongs, a Newcastle firm, used the original drawings.[2]

Turkish Protected Scout, 8 April 1914 (No. 771B)

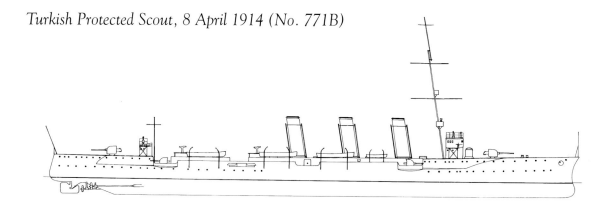

Turkish protected scout cruiser. Two were re-ordered in late 1914 as HMS Centaur *and HMS* Concord. *(Ian Sturton)*

Displacement:	3550 tons
Dimensions:	400 (423 oa) x 41 x 13ft 6in
Armament:	2-6in 50 cal QF, 6-4in 50 cal QF, 2-3in 28cal QF Anti-balloon, 4-3pdr QF, 2-21in TT
Armour:	Nickel steel, 2.5in slopes amidships, 1.5in flats, deck at ends 1.5in, CT 6in
Machinery:	3 sets Parsons Turbines 11 Yarrow boilers, mixed firing, 24000shp =27kts
Fuel:	700 tons coal, 250 tons oil

Two were ordered in May 1914 and assigned yard numbers 877 and 878; material was collected but they were never laid down, the war intervening.[3]

Japanese Light Armoured Cruiser, 10 December 1914 (No. 798)

This design was identical to 771B but had side instead of deck armour.

Armour:	Total of 3in HT steel in wake of engine and boiler rooms, extending from three feet below waterline to upper deck. Forward 2in and 1.5in from 3ft below main deck to 3ft below wl. Aft 2in and 1.75in with the same width as forward. Lower deck 3/8in on slopes and flats. Upper deck 1in gradually reducing towards the ends.

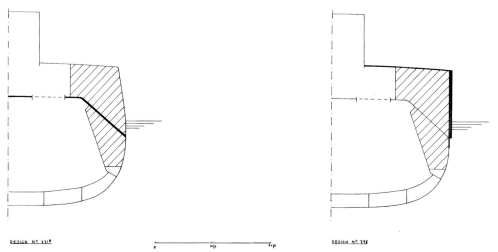

Midships section of Turkish Scout. (Ian Sturton)   *Midships section of Japanese light armoured cruiser. (Ian Sturton)*

Battleship Design for Holland Design, 26 May 1914 (No. 793)

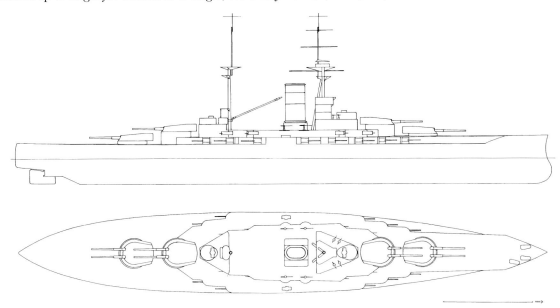

Netherlands Battleship Design. (Ian Sturton)

Displacement:	25,000 tons
Dimensions:	560pp (597oa) x 89ft x 28ft
Armament:	8-14in 45cal, 16-6in 50 cal, 8-3in, 4-3in 28cal anti balloon guns, 5-21in submerged TT
Armour:	Belt 10-7in amidships, 6-4in at ends, Upper belt 7in; Barbettes 12,10,8,5 and 3in; CT 12in; Decks, Lower 2.5-2in, Upper .75-1in
Machinery:	Four shaft turbines
Boilers:	Small tube Yarrow type
Speed:	22kts
Oil:	2000 tons max

Armour sacrificed for speed and heavy armament, on a relatively small displacement. Small tube boilers proposed some two years before their introduction by the Royal Navy.

Stock Battleship Design, 20 Oct 1914 (No 797)

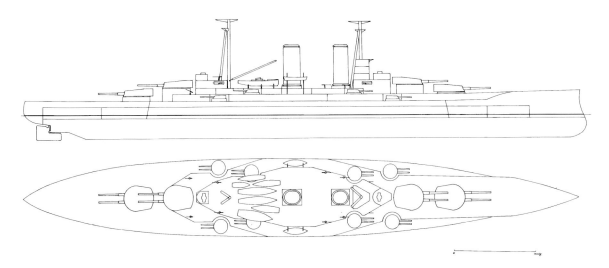

Stock Battleship Design No 797. (Ian Sturton)

Displacement:	30,500 tons
Dimensions:	600pp (688oa) x 95ft x 28ft 6in
Armament:	8-15in, 16-6in housed in armoured gunhouses, 10-3in, 2-3in anti balloon, 4-21in TT
Armour:	Belt 12-6-4in, Middle belt 12-6-4in, Upper belt 6in; 15in barbettes 12 and 10in; 6in barbettes, 6in; CT 12in; Lower deck, forward 1.5in, amidships 1in, Main deck 1-.25in, Upper deck 1.5in; Magazine protection 1.5-1in
Machinery:	Four shaft turbines, Yarrow boilers, half to burn coal, half oil
Speed:	25kts
Fuel:	normal 500 tons coal, 500 tons oil

Roughly contemporary with the *Royal Sovereign* class but despite mixed firing faster by 1kt than *Queen Elizabeth*. Six in gunhouses were not introduced until *Nelson* in 1922. This has the same displacement and main arma-ment as No. 781, one design for the never built Brazilian superdreadnought *Riachuelo*. In fact the latter was more heavily armoured was 2.5kts slower and mounted her 6in guns in an upper deck battery.[4]

Battlecruiser, 18 November 1915 (No. 811)

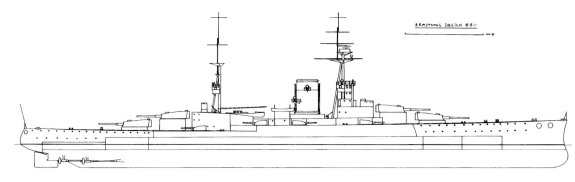
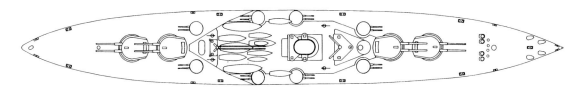

Battlecruiser Design No 811. (Ian Sturton)

Displacement:	33,000 tons
Dimensions:	670pp (710 oa) x 100ft x 30ft
Armament:	8-15in, 16-6in, 4-3in HA, 4-21in submerged TT
Armour:	Main belt 9-6-4in, Upper belt and Citadel 6in; 15in Barbettes 10-6-4-3in; 6in Barbettes 6-1in; CT 12in; Lower deck, For'd 2in, Aft 2.5in, Protective Flat 1in Slope, 2in Middle, 1in Main, 2in Upper, 2in Forecastle, 2in; Wing bulkheads to magazines, Inner .75in, outer 2.5-.5in
Machinery:	Four shaft geared Turbines, Yarrow Boilers
Speed:	28.5kts
Fuel:	Oil, 3500 tons

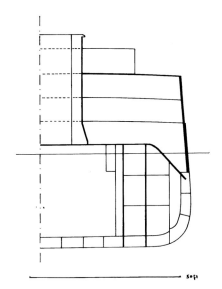

Midships Cross Section of No 811. (Ian Sturton)

Battlecruiser, 29 November 1915 (No. 813)

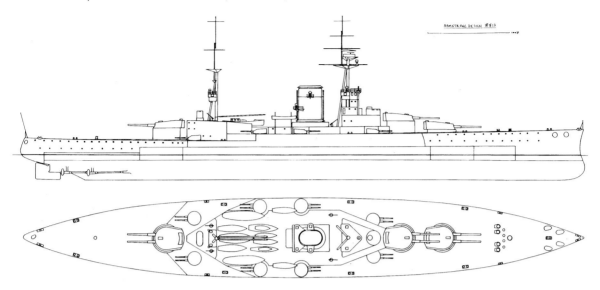

Battlecruiser Design No 813. (Ian Sturton)

Displacement:	30,000 tons
Dimensions:	650pp (690 oa) x 98ft x 29ft
Armament:	6-15in, 16-6in, 4-3in HA, 2-21in TT (broadside submerged)
Armour:	Belt 6-4-3in, Upper belt and citadel 4in; 15in barbettes 7-3in; 6in barbettes 4-1in; CT 10in; Decks, Lower 2-2.5-1in, Protective 2in slopes, 1in flat, Middle 1in, Main 2in, Upper 2in, Forecastle 2in; Wing bulkheads .75in, inner, outer 2.5-3/4in
Machinery:	Four shaft geared turbines, Yarrow boilers
Speed:	28.5kts
Fuel:	3550 tons
Radius:	7000 miles

Decidedly inferior to design 811, losing a quarter of the main armament and with poorer armour protection. All the battlecruisers were pre-Jutland with thin deck armour.

Two designs, 812 and 815 have not been reproduced as they both have a profile similar to 811 except that 812 has only 6-6in gunhouses, the two forward ones on each side mounted at forecastle level.

812 displaced 27,000 tons, mounted 8-14in and 12-6in, Belt 6in, Speed 28kts

815 was 33,600 tons, armament 8-14in, 16-6in, Belt 6in, Speed 29.5kts

Both were poorly balanced designs, reverting to 14in main armament and a thin belt. 812 managed to have the same main armament as 815 on 6700 tons less displacement by sacrificing 1.5kts and 4-6in guns.

Acknowledgements
We gratefully acknowledge the help given to us by the staff of the ships plans department at the Old Brass Foundry, National Maritime Museum, Greenwich.

Notes
[1] P Brook, 'Armstrongs Unbuilt Warships', in A Preston (ed) *Warship 1997-1998*, (London: Conway Maritime, 1997)

[2] E March, *British Destroyers 1892-1953*, (London: Seeley Service, 1966) p.171.

[3] P Brook, *Warships for Export: Armstrong Warships 1867-1927*, (Gravesend: World Ship Society 1999), p.200

[4] *Ibid.*, p.152.

WORLD NAVIES IN REVIEW 2001-2002

Antony Preston looks at current naval developments around the world.

The past year has seen no slackening in the rate of change and renewal. The major navies and many smaller regional navies have clearly decided that the period of retrenchment is over. In fact the drying-up of the flow of second-hand warships has forced these smaller nations to make a choice between new programmes and a steady slide into obsolescence. Given the amount of regional tension, the latter option is one that is politically unaffordable.

Western European Navies

Belgium: The reported enthusiasm for replacing the three remaining trio of *Wielingen* class light frigates seems to have waned. Instead, they are being upgraded piecemeal, with the RIM-7M Sea Sparrow missiles replaced by RIM-7P, enhancing low-altitude performance and incorporating a re-programmable memory. The surviving seven *Aster* class Tripartite minehunters had an upgrade to their propulsion systems in 1999, and a four-year upgrade of capability is planned to run from 2001 to 2004.

Work continues on the four KMV type minesweepers, and M.926 is scheduled to enter service in 2003, while the last, M.929, will be in service by 2007. The long delay in getting this programme under way has been caused by lack of a suitable shipyard, but these problems were solved by the signing of an agreement with SKB Antwerp in October 1999.

The Baltic Republics: The Estonian Navy received the former patrol/fishery protection frigate *Beskytteren* in

June 2000 as an outright gift from the Royal Danish Navy. She retains the full outfit of communications and navigation equipment, as well as the US 3in Mk 22 gun, but not the Lynx helicopter.

The Latvian Coast Guard's ship *Spulga* ran aground off the coast of Sweden on 2 November 2000 while in tow. She was *en route* to Karlskrona to pick unspecified military equipment, and in heavy ship-traffic mistakenly sheered off course.

Cyprus: The Greek part of Cyprus received the former Hellenic Navy patrol boat *Knossos* as a gift in March 2000.

Denmark: Becoming the first navy in the world to adopt commercial classification for all its ships, the Royal Danish Navy (RDN) signed a five-year agreement with the Det Norske Veritas bureau (DNV) on 28 June 2000. Under the agreement DNV assists the Naval Materiel Command in achieving quality-control for both existing and future ships.

The RDN allocates two of its diesel-electric submarines to NATO's Naval Fast Reaction Force, one at a high degree of readiness. After two requests in 1995 and 1999 to deploy a submarine to the Adriatic had to be turned down because the RDN's *Kobben* class were unsuitable for operating in hot climates, the decision was made to 'tropicalise' one. In the first half of 2000 the *Saelen* was given air-conditioning, to improve the environment for the batteries as well as the crew.

Since 13 February 2001 the RDN

has been running the former Royal Swedish Navy submarine *Nåcken*. She was the test-bed for the first seagoing Stirling engine air-independent propulsion (AIP) system, and was bought outright. If the RDN commits itself to buying the four 'Viking' type SSKs in its next five-year plan (2005-2009), the money will be refunded.

Finland: The Frontier Guard ordered two more 50-metre *Telkkä* class from UKI Workboat Ltd in December 2000. They are generally similar to the lead-ship, but are each driven by two of Wärtsilä's latest 12V200 diesels.

France: The *Marine Nationale* lost its back-up carrier when the 38-year old *Foch* was sold to Brazil in August 2000 (see below). The risk was underlined by continuing problems with the nuclear-powered carrier (CVN) *Charles de Gaulle*. She was working up in the Caribbean in mid-November 2000 when she lost a 1-metre section from the blade of one of her two propellers, and had to return to Toulon for repairs. Unfortunately propellers are cast and machined individually and the process takes up to a year. As a short-term measure DCN Toulon decided to replace both propellers with two spares for the old *Clemenceau* and *Foch*, allowing a return to service in March 2001, but with reduced speed. The history of propeller-changes is not a happy one, and if this expedient is unsuccessful the CVN's return to service will be delayed until 2002. The *Charles de Gaulle*, intended to be a prestige ship exemplifying France's ability to project power world-wide, has become an object-lesson in how not to build a carrier. Many in the French Navy and outside it criticise the way in which her total cost of FFr20 billion (about US$2.67 billion) has been paid for by getting rid of the bulk of the surface fleet.

On the positive side, two 'Horizon' type anti-air warfare (AAW) frigates were ordered in September 2000, to replace the ageing *Duquesne* and *Suffren*, with planned delivery in 2006 and 2008 respectively. They will be armed with the same PAAMS vertically-launched AAW missiles selected for the Royal Navy's Type 45 destroyers, eight MM-40 Exocet anti-ship missiles, Sadral short-range AAW missiles and three single Otobreda 76mm Super Rapid guns. The fifth and last *La Fayette* class frigate, the *Guépratte*, was running trials at the beginning of 2001, and will be operational before the end of the year. The fourth *Triomphant* class nuclear-powered strategic submarine (SSBN) *le Terrible*, was ordered from DCN Cherbourg in October 2000. She will be delivered in 2008, and will have the new SET tactical data system and the M51 missile.

At the end of January 2001 two amphibious dock transports (LPDs) were ordered from DCN to replace the ancient *Orage* and *Ouragan*. The ships, to be named *Mistral* and *Tonnerre*, will enter service in 2004 and 2005 respectively, and will be built by the commercial shipbuilder Chantiers de l'Atlantique. This is a major change of policy, away from the expensive state-owned DCN shipyards, which have previously monopolised naval shipbuilding.

Germany: The *Deutsche Marine* is still beset by financial stringency, and struggles to sustain its modernisation plans. The first Type 212A submarine, *U.31*, is to be launched in October 2001, and commissioned in September 2003. Her sisters will enter service between May 2005 and September 2006, a long time after completion of the design in 1992.

Work on the Type 124 *Sachsen* class AAW frigates progresses. Commissioning of the *Sachsen* is planned for December 2002, and the keel of the second, the *Hamburg*, was

The BAE Systems proposal for the Royal Navy's CVF. (BAE Systems)

laid on 1 September 2000 at HDW's Kiel yard. She will be delivered in December 2004. The *Hessen* will be delivered in December 2005 by TNSW's Emden yard.

The first five Type 130 corvettes were approved in July 2000, and will be armed with the Norwegian NSM anti-ship missile as well as the fibre-optic guided Polyphem missile and the Rolling Airframe Missile (RAM) for defence against missiles. It remains to be seen if the full total of 15 will be built. The second Type 404 *Berlin* class combat support ship, the *Frankfurt am Main*, was launched by the Lürssen yard in Bremen on 5 January 2001, marking a new willingness on the part of the German Government to undertake peacekeeping operations outside the NATO area.

Great Britain: Design work continues on the Future Aircraft Carrier (CVF) project, with two consortia competing: one led by BAE Systems Marine and the other by the French Thales Group (formerly Thomson-CSF). The final design rests on a decision about the Joint Strike Fighter (JSF); if the Short Takeoff and Vertical Landing (STOVL) variant is abandoned to cut cost, BAE Systems says the displacement will rise to 60,000 tons to accommodate conventional aircraft. In May 2001 HMS *Ark Royal* was close to recommissioning after her £118 million refit. Sea trials started in July, with a rededication service to be held at

Portsmouth in November. Her sister *Invincible* was reduced to a low level of readiness in May 2001, before starting her refit at the end of the year; she returns to service in 2003. HMS *Illustrious* starts her own 23-month refit in the third quarter of 2002.

The Royal Navy's (RN) nuclear submarine force suffered a severe setback with the discovery of a faulty weld in the cooling circuit of the reactor in HMS *Tireless* in mid-2000, while visiting Gibraltar. As a result all attack submarines (SSNs) were 'grounded' to allow comprehensive checks to be made. On 11 July 2000 the Ministry of Defence (MoD) made a statement to the effect that six of the 12 SSNs were operational: *Sovereign, Splendid, Superb, Trafalgar, Triumph* and *Turbulent*, with two refitting at Rosyth, three at Devonport and one at Gibraltar. Yet the *Sovereign* and *Superb*, based at Faslane, were withdrawn from service. In fact *Sceptre* had displayed the same problem in 1998, and the MoD was finally forced to subject all SSNs to the checks. On 24 January 2001 an official statement admitted that repairs to seven were 'running to schedule'. The work on *Tireless* was not delayed by Gibraltarian fears about nuclear radiation but by their attempts to have all the work done by local shipyard workers, rather than RN specialists brought in. HMS *Trafalgar* is the third SSN armed with the Tomahawk Land Attack Missile (TLAM), and carried out a live firing in the Gulf of Mexico on 7 August 2001.

According to a separate statement the final decommissioning dates for current SSNs are:

Splendid	2003
Sovereign	2005
Superb and *Spartan*	2006
Trafalgar	2007
Turbulent	2008
Sceptre	2010
Tireless	2011
Talent	2015
Triumph	2017
Torbay	2020
Trenchant	2022

The early demise of so many of the *Swiftsure* class explains why the RN is so keen to get the first of the *Astute* class into service by 2005. The keel-laying of *Astute* herself at Barrow in Furness on 31 January 2001 was cosmetic, in that a large amount of fabrication was already in hand. At a submerged displacement of 7200 tonnes she is twice the size of existing SSNs, but the size makes for quicker and cheaper construction as well as lower through-life cost. It has also been claimed that building more *Astutes* will be cheaper than upgrading the *Trafalgar* class, and a case for building at least eight has been studied.

In March 2001 BAE Systems Marine revealed a number of details about the Type 45 AAW destroyer programme, including the fact that the RN has given priority to endurance. The combat management system has been selected, as well as the integrated communications system and the propulsion (full electric, using the WR-21 turbine as the power-source). There are still some matters to be resolved; the forward PAAMS missile silo can be extended to accommodate-land-attack weapons, but this would preclude a larger gun than the new 4.5in (114mm) Mk 8 Mod 1 planned. There was a wrangle between the prime contractor and Vosper Thornycroft, who wanted a share of the work, starting with a contract to build No.2, but on 10 July 2001 six were ordered from BAE Systems Marine, with Vosper Thornycroft guaranteed major structural work on all six. Names announced to date are *Daring*, *Dauntless* and *Diamond*.

Those stalwart old warriors, the Type 42 destroyers, will have to bear the brunt of air defence until long after their first successor arrives on the scene in 2007. As *Birmingham* has been sold, we should logically refer to the seven survivors of Batches 1 and 2 as the *Newcastle* class. One of the

Batch 3 ships, HMS *York*, shipped a SeaRam missile-launcher on 1 February 2001, for evaluation of Raytheon's Rolling Airframe Missile (RAM) as an anti-missile system. The virtues of SeaRam are that it replaces the 20mm 'gatling' gun in the Mk 15 Phalanx mounting, and engages an incoming target at roughly three times the range of the Phalanx gun. The trials are funded by Raytheon, as there is no current RN requirement for a replacement for Phalanx.

The 15th 'Duke' class anti-submarine warfare (ASW) frigate, HMS *Portland*, was handed over to the RN just before Christmas 2000. The last of the class, *St Albans*, was launched on 6 May 2000 and is planned to be handed over in April 2002. The first of the class, HMS *Norfolk*, recommissioned in March 2001 after being rearmed with the 4.5in Mk 8 Mod 1 gun. This mounting has a new faceted cupola to reduce radar cross-section and fires a High Explosive/Extended Range (HE/ER) base-bleed round to extend range from 22km to 27km. HMS *Grafton* ran aground in Oslofjord on 11 September 2000, losing her sonar dome in the process.

The 11th *Sandown* class mine-hunter, *Blyth*, was launched at the

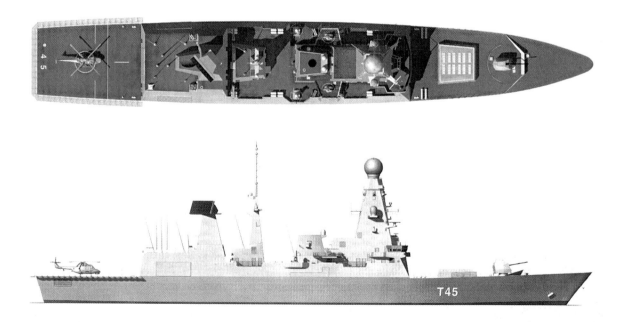

The Type 45 Daring *class air defence destroyer.* (BAE Systems)

The first helicopter landing aboard the trimaran RV Triton, a Lynx Mk 8. (Qinetiq)

HMS York with a SeaRam missile-launcher mounted on the portside Mk 15 Phalanx mounting. (Raytheon)

Vosper Thornycroft's design for the new 'River' class offshore patrol vessels. (Vosper Thornycroft)

Vosper Thornycroft yard in Woolston on 4 July 2000, and accepted by the RN on 7 March 2001. The 12th, *Shoreham*, was launched at the same yard on 9 April 2001. HMS *Walney* completed a major upgrade by Babcock Rosyth in January 2001, being fully 'tropicalised', both diesels replaced, a transportable decompression chamber added, and a second crane.

The amphibious forces have done well, with the helicopter carrier (LPH) *Ocean* proving her worth in supporting operations in Sierra Leone. The new amphibious dock transport (LPD) *Albion* was launched at Barrow in Furness on 9 April 2001, and is expected to enter service in March 2003. In theory HMS *Intrepid* is still available, but she is at a low degree of readiness, and could only be recommissioned at the cost of 'cannibalising' her sister *Fearless*. Four Alternative Logistic Landing Ships (ALSLs) are planned, of which *Lyme Bay* and *Largs Bay* were ordered from Swan Hunter on 19 December 2000. According to the *Daily Telegraph* they were to have been named *Aboukir Bay* and *Quiberon Bay*, but the politicians vetoed the names for fear of offending the French! They may be the first Royal Fleet Auxiliary ships (RFAs) to be driven by podded electric propulsion units.

The remaining five 'Island' class offshore patrol vessels (OPVs) Mk 1 are to be replaced by three new 'River' class ordered from Vosper Thornycroft in May 2001. They will be easier to maintain and will be available for 340 days in each year,

using a rotating watch system. The ships will be leased from the builders for a five-year period, and the contract includes full support. They will be named after rivers: HMS *Tyne* will be in service in September 2002, followed by HMS *Severn* in March 2003 and HMS *Mersey* in September 2003.

Greece: The Hellenic Navy is responding to the threat from Turkey as relations sour over border disputes in the Aegean. Welding of frames for the first Type 214 submarine started at HDW's Kiel yard on 28 February 2001. She will be handed over in 2005, and will be followed by two more built in Greece (with an option for a fourth).

A seventh *Kortenaer* class frigate, the *Pieter Florisz*, was bought in 2001 from the Royal Netherlands Navy. This brings the frigate force up to ten ships.

Work is in hand on the three Vosper Thornycroft 62-metre fast attack craft (FACs) building at Elefsis. Vosper Thornycroft and other yards have also submitted designs to meet a new requirement for three corvettes. The Navy took delivery of the former RN minehunter *Bicester* at Portsmouth on 31 July 2000 and renamed her HS *Evropi*. A second, the former *Berkeley*, was handed over in February 2001 and renamed *Kallisto*. On 16 January the first Russian-built Project 1232.2 'Pomornik' (*Almaz*) type assault hovercraft, HS *Kefallonia*, was handed over.

Ireland: Appledore Shipbuilders in UK launched a second *Roisin* class

offshore patrol vessel, the *Niamh*, on 10 February 2001. She was to be delivered to the Irish Naval Service in March and may be followed by four more. LE *Niamh* was handed over on 19 July at Appledore in Devon, UK by her builders Appledore Shipbuilders. She will be sailed to Ireland by an Irish naval crew, and was formally commissioned in September.

Italy: The long-delayed *nuova unitá maggiore* (NUM) *Andrea Doria* was ordered from Fincantieri in December 2000. She was laid down at Riva Trigoso, south of Genoa, in June 2001 and she will be commissioned in 2007. Work on the Type 212A submarines is proceeding slowly at Fincantieri's Muggiano yard, outside La Spezia. The first was to have been started in January 2001 and will be commissioned in 2005.

Two 'Horizon' type AAW frigates were ordered in September 2000 at the same time as the French pair; they will also be built at Riva Trigoso, and will be delivered 2007 and 2009 respectively. The first of a new class of 1520-tonne corvettes, the *Comandante Cigala Fulgosi*, was launched at Riva Trigoso on 7 October 2000, followed by the *Commandante Borsina* on 17 February 2001.

The Netherlands: The AAW frigate *de Zeven Provincien* is fitting out, and will be commissioned in March 2002, followed by her three sisters in 2003-2005. The old AAW destroyer *de Ruyter* will be paid off in 2003.

Norway: The contract to build five new frigates was signed in June 2000 with Spanish builders IZAR (formerly Empresa Nacional Bazán), the largest defence contract in Norwegian history. The ships will be built at Ferrol in NW Spain and the electronics, including the Aegis weapon direction system, will be integrated by Lockheed Martin. The *Frithjof Nansen* (F-310) is to be delivered in 2005, and the *Roald Amundsen* (F-311), *Otto Sverdrup* (F-312), *Helge Ingstad* (F-313) and *Thor Heyerdahl* (F-314) by 2009.

Norway is a partner in the 'Viking' submarine project, but plans to buy four to follow the *Ula* class from 2007 onwards have been vetoed by Parliament. It seems likely that the *Ula* class mid-life modernisation will be cancelled, and six 'Vikings' will be ordered. The six surviving *Kobben* class are now over 30 years old, and two were supposed to pay off in 2000; they will not be replaced.

The modernised fast attack craft (FAC) KNM *Stegg* (P-994) started trials in November 2000, the first of 14 *Hauk* class to receive the SENIT 8 combat system. It is hoped to replace the Penguin missiles with the new NSM missile system, and five more of the surface-effect *Skjold* class have been ordered.

Poland: The correct names for the two ex-US Navy frigates acquired in 2000-2001 are *General Kasimir Pulawski* (ex-*Clark*) and *General Kosciuscko* (ex-*John H Sides*), with pennant numbers 272 and 273 respectively. As yet there is no further news of an order for the planned six Project 924 missile-armed corvettes. They will be built in Poland to a Western design, believed to be a variant of the Blohm+Voss MEKO 200. A contract was signed on 6 August 2001 with Thales to modernise the three Project 660 *Orkan* class corvettes.

No news either of projected replacements for the Project 641 'Foxtrot' type submarines *Dzik* and *Wilk*, and several offers have been received, including second-hand *Agosta* class from France, Type 206A boats from Germany, and two *Gal* class from Israel.

Romania: The flagship of the Romanian Navy, the former destroyer *Marasesti*, has been reclassified as a frigate to achieve commonality with NATO designations.

Spain: The AAW frigate *Alvaro de Bazán* (F-101) was launched at Ferrol on 27 October 2000, about two months after Lockheed completed testing and integration of her Aegis weapon direction system. Her sister *Roger de Lauria* (F-102) was expected to be laid down in February 2001, for completion in November 2003, while the *Blas de Lezo* and *Mendez Nuñez* will be completed in 2004 and 2006 respectively.

No announcement has been made about an order for up to four 'Scorpène' type submarines, which makes the in-service date of 2005 for No.1 unlikely to be achieved.

The minehunter *Tambre* (M-33) was commissioned on 18 February 2000 and her sister *Turia* (M-34) on

Launch of the Spanish Navy's first Aegis frigate, the Alvaro de Bazán, *at Ferrol on 27 Otober 2000.* (IZAR)

18 October 2000, but the planned order for the next four *Segura* class has not yet materialised.

The second *Galicia* class assault ship, the *Castilla* (L-52) was completed in June 2000, marking a significant improvement in the Spanish Navy's amphibious warfare capability.

Sweden: The corvette *Visby* was launched at the Karlskrona yard of Kockums AB on 8 June 2000 and contractors' sea trials were scheduled for mid-2001. She will be operational with the Royal Swedish Navy in 2004, and the remaining five ships, *Helsingborg, Härnösand, Nyköping, Karlstad* and *Uddevalla*, will follow at yearly intervals.

The older corvettes *Stockholm* and *Malmö* have started their mid-life upgrade at Karlskrona, to reduce their radar cross-section and renew the propulsion system. The two MTU TB 93 diesels will be replaced by TB 94s, and the Allison 570KF gas turbine on the centre shaft will be replaced by a TF50 gas turbine. The two ships are expected to rejoin

the fleet in May 2002. In June 2001 a contract was awarded for similar modernisation of all four *Goteborg* class.

The 'Viking' submarine project reached tendering stage in February 2001, the Danes and Norwegians having submitted their specifications. It was hoped to fund ten submarines, four each for Denmark and Norway and two for Sweden, to be ordered not later than 2005, but internal problems may delay the partners' decisions. The submarine force is down to seven boats, with the sale of the *Nåcken* to Denmark.

Turkey: No fewer than 24 ships were commissioned in a ceremony on 8 June 2000, including the frigate TCG *Kemalreis*, the FAC *Mizrak* and an assortment of naval auxiliaries and Coast Guard vessels. A sixth *Oliver Hazard Perry* class frigate, the former *John A Moore*, was transferred in February 2000 and renamed TCG *Gediz*, and the ex-*Flatley* was acquired in July 2001. Approval has been given for the construction of six

TF-2000 type frigates, but no design has been selected so far.

The four IKL Type 209/1400 submarines are all in service, and the *Gür* and *Canakkale*, first and second of a new class, are under construction. They and the other two successors may be repeat Type 209/1400s, but in the light of the Greek order for Type 214 boats with air-independent propulsion it seems unlikely that the Turks will be content with the older and less capable design. As Gölcük Shipyard is already experienced in building IKL/HDW designs, a switch to Type 214 boats seems likely.

Six redundant A69 type *d'Estienne d'Orves* class coastal corvettes were bought in November 2000, and the first was to be delivered in February 2001. Names are: *Bafra* (ex-*Second Maitre le Bihan*), *Bodrum* (ex-*Drogou*), *Bandirma* (ex-*Quartir-maitre Anquetil*), *Bozcada* (ex-*Commandante le Pimodan*), *Beycoz* (ex-*d'Estienne d'Orves*) and *Bartin* (ex-*Amyot d'Inville*). TCG *Bozcada* was commissioned on 25 July 2001.

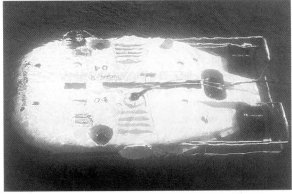

Royal Swedish Navy mine clearance operations off the coast of the Baltic Republics, using the Double Eagle robot. (RSwN)

The Turkish 'stretched' MEKO 200 type frigate TCG Oruç Reis. (Turkish Navy)

The United States, Canada and Latin America

United States: The aircraft carrier *Ronald Reagan* (CVN-76) was formally christened on 4 March 2001 by Mrs Nancy Reagan at Newport News, VA, and will join the fleet in December 2002. It has now been decided to build three more CVNs to the basic CVN-77 design, to allow time for the development of new technologies such as electric catapults and a possible alternative to nuclear propulsion.

On 12 October 2000 the destroyer USS *Cole* (DDG-67) was rammed by a suicide boat in Aden and hit full amidships by the equivalent of 600lbs of C4 explosive (the equivalent of two heavyweight torpedoes). Despite much ill-informed criticism, the incident showed how battleworthy the *Arleigh Burke* class destroyers are. The *Cole* was capable of making her way back to the US on one set of gas turbines, although the US Navy decided not to take any risks with North Atlantic autumnal gales, and was taken back to her builders in the Gulf of Mexico on a heavy-lift transporter.

Two *Ticonderoga* (CG-47) class cruisers completed trials of the Baseline 6 Phase 1 improved Aegis weapon direction system in May 2000. Baseline 6, which will be retro-

fitted to all but the oldest cruisers, handles the Evolved Sea Sparrow Missile (ESSM), Co-operative Engagement Capability (CEC) and the ability to provide defence against Tactical Ballistic Missiles (TBMs).

The name *Zumwalt* was announced for the first land-attack DD-21 destroyer in July 2000. The 34th *Arleigh Burke* (DDG-51) class Aegis destroyer *Bulkeley* (DDG-84) was christened on 24 June 2000. The first Flight IIA ship, the USS *Oscar Austin* (DDG-79), was commissioned at Norfolk, VA in August 2000, followed by the USS *Roosevelt* (DDG-80) in October the same year, and the USS *Lassen* (DDG-82) in April 2001. The name *Nitze* (DDG-94) was announced for the 44th unit, while the *Shoup* (DDG-86) was christened in February 2001. The USS *Winston S Churchill* (DDG-81) was commissioned on 10 March 2001 at Norfolk, having fired the first rounds from her 5in Mk 45 Mod 4 62 calibre gun in July the previous year. She fired 132 rounds of conventional and extended-range guided munitions (ERGM) to test for shock and hull-stress. The latest names allocated are *Mason* (DDG-87) and *Preble* (DDG-88). Three Aegis SPY-1D(V) radars and Mk 99 trackers were ordered for DDG-99/100 and 101 in March 2001.

The attack submarine USS

Greeneville (SSN-772) collided with and sank the Japanese fishing vessel *Ehime Maru* off Hawaii on 9 February 2001. The official enquiry revealed that the SSN was about 1.5 nautical miles (3000 metres) outside the designated exercise area, that the control room had sixteen civilians in it during the crucial period of coming to periscope-depth, and other serious shortcomings in procedures.

The renewal of the amphibious forces continues, with two more *San Antonio* (LPD-17) class amphibious dock transports ordered in 2000, LPD-19/20. The seventh *Wasp* class amphibious assault ship has been named *Iwo Jima* (LHD-7), and design work on the eighth *Wasp* class amphibious assault ship, LHD-8, has been started. She will be the first of the class to be driven by gas turbines rather than steam turbines. The plant will comprise a pair of 35,000shp LM 2500+ gas turbines, and a unique hybrid electric drive for 'loitering' at low speed.

Canada: The former destroyer escort (DDE) *Yukon* was scuttled on 15 July 2000 off San Diego, CA to form an artificial reef. All twelve *Halifax* class frigates will have their Sea Sparrow missiles replaced by the Evolved Sea Sparrow Missile Systems (ESSM) in 2003, the first phase of a major upgrade programme. Unconfirmed

The USS Enterprise *(CVN-65), oldest of the nuclear-powered aircraft carriers, will remain in service until 2013. (USN/USS Enterprise)*

The Enterprise Carrier Battle Group *in close formation, with an amphibious assault ship astern. (USN/USS Enterprise)*

Cutaway model of the Chilean Navy's French-designed 'Scorpène' submarines. (Adrian J English)

reports suggest that four ships may be given the Dutch APAR 3-D radar as part of a conversion to AAW ships. At the end of December 2000, however, the AAW destroyer HMCS *Huron* was laid up, apparently because the Navy can no longer afford to operate her. Most of her crew and essential equipment were transferred to other ships.

In the submarine branch things are looking better. HMCS *Victoria* (ex-HMS *Unseen*) was handed over at Barrow in Furness on 6 October 2000, and HMCS *Windsor* (ex-HMS *Unicorn*) followed on 5 July 2001. The *Cornerbrook* (ex-HMS *Ursula*) and *Chicoutimi* (ex-HMS *Upholder*) will follow by July 2002. The last *Oberon*, HMCS *Onondaga*, was paid off in August 2000.

Argentina: The ASMAR shipyard at Talcahuano in Chile completed a major part of the refit of the Type 42 destroyer ARA *Hercules* in November 2000. She was given a new hangar capable of accommodating a Sea King helicopter, but has returned to Argentina for the rest of the refit.

Brazil: The old French carrier *Foch* was bought in August 2000, handed over on 15 November 2000 and underwent a detailed overhaul and refurbishment by DCN Brest. Under her new name, BNS *São Paolo* (A-12), she left Brest for Rio de Janeiro on 1 February 2000. The 55-year old carrier *Minas Gerais* (ex-HMS *Vengeance*) will be sold for scrapping and her air group will transfer to her successor.

The submarine BNS *Tonelero* sank at her moorings in the submarine base at Rio de Janeiro on 24 Decembr 2000. She was refloated on 4 January 2001 but is unlikely to be repaired as she is already over-age.

Chile: *Proyecto Tridente* is an ambitious project to build a series of up to a dozen frigates, and after long deliberation the Blohm+Voss MEKO 200 design was chosen as the basis. However, the Defence Minister gave only qualified approval, bearing in mind the dismal track record of indigenous warship-building in Argentina, Brazil and Peru. The AAW destroyer *Capitan Prat* completed a ten-month refit to convert her into a helicopter-carrying destroyer (DDH) at the end of 2000.

The after sections S1 and S2 of the first 'Scorpène' type submarine, the *O'Higgins*, left DCN Cherbourg for Cartagena in July 2000; they will be united with other sections fabricated by Empresa Nacional Bazán.

Uruguay: The patrol boat *Valiente* (32), a former East German 'Kondor II' type minesweeper sank with the loss of 11 lives, following a collision with merchant ships in August 2000.

Russia

The Project 649A *Antey* class ('Oscar II') nuclear-powered cruise missile submarine *Kursk* was lost in tragic circumstances in the Barents Sea on 12 August 2000. The Royal Navy and the Royal Norwegian Navy both promised the assistance of their own submarine salvage specialists, but the Russian authorities stalled for time,

claiming that strong cross-currents and poor visibility, combined with damage to the after escape hatch made any attempt to rescue survivors useless. Later the flag-office in charge of the Norwegian team denied all this, saying that his divers could easily have searched the after section of the *Kursk* but were repeatedly blocked by the Russians. An international consortium hopes to raise the wreck in mid-September 2001 (see more detail in Warship Notes).

The Northern Fleet has taken 109 nuclear submarines out of service, and nearly all first- and second-generation boats are being scrapped at the Severodvinsk shipyard. Nuclear waste is taken by train from the shipyard to the Mayak plant in the Chelyabinsk Region for processing. According to a statement by Itar-Tass in December 2000 Severodvinsk can scrap eight to ten nuclear boats a year. The second Project 971M *Bars* ('Akula II') class SSN, the *Gepard*, started sea trials in the White Sea in November 2000.

Two Project 1155R *Udaloy* class destroyers of the Pacific Fleet, the *Admiral Vinogradov* and *Admiral Panteleyev*, set out on a cruise in the Far East on 15 January 2001. Up to that point the Pacific Fleet had been unable to undertake extended operations because of a chronic shortage of cash.

And now, one for the *Guinness Book of Records*: the 85-year old submarine salvage vessel *Kommuna* (ex-*Volkhov*), believed to have been scrapped some fifteen years ago, turns out to be still active (possibly under her original name). In 1973 she was converted to a midget submarine carrier at Sevastopol and was also equipped to operate deep-submergence rescue vehicles (DSRVs). In 1974 she established a record when the AGA-6 autonomous DSRV made a record dive to 2026 metres. She is to become a floating memorial to submarine rescues of all navies.

Middle East and Indian Ocean Navies

Egypt: After many years of good intentions but no action, the Navy ordered two 'Moray 1400' conven-

INS Viraat *(ex-HMS* Hermes*) at the Fleet Review in Mumbai.* (Commodore Rai)

The air defence destroyer INS Rajput *at the Fleet Review.* (Commodore Rai)

The new destroyer INS Delhi *launches a Kh-35 Uran missile.* (Indian Navy)

tional submarines from RDM in Rotterdam on 15 September 2000. They will, however, be built by Ingalls at Pascagoula, MS to qualify for Foreign Military Sales (FMS) funding, and will have an AIP plant of unspecified type, possibly RDM's own Spectre. With four Chinese Project 033 'Romeos' to be replaced, an order for two more is likely.

Four 'Ambassador Mk III' 61-metre FACs were ordered in January 2001 from Halter Marine. They will have a Lockheed combat system and Harpoon anti-ship missiles. The contract awarded to Alenia Marconi Systems (AMS) in March 2000 covered the modernisation of the combat systems of the six *Ramadan* class FACs. In April 2001 two more contracts were won by AMS, one to upgrade the *Ramadans'* Otomat missiles and the other to refurbish and upgrade the S820 surveillance radars and ST802 trackers in four of the vessels.

India: In October 2000 the Indian and Russian governments finally signed the agreement for the purchase of the Project 1143.4 hybrid cruiser-carrier *Admiral Gorshkov*. She will be delivered free but will undergo a two-year refurbishment and repair in a Russian shipyard at a cost of US$1.5 billion. She will operate about 24 MiG-29K fighters. In parallel, design work continues on the Air Defence Ship (ADS), the outcome of the original over-ambitious plan to build three carriers, the first to be ready in 1997. The first design was cancelled, then a variant of the Italian LPD was proposed, then a French design, but the Defence Ministry seems serious this time.

The *Mumbai*, last of three *Delhi* class AAW destroyers, was launched on 23 January 2001 by Mazagon Dock at Mumbai. The first Project 1135.6 'Krivak III' type destroyer was launched on 12 May 2000 at the Baltiisky Zavod shipyard in St Petersburg and named *Talwar*. Work started on the third unit on 26 May 2000, to be named *Toofan*, and the second, *Trishul*, was launched on 24 November the same year. The names *Kashmir*, *Arunachal Pradesh* and *Sikkim* were originally earmarked for the indigenous Type 17 Project, but some were considered politically sensitive. The *Talwar* is to be delivered in April 2002, followed by the Trishul in June 2003, and three more may be built locally.

The Project 877EM 'Kilo' type submarine *Sindhushastra* was commissioned at the Baltiisky Zavod yard on 16 July 2000. She is the tenth and last of the class. Two of the early boats were sent to St Petersburg for overhaul in May 1999, and the first was refloated in April 2001.

Rumours of more IKL Type 1500 boats and a switch to the Project 636 Improved 'Kilo' seem to have been off beam, as the Admiralteyskiye Verf shipyard announced on 23 April 2001 that it will probably deliver the prototype Project 677 *Amur* 1650 boat. But a successful bid has also been received from Thales in France for Project 75, the 'Scorpène' design.

The government was reported in February 2001 to be close to finalising an agreement to lease a nuclear attack submarine from Russia. This seems likely to be a Project 971 or 971U *Schuka-B* ('Victor III') type, and it would effectively checkmate Pakistan's modern *Khalid* class.

The second *Kora* class corvette *Kirch* was launched on 23 January 2001 at Garden Reach in Calcutta. The *Pralaya*, first of a new class of missile-armed corvettes, was commissioned in December 2000. The 477-ton vessel is armed with Kh-35 *Uran* ('SS-N-25') anti-ship missiles and is driven by four gas turbines at a maximum speed of 35kts. The displacement suggests that she may be a development of the *Veer* class, which is a local variant of the Russian Project 1241RE 'Tarantul' design.

The three *Samar* class Coast Guard offshore patrol vessels have been refitted with Radamec 2400 electro-optical fire control systems.

Iran: The first of a new type of missile-armed craft, locally-built and armed with 'rocket launchers' was delivered to the Islamic Revolution Guard Corps (IRGC) in April 2001. At the same ceremony a *Karbala* class tank landing ship was launched. One of the three 'Kilo' class submarines has been given a four-month refit locally.

The corvette INS Ajay *at the Fleet Review.* (Commodore Rai)

The acoustic research ship INS Sagardhwani *at the Fleet Review.* (Commodore Rai)

Israel: A *Times* report on 18 June 2000 raised the spectre of Israeli submarines launching nuclear-tipped cruise missiles for land-attack. The report claimed that two new submarines, presumably the *Dolphin* and *Leviathan*, had fired missiles a distance of 930km (about 430nm) off the coast of Sri Lanka. The range is suspiciously identical to that given for Israel's Jericho intermediate range ballistic missile (IRBM), about six times the range of the boats' UGM-89 Harpoon anti-ship missiles. Putting a nuclear warhead on Harpoon would deliver a modest 6kg (2.7lb) payload. Like most media scare-stories, it has a grain of truth, but was almost certainly a test-firing of standard Harpoons. Sri Lanka buys a great deal of military equipment from Israel, and the Israelis are always looking for range facilities well away from 'snoopers' in the Eastern Mediterranean.

Kuwait: The arrival of the last four

42-metre FACs at the Mohammed al Hamad base in Kuwait City in October 2000 marks the return of the Kuwait Navy to its strength in 1990, before the Iraqi invasion. Plans to build three 88-metre offshore patrol vessels or corvettes have been delayed.

Pakistan: Four frigates, reported to be 'Jiangwei' type, are to be ordered from mainland China, the first to be built in a Chinese yard and the remainder to be built at Karachi.

With the new submarine *Khalid* now in service and the *Saad* to be launched at Karachi in 2001, one of the four *Hangor* class (*Daphné* type) will be taken out of service shortly.

Saudi Arabia: The frigate *Taif* left DCN Toulon on 21 March 2000, following a major refit. This brings to an end the *Mouette* programme to modernise all four *Madina* class.

The *Riyadh*, first of three modified *La Fayette* class AAW frigates ordered under the Sawari II project, was launched on 1 August 2000 at DCN Lorient. She will be commissioned in July 2002, followed by the *Makkah* in April 2003 (launched on 20 July 2001) and the *Damman* in January 2004. In general the design is similar to the *La Fayette*, but with vertically launched Aster-15 missiles forward and the Arabel multi-function radar on a stump mast aft.

Sri Lanka: The Sri Lankan Navy continues to fight a bloody war against the Liberation Tigers of Tamil Eelam (LTTE) separatists. On 20 March 2001 an Israeli-built 'Dvora' or 'Super Dvora' type coastal patrol craft was sunk 250km NE of Colombo, and on 23 May thirteen naval personnel were killed by a land mine near Trincomalee on the east coast.

On a more positive note, the first helicopter-operating ship, an Indian-built *Sukanya* class offshore patrol vessel, was delivered in December 2000. She will be followed by a second vessel of this type shortly.

United Arab Emirates: In March 2001 the UAE announced an order for six 58-metre FACs from Constructions Mécaniques de Normandie (CMN). In fact the programme will be a partnership between CMN and the Abu Dhabi Shipbuilding (ADSB) yard, with ADSB acting as prime contractor.

At the IDEX 2001 exhibition in March 2001 the UAE Navy unveiled

The frigate HMAS Arunta *at Fremantle in December 2000.* (Antony Preston)

two locally built swimmer-delivery vehicles, the Class 4 and Class 5 two-man Long Range Submersible Carriers (LRSCs). The smaller Class 4 LRSC carries a payload of 200kg, while Class 5 carries 450kg.

Asia-Pacific Regional Navies

Australia: HMAS *Warramunga*, third of the *Anzac* class frigates, was commissioned on 31 March 2001. Plans to design a 6000-tonne Future Surface Combatant seem to have cooled somewhat, and reports suggest that a number of foreign off-the-shelf designs have been looked at. According to some sources the Spanish F-100 design comes out best, with its Aegis weapon direction sys-

tem, SPY-1D or -1F radar and Standard SM-2 missiles.

In September 2000 it was confirmed that the Royal Australian Navy's (RAN) *Collins* class submarines, HMAS *Sheean* and HMAS *Dechaineux*, have received upgrades to rectify many of the faults affecting the class. In addition, funds were made available to upgrade HMAS *Farncomb* and the then-incomplete *Rankin* to the same standard. On 8 December 2000 the upgraded *Collins* and *Waller* docked at Fleet Base West in Fremantle, WA, after a marathon 183-day deployment to Hawaii and Alaska. The US Navy is to make elements of its latest BSY-2 command system to bring the *Collins* class to full operational capability. On 15 December 2001 HMAS *Otama*, last of the RAN's *Oberon* type, was paid off at Fleet Base West.

HMAS *Norman*, third of the *Huon* class coast minehunters, was handed over to the RAN in August 2000. *Gascoyne* was launched in March the same year; *Diamantina* and *Yarra* are still under construction.

Brunei: The first of the new 'offshore patrol vessels' (corvettes) was launched on the Clyde on 13 January 2001. Work on the second ship started in November 2000, and assembly of material for the third began after the launch of the first ship. Tenders are being sought for the replacement of all fifteen *Fremantle* class patrol vessels.

China: The People's Republic of

The former RN Type 21 frigate PNS Tippu Sultan *at the Indian Fleet Review.* (Commodore Rai)

China signed an agreement with the Russian Government in mid-July 2000, to order two more Project 956E *Sovremenny* class destroyers for the People's Liberation Army-Navy (PLAN). The ships will be built by the Northern Shipyard in St Petersburg. The second ship of the original order was handed over on 25 November the same year.

The PLAN is building a new Project 094 SSBN, and a new Project 093 SSN, and production of the Project 039 'Song' diesel-electric boats continues slowly. In June 2000 the Zvezda shipyard in the Pacific town of Bolshoi Kamen won its first foreign order, to refit a PLAN submarine.

Indonesia: In November 2000 the Navy Chief Admiral Indroko announced his plan to modernise the Navy's ships and weapon systems. At least two submarines will be bought and a number of surface warships.

Japan: The Self Defence Force added the *Oyashio* class submarine *Makishio* to its strength in March 2001 and the *Murasame* class destroyer *Ikazuchi*. New construction includes three more *Oyashio* class submarines, two more *Murasame* class destroyers and three Improved *Murasame* class.

Korea (South): In November 2000 the Republic of Korea Navy (RoKN) announced its choice for the submarine design to follow the IKL Type 209/1200 boats. The KSS II programme will be three IKL Type 214 boats, to be delivered before the end of 2009. This marks a major advance in RoKN capability; the Type 214 can dive to 400 metres and has a fuel-cell AIP system.

Malaysia: The first of two ex-Royal Netherlands Navy submarines, the ex-*Tijgerhaai*, arrived at Lumut in Perak on 16 January 2001. This would seem to presage the purchase of 'Moray' type boats from RDM, but the market is very competitive.

New Zealand: Times are hard for the armed forces of New Zealand, and the Royal New Zealand Navy was told in March 2001 by Prime Minister Helen Clark that there is no

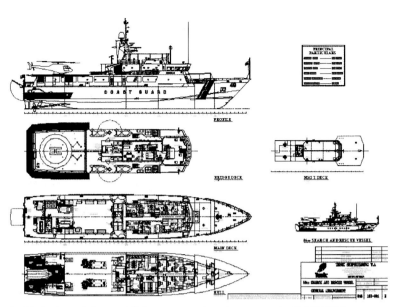

Builder's plan of the new Philippines search and rescue craft. (NAVINT)

question of buying a third *Anzac* class frigate. The old *Leander* class frigate *Waikato* was scuttled on 25 November 2000 off Tutukaka Harbour. The military sealift ship HMNZS *Charles Upham* is to be sold.

Singapore: The submarine RSS *Chieftain* (ex-Swedish *Sjöhunden*) was re-launched and named at Kockums' Karlskrona shipyard on 22 May 2001, bringing the final stage of the 'Riken' Project to an end. The third boat, RSS *Conqueror* (ex-*Sjölejonet*) had been commissioned at the Tuas naval base in July 2000. Work has started on the first of six French-design 'corvettes' based on the French *La Fayette* design. RSS *Endeavour*, last of four *Endurance* class LPDs, was completed in the first quarter of 2001.

Taiwan: In December 2001 the Republic of China Navy announced an order for the eighth *Cheng Kung* class frigate, *Tien Tan*, to be placed with the China Shipbuilding Corporation. She may have Harpoon missiles in place of the Hsiung Feng II weapons in the first seven ships. The four redundant *Kidd* (DDG-993) class AAW destroyers are to be acquired from the US Navy.

A request to the US Government for permission to buy the Aegis weapon direction system was vetoed by the Bush Administration (temporarily at least), but surprisingly a

request for eight submarines was agreed. They will be supplied by Ingalls Shipbuilding, either direct or under a technology-transfer agreement, unless a European design is involved, in which case there will be political repercussions.

Thailand: Once again the Royal Thai Navy has changed its mind about submarines. A lease of one or two boats was discussed in January 2001, but was later vetoed by the government in the light of serious financial problems.

African Navies

South Africa: The South African Navy is virtually the only African navy showing any signs of activity. Four MEKO A200 corvettes have been ordered from Blohm+Voss in Hamburg and HDW in Kiel, to be delivered as 'bare hulls' in 2002-2003. They will be armed with Exocet MM-40 Block 2 anti-ship missiles and the new Umkhonto vertically-launched air defence missile system.

The three IKL Type 209/1400 submarines will be delivered in 2005-2007, and first steel was cut on 22 May 2001. The old submarine *Spear* (ex-*Maria van Riebeeck*) has been deleted, leaving only two of the French-built *Daphné* type to bridge the gap.

WARSHIP NOTES

This section comprises a number of short articles and notes, generally highlighting little known aspects of warship history.

ARCHAEOLOGICAL SURVEY AT SCAPA FLOW

Daniel Mersey reports on recent underwater investigations at Scapa Flow

In June 2001, an archaeological survey took place around the warship wrecks of the scuttled German High Seas Fleet in Scapa Flow, Orkney. Marine survey techniques, operating by multi-beam sonar, allowed the surveyors to construct images of the vessels themselves and the debris around them.

A number of academic institutions and marine technology companies worked together on the survey, including Heriot-Watt University's Department of Civil & Offshore Engineering and International Centre for Island Technology (Edinburgh); the Joint Hydrographic Center of the Center for Coastal and Ocean Mapping of the University of New Hampshire; and Reson Offshore Ltd (Aberdeen), who provided marine survey expertise. The survey utilised Reson's innovative *SeaBat* 8125 technology. The underwater work was carried out from the survey vessel of the Archaeological Diving Unit, University of St Andrews.

The survey revealed that seven wrecks of major warships remain, measuring up to 25,000 tons and over 200 metres in length, in an area of 8km² of flat, muddy seabed, at depths of between 30-50 metres. Between these seven wrecks lay wreckage asso-

ciated with salvage activities on the existing wrecks and the vessels that had previously been raised (and scrapped after this recovery).

The remains of the German High Seas Fleet at Scapa Flow represents an important archaeological and historical resource which, although the subject of salvage, amateur investigation, and recreational diving in the past, remains largely untapped by reliable archaeological investigation. Looking after the site in the future will require a high level of environmental marine information, the need to promote future protection, and, as with all sites of our heritage, access by the widest possible community to encourage understanding and interest. These hopes may not just remain forlorn, in May 2001 Historic Scotland scheduled the seven wrecks under the Archaeological Monuments and Areas Act (1979).

Further information and images of the wrecks can be seen on Heriot-Watt University's Orkney campus website:

http://www.icit.demon.co.uk

RN SUBMARINE CENTENNIAL STAMPS

Martin Robson details the Royal Navy Submarine Service Centennial stamps available from the Royal Mail

On 10 April 2001 the Royal Mail issued a special set of commemora-

tive stamps to coincide with the start of a series of celebratory events by the Royal Navy Submarine Service.

The 2nd class stamp features HMS *Vanguard*, the most recently developed class of submarine in service.
The 1st class stamp depicts HMS *Swiftsure*, typical of the Cold War period.
The 45p stamp remembers the *Unity* Class, a small but highly successful design that was employed in the Mediterranean during the Second World War.
The 65p stamp features the first RN submarine; *Holland* One first launched in 1901.

The set was designed by Dick Davis, who worked closely with the Royal Navy Submarine Museum Gosport in the development of the stamps. After an extensive research period in the Museum's excellent photographic archive he selected a four archive photographs which symbolised significant eras in the history of the RN Submarine Service. Davis also created the interesting icons; a blueprint drawing of a submarine, a view from a periscope, a depth meter and a sonic wave. Finally, he added a waterline and silhouettes of the featured submarines, suggesting the depth at which they typically operated.

A further set of submarine-related stamps and a special stamp book will be released by the Royal Mail in October 2001.

Postage stamps issued in 2001 to commemorate the RN submarine centenary. (Royal Mail)

SÃO PAULO HEADS FOR HER NEW HOME
Antony Preston reports on a major refurbishment for the Brazilian aircraft carrier São Paulo

The aircraft carrier *São Paulo* left Brest for Rio de Janeiro on 1 February 2001 following refurbishment work by DCN. The French Navy sold the vessel to its Brazilian counterpart under a contract signed in September 2000. Following the official hand-over to the Brazilian Navy on 15 November 2000, DCN's Brest facility began overhauling the vessel's propulsion system, catapults and arresting gear under a contract between the Brazilian Navy and DCN International signed in October 2000. All tasks were completed on time and to the client's satisfaction. Sea trials were undertaken on 25 and 26 January 2001 which confirmed the vessel's capabilities.

São Paulo
Characteristics

Length	265 m
Beam	31.72 m
Height	51.20 m
Displacement	7.50 t
Maximum speed	32 kts
Maximum range	13,500 km
Complement	
With air wing:	around 1500
Without air wing:	around 1200

Flight deck
The flight deck features a main runway measuring 165.50m by 29.50m and length-wise runway measuring 93m by 28m. The main runway is angled at 8.5° to the ship's longitudinal axis. There are two lifts, each with a load capacity of 15 tons. The main runway and axial launch area are equipped with catapults capable of accelerating a 12 to 15-ton aircraft to 150kts.

Propulsion
The *São Paulo* is equipped with six oil-fired superheated boilers rated at 45 kg/cm². Superheated steam at 450°C is delivered to two Parson turbines, each rated at 92,640 kW (126,000 HP), driving two propellers.

The Brazilian aircraft carrier BNS São Paulo *(formerly the French* Foch*) left Brest on 1 February 2001. (DCN International)*

THE FIGHTER SUPPORT SHIP
George L Moore reports on drawings of a Fighter Support Ship held in the National Maritime Museum, Greenwich

The origins of this ship go back to October 1941 when the type first emerged in discussion at a Controllers meeting. On 30 December 1941 the Controller instructed the Director of Naval Construction to design a carrier without protection to develop a speed of 25kts and to carry at least 15 fighters. On 7 January 1942 a statement of requirement was taken to Vickers Armstrongs, Barrow who were to undertake the design. Two sketch designs were produced in January 1942; it seems likely that this undated and unnumbered drawing is the first of these sketches. It was discussed at a Controller's meeting on 14 January 1942. Among alterations sought were the movement of the lifts in order to create bays forward and abaft the lifts, the two main boilers to be in separate compartments and the engine room, moved aft to reduce the length of the propeller shafts. The length was to be increased by 20ft. Dimensions scaled from the drawing were: length at water line 632ft, length of flight deck 637ft, length overall 655ft, width of flight deck 77ft, maximum beam (over sponsons for Mark M. Pom

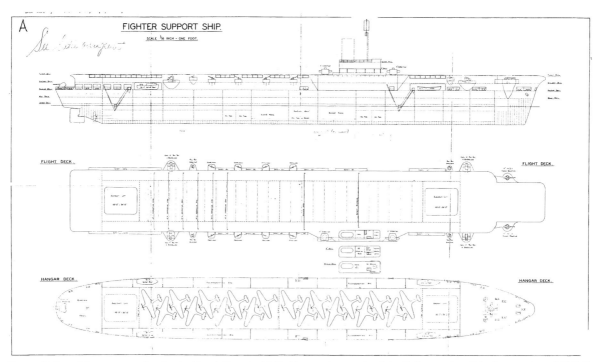

Proposals for a fighter support ship for the Royal Navy in 1941-42 were the genesis of the Colossus *class light fleet carriers.* (NMM)

Poms) 101ft, hanger length 488ft, hanger width 56ft.

A further sketch was submitted by 23 February 1942, the result of discussions being a requirement for a more elaborate design. By February the basis of the new carriers was clear, the vessels being 14,000 tons (standard), length 682ft and capable of operating 24 fighters. At this time the fighter support ship became known as the intermediate carrier which in turn was to give way later to the term light fleet carrier.

The drawing was originally held in ADM 138/666 'The *Colossus* Class' Ships Cover but it is now kept in a separate file at the National Maritime Museum.

My thanks are due to Bob Todd and Michael Lewis of the National Maritime Museum for their support.

KURSK UPDATE

Antony Preston provides an update on the loss of the Russian SSGN Kursk

Although conspiracy theorists in Russia maintained for months that the *Kursk* was in collision with an American or British submarine, and others claimed that the nuclear cruiser *Pyotr Veliky* scored an 'own goal' with an anti-ship missile, the former accusation was strongly denied by the Royal and the US Navy. Western experts are convinced that something triggered off an explosion of a high-test peroxide (HTP) fuel tank in a torpedo, and the fire which followed detonated all the torpedoes. The Russians themselves have finally come to the same conclusion, but whatever the cause, the entire front end of the boat was destroyed.

Preparing to raise the sunken SSGN is taking longer than hoped because divers have to do much of the work by hand instead of using robots, according to the operation's director. 'In the beginning of the operation we thought everything would be considerably quicker and smoother', said Vice Admiral Mikhail Motsak in an interview on the pro-Kremlin *Strana.ru* website on 31 July.

Divers continued work on Wednesday 1 August 2001, cutting holes in the *Kursk*'s double hull, to which 26 huge cables will be attached to lift the submarine from the bottom of the Barents Sea in mid-September. Vice Admiral Motsak said that planners had hoped to cut the holes, mostly using remote-controlled robotic equipment. But clearing out the space between the inner and outer hulls, filled with pipes, air pressure bottles and struts, has proved too difficult, and instead divers have been operating cutting equipment by hand, he said. Motsak also warned that the canisters enclosing torpedoes in the bow section of the submarine may have been damaged. Divers will slice off the mangled bow compartment, where the main explosion took place, before lifting the rest of the submarine; this is because of concerns about remaining torpedoes inside.

Expressing irritation, Motsak said foreign naval and air surveillance have been active in the region, even though Russian Navy officials have cordoned off an area around the salvage site 20 nautical miles in diameter. The seas have been rough in the region and winds are forecast to get stronger in coming days, according to Russian Navy spokesman Capt 1st Rank Igor Dygalo.

Meanwhile, the yard that built the *Kursk* is working out ways to re-use her weapons systems after the wreck is raised, said Raisa Elimelakh, spokeswoman for the Sevmash factory in the northern city of Severodvinsk. She said on 1 August that the project was still in an early stage and could provide no details. Russian officials have said that a key reason for the costly lifting operation is to try to determine what caused the disaster. Russian officials have said in the past that the explosion was set off by a practice torpedo, which they said was likely to have been triggered by a collision with another submarine, although it is now widely admitted that the explosion was almost certainly caused by an internal malfunction.

In a much-puffed documentary shown by the BBC's Channel 2 on 9 August, the loss was attributed to HTP thermal fuel in the torpedoes. 'Hitherto secret' seismic reordings from a UK research centre were revealed, although virtually identical readings from a Norwegian seismic research centre were released six months ago. Usually reliable US sources stated that the initial cause was probably a lithium battery intended to warm the thermal fuel. This battery, according to the same sources, 'ran hot' and ignited the fuel in its parent torpedo (creating the initial explosion), and the resulting fire set off the fuel tanks in the remaining torpedoes.

Another aspect which may be relevant is the fact the former Soviet Navy introduced a kerosene-HTP mixture for its thermal-fuelled torpedoes over 25 years ago (substantiated by retired Russian flag-officers in the BBC 2 documentary), without suffering accidents. Western navies use thermal fuels for their latest torpedoes (Otto II in the US Mk 48 ADCAP, HAP-Otto in the British Spearfish, and straight HTP in the Swedish Tp 61 and Tp 62 series), but these achieve safety by the addition of a stabiliser. Such stabilisers add considerably to the cost of the torpedo, and it has been suggested that the Russians have tried to dispense with a stabiliser for their latest thermal torpedoes, on the grounds that it was an expensive luxury, in the light of the good safety record of the original fuel.

What is remarkable is that the HTP theory matches the tragic sinking of HMS *Sidon* in Portland on 16

June 1955. She was destroyed by the explosion of an HTP-fuelled Mk 12 'Fancy' torpedo as it was being loaded. As with the *Kursk*, the entire bow section was destroyed, and the official enquiry recommended that the Mk 12 be withdrawn. A quarter of a century was to pass before the Royal Navy could contemplate thermal fuel for its torpedoes.

MEMORIAL SHIP MIKASA
Martin Robson and Dan Soares USN report on a recent visit to the Japanese predreadnought battleship Mikasa *at Yokosuka*

Mikasa was the last of four Japanese battleships ordered under the Ten Year Programme of 1896, which had authorised the building of four battleships, twelve cruisers and eighty-six destroyers and torpedo boats. *Mikasa* was built by Vickers at Barrow and was designed as an improved version of the Royal Navy's *Majestic* class. She was armed with 4-12in housed in two turrets (actually hooded barbettes) located fore and aft which could fire three times in two minutes with magazine storage for 240 rounds. A secondary battery consisted of 14-6in, in a break from previous designs 10-6in were located in casemates on the main deck (similar to *King Edward VII* class, see pp.63-69),

HIJMS Mikasa *with the memorial to Admiral Togo in the foreground.* (Martin Robson)

Fore turret and 12in guns looking into Yokosuka harbour. (Martin Robson)

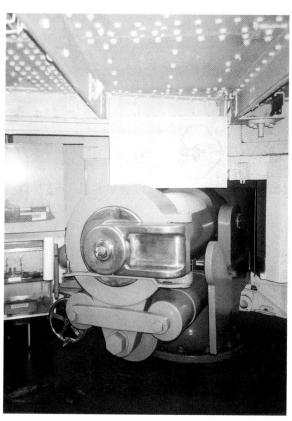

Left: Stern, showing how Mikasa is now cemented into the dock. Right: Interior of 6in casemate. (Martin Robson)

which provided additional protection from rear penetrating shells, while the other four were in casemates on the upper deck. 8-12pdrs were grouped into batteries on the upper deck and received some protection from the 1in shelter deck. Unlike the previous three ships of her class, Shikishima, Hatsuse and Asahi, Mikasa's belt was 9in Krupp Cemented armour.

Mikasa was the flagship of Admiral Heihachiro Togo, Commander of the Grand Fleet during the Russo-Japanese War and was present at the blockade of Port Arthur where she received 3 hits. At the Battle of the Yellow Sea, 10 August 1904, Mikasa was hit 22 times and had almost all her guns damaged, with 32 dead and over 80 wounded. Mikasa underwent damage repair at Sasebo and again served as Togo's flagship at Tsushima on May 27 1905. At Tsushima Togo allowed the Russian fleet to close before suddenly implementing an unorthodox 180° turn which, capped the 'T' of the Russian fleet and blocked their retreat to Vladivostock and placing the Japanese fleet in a position of tactical and strategic superiority. The Japanese fleet captured, sunk or disarmed 35 out of 38 Russian ships, one of the most decisive naval battles in history. Mikasa again suffered from Russian fire, she was hit 32 times, causing 113 casualties.

Mikasa sank at Sasebo on 12 September 1905 after an ammunition explosion in her aft 12in turret or magazine but was raised and repaired. Disarmed in 1922, following the Second World War she was completely stripped down in accordance with Japanese demilitarisation. After a public campaign to restore the ship work was undertaken with the help of the US Navy. Mikasa was finally

Starboard shelter deck showing the bridge, wheelhouse and compass platform.
(Martin Robson)

Starboard shelter deck looking aft. (Martin Robson)

Aft pair of 12in guns, in the foreground are the skylights above the Admiral's cabin. (Martin Robson)

opened as a museum ship exactly 56 years to the day after Tsushima in 1967 by USN Fleet Admiral Chester Nimitz.

With a memorial and statue to Togo on the approach to the ship, upon entering the memorial park *Mikasa*, although cemented into the dock, looks extremely impressive. Visitors can walk round most parts of the ship including Togo's cabin and the bridge. The ship serves as a museum to the Japanese victory at Tsushima and contains many interesting and well-preserved exhibits, varying from 12in, 6in and 12pdr shells to Naval Ensigns and uniforms. There are also many well drawn plans of *Mikasa* and her armaments on display, including a cut away drawing of a 12in gun turret, and a 6in casemate. However, the centrepiece of the museum is an excellent model (complete with Japanese commentary and lighting effects to simulate gun fire and explosions!) of Tsushima, which portrays Admiral

Port side showing clearly the casemate arrangements of the 6in secondary armament on the main and upper decks. Also clearly shown on the upper deck is the 12pdr battery under the shelter deck. (Martin Robson)

Togo's famous turn. Throughout the ship are patches of green and red hatched paint to mark where the ship received hits at Yellow Sea and Tsushima. Many of the various artefacts contained in the ship are accompanied by English language annotations.

Upper deck, 12pdr battery looking forward. On the extreme left is an example of the hatched painting locating damage inflicted at Tsushima. Despite the presence of the shelter deck, this position remained relatively exposed. (Martin Robson)

For more details contact:
Mikasa Preservation Society
Yokosuka, Kanagawa, Japan
Tel: (0468) 22-5408(5225)
Fax: (0468) 11-9822
Open daily: 09:00-17:00
  (with seasonal variations)
Admission: Adult ¥500, Child ¥200

HIJMS *Mikasa*
Laid down: 24.1.1899
Launched: 8.11.1900
Completed: 1.3.1902
Builder: Vickers, Barrow

The Review, *the quarterly journal of the NHCRA. (Steve Dent)*

Displacement:	15,140 tons normal, 15,194 full load
Dimensions:	415ft wl, 432ft oa x 76ft x 27ft
Machinery:	2-shaft reciprocating VTE, 15,000ihp
Speed:	18kts
Coal:	700/1521 tons
Armour:	Krupp Cemented: Main belt 4-9in, upper belt 6in, deck 2-3in, barbettes 8-14in, casemates 2-6in
Armament:	4-12in, 14-6in, 20-12pdr, 8-3pdr, 4-2 1/2pdr, 4-18in TT
Complement:	40 officers and 790 enlisted (930 as a flagship)

CALLING ALL NAVAL ENTHUSIASTS
Martin Robson reports on The Naval Historical Collectors & Research Association (NHCRA)

The NHCRA was formed in 1988 by a group of naval enthusiasts, many of whom were retired naval officers and ratings, who did not feel that any existing organisation catered for their interests. The Association covers a wide range of subjects including warships, merchant vessels, memorabilia, medals and naval genealogy. The Association also has its own research service which will search service records for officers and ratings, honours and awards, action reports and chronologies of ships' WWII service.

The NHCRA's quarterly *Review* contains a wide range of articles on naval history from the eighteenth century to the present day. The *Review* also includes medal rolls, casualty lists, news from museums and the PRO, plus book reviews. There is also a free facility to place notes and appeals for information.

Annual membership is £12 (UK & BPFO, £14 (EUROPE & EIRE), £17 ($25) (OVERSEAS). Cheques made payable to NHRCA. For more details please contact:

Membership Secretary,
NHCRA
17 Woodhill Avenue
Portishead
North Somerset
BS20 7EX
UK

AUSTRALIA'S MARITIME HERITAGE
The two Warship *articles by Colin Jones examining the pre-Federation Australian Navies have highlighted some of the fascinating vessels that provided defence for the region. Utilising information supplied by Vic Jeffrey, Martin Robson provides a brief overview of Australia's rich naval heritage.*

Preserved Ships

HMAS *Diamantina*
River class frigate built for the RAN during the Second World War is currently undergoing restoration at the Queensland Maritime Museum.

John Oxley
A pilot steamer, the *John Oxley* was acquired by the RAN in 1943 to prove the identity of ships entering Queensland harbours. She is undergoing preservation work at the Sydney Maritime Museum.

Krait
Captured from Japan during the Second World War, *Krait* was used

The hulk of the former South Australian Naval Forces' 'cruiser' Protector, *serving as a breakwater at Heron Island, Queensland.* (RAN)

for Special operations against the Japanese and carried out raids against Singapore Harbour and later in Borneo. She is preserved as part of the National Maritime Museum's fleet in Sydney.

HMAS *Advance*
Star of the ABC television series Patrol Boat, *Advance* was one of twenty *Attack* class boats built for the RAN. Acquired by the National Maritime Museum in 1988 and can be seen in Sydney Harbour.

Tortoise
Built for the RAAF, she was transferred to the RAN in 1962 and converted to a diving tender. Lying derelict in Sydney Harbour, she was restored by the Naval Reserve Cadet Unit T. S. *Hawkesbury* and is now based at Gosford.

HMAS *Castlemaine*
Castlemaine was one of 60 *Bathurst* Class corvettes built in Australia during the Second World War. After the war she served as a training ship and in 1973 was transferred to the Maritime Trust of Australia and is now a museum ship at Williamstown, Victoria.

HMAS *Vampire*
Commissioned into the RAN in 1959 this *Daring* Class destroyer is

now on display at the National Maritime Museum, Sydney.

HMAS *Whyalla*
Sister of *Castlemaine*, she was commissioned in 1942, undertaking survey duties and then to maintain navigation markers in Port Philip Bay. Acquired by the City of Whyalla, restoration work is underway.

Wattle
Launched in 1933 the ex-naval tug is preserved by the Victorian Steamship Association in Port Philip Bay.

Falie
The sailing ketch *Falie* was built in the Netherlands and requisitioned as an examination vessel and stores carrier by the RAN. Now restored she is a fully operating museum ship in South Australia.

Sleuth
Built in Sydney in 1901 utilising wood from HMVS *Nelson*, this steam yacht was requisitioned during the First World War. Renamed *Ena*, she sank but was raised and restored and can now be seen in Sydney Harbour.

Martindale
Motor yacht loaned by the RAN as a naval patrol boat, she was armed with a .303in Vickers machine gun and two depth charges. She can also be

The remains of Cerberus, *once the pride of the Victorian Naval Forces, lying derelict off Black Rock in Port Phillip Bay, Melbourne.* (RAN)

seen in Sydney Harbour.

S 70 *Ovens* (1967 Oberon Class)
During her 26 years of service *Ovens* covered more than 420,000nm. In 1986 she had the distinction of being the first conventional submarine in the world to fire a Harpoon anti-ship missile. In May 1995 she was Gifted to the Western Australian Maritime Museum, Fremantle, and was officially opened to the public in December 1999.

S 59 *Otway* (1966 Oberon class)
Holbrook is a tiny rural town of some 1,500 people located 500km southwest of Sydney and the fascination of the locals with submarines dates back to the First World War, when the town was named 'Holbrook' after Commander Norman Holbrook, VC. A replica of Holbrook's original B11 submarine and a statue of Commander Holbrook are located at the town main square. In 1995 the

RAN donated a decommissioned *Otway* submarine (fin and superstructure) and the memorial was opened in June 1997.

S 60 *Onslow* (1968 Oberon class)
Onslow arrived at Australian National Maritime Museum for permanent display just weeks after her decommissioning ceremony in March 1999 with the official opening following in June. *Onslow* is complete and is preserved very close to operational condition.

Hulks and Wrecks

Gayundah
Built in 1884 for the Queensland Government, *Gayundah* participated in early Australian ship to shore radio experiments and saw service during the First World War. Her remains are still visible at Woody Point, Redcliffe on Moreton Bay.

Protector
Ordered in 1884 by the South Australian Government, *Protector* was the only light cruiser operated by an Australian colony. She saw active service in China during the Boxer Rebellion and during the First World War. She now serves as a breakwater on Heron Island, Queensland.

Cerberus
The forerunner of the modern battleship *Cerberus*, once the pride of the Victorian Naval Forces has, for the past 70 years, served as a breakwater off Black Rock in Port Phillip Bay. Unfortunately her condition is deteriorating.

'J' Class Submarines
Six 'J' class submarines were transferred to the RAN after the First World War but were paid off and sold for scrap. Sunk as breakwaters, *J3* is still visible at Swan Island and *J7* at Hampton both in Port Phillip Bay.

Parramatta
Launched in Scotland in 1910 she was the first warship built for the Commonwealth Naval Forces and saw service during the First World War. Her bow and stern were removed, the bow is on display at Garden Island, the stern on the banks of the Parramatta River at Parramatta.

Kangaroo
A boom defence vessel, she was commissioned in 1940 was at present when the Japanese raided Darwin in 1942. Operating post-war as a minesweeper, she was scuttled in Hombush Bay.

Useful Contacts

Vic Jeffrey
Director
DPACC
HMAS Stirling
Rockingham WA 6958
Australia

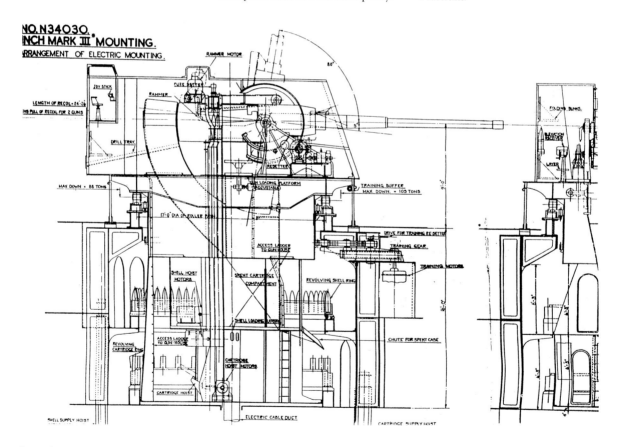

General arrangement of a proposed 5.25in Mk IV mounting with electric drive. Neither the gun nor the mounting became reality, not least because the original 5.25in twin mounting in the Dido class cruisers fired a shell which was too heavy for rapid fire and too light for surface action. (Antony Preston)

Western Australian Maritime Museum

Cliff Street, Fremantle, Western Australia, WA 6160
Friday and Saturday 11.00 - 16.00
Sunday 10.00 - 16.00
Anzac Day: 13.00 - 17.00
Closed Good Friday, Christmas Day and Boxing Day
Tel: (08) 9430 6756
Fax: (08) 9431 8490
http://www.mm.wa.gov.au

Australian National Maritime Museum

Street Address: 2 Murray Street, Darling Harbour, Sydney, NSW 2000, Australia
Postal Address: GPO Box 5131, Sydney, NSW 2001, Australia
February to December:
  Daily 9.30 - 17.00
January: Daily 9.30 - 18.00
Closed Christmas Day
Tel: (61) (0)2 9298 3777
Fax: (61) (0)2 9298 3780
www.anmm.gov.au/

Commander Holbrook Submarine Memorial

Holbrook NSW (New South Wales) 2644, Australia
Tel: (02) 6036 2131

ANTI-POLLUTION MEASURES ON THE *ROYAL OAK*
Antony Preston examines a new attempt to stop pollution leaking from the wreck of Royal Oak

A new attempt was to be made in June 2001 to prevent pollution caused by oil seeping from the wreck of the torpedoed battleship HMS *Royal Oak*, lying in Scapa Flow in the Orkneys. She was torpedoed by *U-47* in October 1939 and sank with heavy loss of life. An estimated 900-1800 tonnes of fuel remain aboard.

Earlier efforts to patch the hull and attach a containment canopy failed when the canopy became detached during storms two years ago. The new plan will use a different method, 'hot tapping' to remove the oil with minimum intrusion and disturbance to the bodies still in the wreck (the

Royal Oak is a war grave). The technique was developed in the offshore oil industry, and involves the joining of a valve or flange to a pipe or space containing a substance under different pressure or temperature. Taps will be attached by drilling holes in the side of the battleship to reach the fuel bunkers. Once attached, they will provide an easy escape-route for the oil, so that it can be drawn off in a controlled way.

The work will be done by the UK Ministry of Defence Salvage and Mooring Organisation (SMO) within the Naval Bases Supply Agency. SMO staff will work with commercial staff.

THE SUBMARINE CSS *HUNLEY*
Antony Preston updates last year's note on the CSS Hunley

The wreck of the Confederate submarine CSS *Hunley*, the first submersible to sink an enemy warship in battle, was raised on 8 August 2000 off the South Carolina coast. The 12-metre *Hunley* attacked and sank USS *Housatonic* during the American Civil War on the night of 17 February 1864, a mission from which she never returned.

WRECK OF THE 'MIGHTY *HOOD*' FOUND
Antony Preston and Martin Robson report on 'The Hunt for the Hood*'*

In July 2001, Channel 4 launched an expedition led by David Mearns to find and film the wreck of HMS *Hood*. Previously the UK Ministry of Defence listed the wreck as a war grave and has forbidden any attempts to examine it, but the unique historical importance of the loss of the *Hood* has resulted in the ban being lifted. On 23 July the expedition located the wreck in the Denmark Strait at 63° 20'N, 31° 50'W. Magellan 725 a remotely operated vehicle (ROV) has examined the wreck, which lies at a depth of about 5000ft (1500 metres).

Experience with other catastrophic losses suggested that the hull would be so badly damaged that detailed analysis regarding the cause of the loss would be impossible. This assertion has been borne out by the expedition, which has confirmed the poor condition of the wreck.

The wreck lies in at least three pieces: a large centre section comprising 'A' turret to the forward engine room which is inverted, the bow, which is in poor condition and the stern, the best-preserved section of the ship. The bow and stern are close together about 750 yards from the inverted hull section while two other substantial sections of the hull now make up the debris scattered across the site; the result of the explosion and collapse of the superstructure.

The expedition was accompanied by Ted Briggs, the last survivor of *Hood*'s sinking. A bronze commemorative plaque and a CD containing the Roll of Honour of those who died, was left close to *Hood*'s bow.

Two 90 mins documentaries on the *Hood*, and the search for the wreck, will be broadcast on Channel 4 in December.

For more information see
http://www.channel4.com/hood/
http://www.hmshood.com/

***The Battlecruiser* Hood** by John Roberts is now available in a revised edition from Conway Maritime Press, ISBN 0 85177 900 X, price £25.00
The World's Worst Warships by Antony Preston includes an examination of the 'Mighty *Hood*', available from Conway Maritime Press, April 2002, ISBN 0 85177 754 6, price £19.99

BRASSEY'S NAVAL ANNUAL OF 1901
Martin Robson presents an RN submarine service excerpt from the 1901 Brassey's Naval Annual

Continuing the series of excerpts from various issues of *Brassey's Naval Annual*, in the Royal Navy's Submarine Service centennial year attention was inevitably drawn to the

1901 issue. In examining the 'Progress of the British Navy', Commander C N Robinson had the following to say regarding the 'submarine boats':

The most interesting item in the new programme is five submarine boats, which were ordered from Messrs. Vickers, Son, and Maxim in 1900, when work was at once commenced upon them. The secret of their construction was kept for some time, and when it did leak out did not obtain universal credence. In the First Lord's memorandum, 1901-1902, it is stated that the first of them will be delivered next autumn, and the following explanatory paragraph is added:- "What the future value of these boats may be in naval warfare can only be a matter of conjecture. The experiments with these boats will assist the Admiralty in assessing their true value. The question of their employment must be studied, and all developments in their mechanism carefully watched by this country."

The dimensions of the boats are 63 ft. 4 in. length over all, 11 ft. 9 in. beam, and 120 tons displacement submerged. They will be provided with means of expelling torpedoes either with the boat stationary, during the run on the surface, or submerged at full speed. The armament consists of one torpedo expulsion tube situated at the extreme forward end of the vessel, opening outward 2 ft. below the water-line. Interlocking

safety devices are employed to prevent accident while operating valves &c. on the expulsion of the torpedo. The general construction of the vessels is such that all portions of the exterior of the hull are free from projections of a nature to be entangled by ropes or other obstacles when submerged, and the lines of the vessel are specially designed to minimize resistance for surface cruising. The propulsion of the vessel on the surface is effected by a gasoline type of main engine, which is supplied with a sufficient amount of fuel for a run of about 400 knots with a maximum speed of about 9 knots. An electric main motor is provided for giving the vessel a speed of 7 knots when submerged. It is worked by storage batteries having a capacity which will admit of a speed of 7 knots for four hours' submerged run. Gearing is provided to allow for the charging of the battery, driving the propeller from the main engine, or moving the engine from the main motor, these combinations being effected through clutches which are operated as desired. The lighting of the vessel is effected by portable incandescent electric lamps. The ballasting system consists of apparatus and means for quickly changing the vessel from light to a diving condition and for keeping her displacement constant in different waters. Also for keeping the longitudinal trim under the control of the navigator, and for compensating for the variable weights installed

or expended from time to time, such as discharging torpedoes, &c. The air supply and ventilation are secured by compressed air stored on board the vessel, the gasoline vapours from the engines being carefully excluded by suitable arrangements. Safety valves are arranged to relieve any excess of pressure in the vessel over that of the atmosphere. The steering and diving engines are provided with automatic means of moving the rudders to the desired positions to prevent the vessel from inclining to excessive angles during diving or rising, and to keep the depth of submergence constant, as well also as to bring the vessel to a horizontal position at the required depth, and to prevent diving to excessive depths. Steering and diving can be executed by hand gear if desired. The compasses are compensated and adjusted so that the boat can be steered with equal accuracy submerged as on the surface. The type is that which has been invented by Mr. Holland, and has been tried in America.

USS VINCENNES IN YOKOSUKA, JAPAN
Martin Robson and Dan Soares USN report on the US Navy vessels to carry the name USS Vincennes.

The Sloop of War *Vincennes*

The first *Vincennes* was rated an 18-gun sloop of war named after the fort that George Rogers Clark captured (twice) during the American War of Independence. She was built in the New York Naval Yard at Brooklyn and was commissioned on 26 August 1826. Sailing to the Pacific, Manila and Cape Town then back to New York the *Vincennes* was the first US warship to circumnavigate the globe, in fact she would carry out a further two circumnavigations!

Between 1838 and 1840 she served as the flagship of Lt Charles Wilkes Antarctic exploration expeditions and in January 1840 was the first ship to sight land in the Antarctic. She then saw service in the warmer climes of the West Indies until 1844

Stern view of USS Vincennes *(CG-49). (Martin Robson)*

The Vincennes' *forward 5in 54 cal Mk 45 gun, with one SPY-1 fixed planar radar array on the forward face of the superstructure.* (Martin Robson)

Another view of the Vincennes' *forward superstructure and one of the SPY-1 radar arrays linked to the Aegis weapon direction system.* (Martin Robson)

and then in Japanese waters in an unsuccessful attempt to open trade links. More voyages of exploration followed in 1849, this time in the North Pacific. In 1857 she undertook anti-slavery duties on the African coast. During the American Civil War she was part of the Federal fleet blockading the Gulf Coast. After a career of over 41 years she was sold at public auction for $5000 on 5 October 1867.

Sloop of War Vincennes
Built: NY Navy Yard, 1826
Displacement: 780t
Dimensions: 127ft x 33.8ft x 16.5ft
Armament: 20x32pdr
Complement: 80

Heavy Cruiser *Vincennes* (CA-44)

The second ship to be named *Vincennes* was a *New Orleans* Class heavy cruiser commissioned on 24 February 1937. In 1942 she joined the *Hornet's* Task Force 18 (TF-18) and headed for the Pacific, joining *Enterprise's* TF-16 en route. Arriving too late for Coral Sea, *Vincennes* provided important air-defence at

Midway and with her sister ships *Quincy* and *Astoria* participated in the landings at Guadalcanal on 7 August, providing important defence against Japanese aircraft and fire support to the landings. On 8 August she shot down at least seven Japanese attackers, evaded a torpedo and was narrowly missed to port by a bomb. After this eventful day she was stationed off Savo Island, continuing to provide essential cover to the land forces.

In the early hours of 9 August a Japanese fleet under Vice Admiral Gunichi Mikawa comprising six cruisers and one destroyer furiously attacked *Vincennes, Quincy* and *Astoria.* After 20-25 minutes of intense gunfire *Vincennes* had received at least 57 hits from 8in and 5in shells and one or possible two Japanese torpedoes. *Quincy* and *Astoria* had also suffered at the hands of Japanese gunnery and torpedo attack. *Vincennes* began to list dangerously to port as the Japanese retreated from the engagement. After the crew evacuated her, *Vincennes* rolled and sank just before 03:00 in 500 fathoms.

Despite *Vincennes'* short career, her important contribution to the victories at Midway and Guadalcanal was

recognised with the award of two battle stars.

Heavy Cruiser Vincennes CA-44
Built by: Bethlehem, Quincy
Displacement: 10,136t standard / 12,463t full load
Dimensions: 578ft x 61ft 9in x 22ft 9in full load
Machinery: 4 shaft Westinghouse turbines, 8 Babcock & Wilcox boilers, 107,000hp
Speed: 32.7kts
Armament: 9-8in 55 cal (3x3), 8-5in 25 cal (8x1), 8-.05in (8x1), 4 aircraft
Complement: 1042-1121 Officers and Crew

The Light Cruiser *Vincennes* (CL-64)

Launched on 17 July 1943 and commissioned on 21 January 1944 the third *Vincennes* was a light cruiser of the *Cleveland* Class and like her immediate predecessor was built at Bethlehem, Quincy. *Vincennes* participated in a substantial number of engagements during the last year of the Pacific War. After joining TF-58in 1944 she participated in raids on Saipan, Guam, Tinian and Iwo Jima. Further battle honours were won at the Battle of the Philippines Sea, Okinawa and Leyte Gulf on 24 October. In 1945 *Vincennes* provided support against further attacks against Okinawa and then headed for Japanese home waters. *Vincennes* won six battle stars for her contribution to the US victory in the Pacific. Her post-war service was less glamorous; transporting USN and USM personnel back home to the US. Decommissioned in 1966, she met an inglorious, but for many a battle hardened warship a typical end, sunk as a target off Washington State.

The Light Cruiser CL-64 Vincennes

Built by:	Bethlehem, Quincy
Displacement:	11,744t standard / 14,131t full load
Dimensions:	610ft 1in x 66ft 4in x 26ft 6in
Machinery:	4 shaft General Electrics turbines, 4 Babcock & Wilcox boilers, 100,000shp
Speed:	32.5kts
Armament:	12-6in 47 cal (4x3), 12-5in 38 cal (6x2), 24-40mm (4x4, 4x2), 21-20mm (21x1), 4 aircraft
Complement:	1214-1475 Officers and Crew

The Aegis Cruiser *Vincennes* (CG-49)

The present *Vincennes* was laid down on 20 October 1982 by Ingalls Shipbuilding Division of Litton Industries, Pascagoula, Mississippi. Launched on 14 January 1984 and formally commissioned on 6 July 1985 *Vincennes* was the first *Ticonderoga* Class Aegis (the name of Zeus's shield) Cruiser to join the Pacific Fleet in August 1986. After serving as the anti-aircraft warfare (AAW) commander with the *Carl Vinson* (CVN 70) and *New Jersey* (BB 62) Battle Groups she conducted joint operations with the Japanese Maritime Self-Defense Force (JMSDF) and the Royal Australian Navy.

In May 1988, with Iran seemingly installing Silkworm missile systems at the Strait of Hormuz, *Vincennes*, under the command of Captain W C

The two sets of quadruple Harpoon missile-canisters on the Vincennes' *fantail (quarterdeck) and the after 5in 54 cal Mk 45 gun. (Martin Robson)*

Rogers III, was sent to the Persian Gulf. On 3 July three Iranian gunboats fired on one of *Vincennes* helicopters, the gunboats themselves came under attack from the combined fire of *Vincennes* and the frigate *Elmer Montgomery*, two gunboats were sunk and the third damaged. Around five minutes after this incident a seemingly hostile aircraft was detected taking off from a military airbase headed towards *Vincennes*. The aircraft failed to answer seven Military Air Distress (MAD) 'identify friend or foe' (IFF) challenges and was identified by Aegis operators as an F-14 descending towards *Vincennes*. At this point *Vincennes* was left with little choice but to implement defensive measures firing two SAM's at the target. The target turned out to be a flight IR655, an Iran Air Airbus, all 290 on board were killed.

Reports of teething troubles with the Aegis system and a rumour that it had only been subjected to two tests later surfaced. This may explain why the Aegis system identified the aircraft as an F-14 instead of an Airbus and was identified as descending towards *Vincennes* when it was climbing. This certainly gave the impression that the ship was under attack from the air very shortly after coming under attack from the surface; it is only in this context that the tragic accident can be understood.

After this infamous incident

Vincennes served in the Pacific and Indian Oceans joining the *Kitty Hawk* (CV 63) Battle Group, in June 1994 as AAW commander and again cooperated with the JMSDF. For her service CG-49 USS *Vincennes* has been awarded the Navy Meritorious Unit Citation, the Battle 'E' three times, the Combat Action Ribbon, the Armed Forces Expeditionary Medal, the National Defense Medal, and the Sea Service Deployment Ribbon with four stars. Currently based at Yokoskua in Japan, the USS *Vincennes* remains part of the *Kitty Hawk* group and a vital component of the USN's 7th Pacific Fleet.

The Guided Missile Cruiser
CG 49 Vincennes

Displacement:	9,600t
Dimensions:	567ft x 55ft x 33.8ft
Speed:	30+kts
Propulsion:	4 LM2500 Gas Turbine Engines, 2 Controllable Reversible Pitch Propellers, 80,000shp
Armament includes:	MK 7 MOD 5 Aegis Weapons System, 2-MK 45 5in / 54 cal, 2-MK 41 VLS, 2-Harpoon Missile Quad-Canister Launchers, 2-MK 32 TT, 2-Phalanx Close In Weapons System (CIWS) mounts, 2-SLQ 32 V3, 2-SH 60B helicopters
Complement:	27 Officers, 27 Chief Petty Officers, 315 Enlisted

Looking forward along the Vincennes' *superstructure, with the forward funnel offset to port.* (Martin Robson)

The starboard Mk 15 Phalanx 20mm gun mounting, with its distinctive white radome. (Martin Robson)

Overall view of Yokosuka, with the USS Kitty Hawk *(CV-63) refitting (left), the frigate* Gary *(FFG-51) (centre) and the* Vincennes *(far right).* (Martin Robson)

NAVAL BOOKS OF THE YEAR

John Beeler, Birth of the Battleship: British Capital Ship Design, 1870-1881
London: Chatham Publishing, 2001. 224 pages, 120 illustrations and diagrams, £35
ISBN 1 86176 167 8

Many books on battleships have been written in recent years, but this one is rather different. The author has dug deep into archives and contemporary sources concerning the period after the first rush of ironclad construction, when ironclads began to turn into battleships.

After about two hundred years of technical stability, when lessons learnt from great-grandfather's time were still relevant, planners and designers were faced with dazzling progress in armament, machinery (a new concept) and protection, and with the very latest designs becoming obsolete when still under construction. Costs were skyrocketing, which was unnatural to people who could remember a long era when prices hardly changed from generation to generation. Inventions, like Sam Weller's double-fortified gas microscopes, proliferated, but it was almost impossible to tell which ones held real promise.

The international situation was equally confused, France being the only permanent naval threat. America had made prodigious efforts in 1861-65 but had then turned to other concerns, though the potential revealed was not forgotten. The Royal Navy's most recent combat experience was the Crimean War, and one of the author's revelations is that the 'Coast Defence Ships' built in this era were in fact Coast Attack Ships, with St.Petersburg or Constantinople in mind.

Personalities played a considerable part in Research and Development (they probably still do). Up to 1870, the formidable team of Sir Spencer Robinson (the Controller; the 'user' or client) and Sir Edward Reed, that awkward, unscrupulous and very able man, as chief designer and provider, kept up a rapid flow of 'Broadside' ironclads, in succession to *Warrior*. Thereafter, the rapid appearance of bigger and more powerful guns made things very difficult indeed. Materials improved; the British development of malleable iron gave an initial advantage, steel gave the French a chance to recover, but in the longer run, Britain's much stronger industrial base, and France's land frontier, gave Britain a long-tem lead.

Early engines were very uneconomical, and this made sail rational as an auxiliary. For cruising and 'showing the flag' duties, it made sense right up to the turn of the century, but as the *Captain* showed, sail and turrets did not mix. This limited the armament that could be carried by sail-and-steam ships, and meant that they eventually dropped out of the front rank. The coming of compound engines and twin screws made it possible for ocean-going capital ships to abandon sail; the Italians in the Mediterranean did this much earlier. The author does not think much of the 'Banjo' arrangement for hoisting the screw, though it gave good service for many years.

The purse-strings were tight in the 1870s; France had been knocked out by the Prussian Army, and technical progress tended to make the latest and costliest ship obsolete even before completion, which discouraged mass building. Barnaby, the much criticised Chief Constructor of the era, suffered a lot from his colleagues mangling his designs to

incorporate the latest and mightiest guns , engines and equipment, what the Americans call 'Gold-Plating'; he was eventually eased out over the changing of the engines of the *Orlando* class, which was done without his authority.

One very relevant point made by the author is that the ships of that era were built against 'the threat' as foreseen at the time, with the technical resources then available. Seen in this light, they make much more sense than those designed in a more stable era.

K D McBride

Robert P Largess, USS *Albacore*: Forerunner of the Future
Portsmouth, New Hampshire: The Portsmouth Marine Society, 1999. 166 pages, 119 illustrations, price not known
ISBN 0 91581 925 2

It is impossible to deny the importance of the experimental submarine USS *Albacore* (AGSS-569) in the development of the modern submarine. The origin is traced back to an initiative by the Assistant Chief of Naval Operations (ACNO) for Undersea Warfare, Rear Admiral Charles B Momsen USN, to investigate underwater performance independently from any considerations such as weapons or sensors. Also credited with the parentage of the *Albacore* was Captain Frank Andrews, Submarine Project Officer at the David Taylor Model Basin.

Political approval was given in March 1950 for an 'experimental target' submarine designated as AG(SST)-1. A large number of innovative features was incorporated, including low-carbon HY-80 steel, a dynamometer shaft (which gave endless trouble) a revolutionary 'teardrop' hull etc. The boat went through four phases of major design changes, but the common denominator remained outstanding manoeuvrability, and that remains her legacy.

This book is a remarkable tribute to the author (a contributor to *Warship*, incidentally) and the dedication of the Portsmouth Marine Society. The standard of production is excellent. Not for the average ship-lover, but a unique technical record of one of the most influential submarines in history.

Antony Preston

D K Brown, Nelson to Vanguard – Warship Design and Development 1923-1945
London: Chatham Publishing, 2000. 192 pages, 214 photographs, 15 drawings, £35
ISBN 1 86176 136 8.

David Brown adds to his impressive series on the evolution of design in the Royal Navy, bringing it to the end of the Second World War.

Brown bridges the gap between this work and his magnificent *Grand Fleet* volume, examining the intense trials begun after the Armistice to absorb and profit by war-experience. This led to a new generation of warships to meet the potential threat which nobody in public or political life seemed willing to contemplate. He also adds interesting comparisons with contemporary US Navy practice. He adds his invaluable comments on the personalities of the Director of Naval Construction's (DNC) department.

The book is probably at its best in describing the war period, when pre-war concepts and materiel were submitted to the ultimate test. Traditionalists may take exception to his criticism of the 'Flower' class corvette as a 'poor design', but his argument is convincing. What is clear is that a lot more money spent between the wars could have sorted out many problems, but not all of them. Dive-bombing was not seen as the threat it really was, although the pig-headedness of the RAF made it virtually impossible to exercise fleet air defence tactics realistically. Ordnance was generally good, but

the damage done by the Depression to the British maritime industry showed itself in many ways, when the time came to expand in a hurry. Not until late in the war was there time to look at ways of improving ship propulsion.

The Royal Navy was hardly an antiquated organisation, but the heroic efforts of officers, ratings and industrial workers were at times rendered less effective by pre-war Treasury parsimony and damage to the industrial base.

Antony Preston

John Roberts, British Warships of the Second World War
London: Chatham Publishing, 2000. 155 pages, 78 drawings, £30
ISBN 1 86176 131 7

This is the second volume in Chatham's 'Blueprint' series, intended to make available representative reproductions of the plans held in the National Maritime Museum. This volume opens with a chapter on the design process with an emphasis on procedures as opposed to the technical aspects. This is followed by a chapter on the constraints affecting British warship design between the wars such as Treaty limits, and the depressed state of British industry. It could have been mentioned that, though the size and armament of ships was limited, the weapons they had to face were unlimited. The chapters are quite brief but cover the main aspects clearly and correctly.

The remaining chapters deal in turn with major categories of ship for which representative sets of plans are reproduced. Chapter headings and principal ships illustrated (with a few minor omissions) are:
Battleships; *Nelson, King George V, Warspite*
Aircraft Carriers; *Ark Royal, Indefatigable*
Cruisers, *Kent, Ajax, Manchester, Naiad*
Destroyers; *Gloworm, Eskimo, Savage*
Escorts; *Starling, Belvoir, Bryony, Swale, Winchester, Attacker*
Submarines; *Osiris, Thunderbolt* (ex *Thetis*)
Minelayers; *Latona*

Others; *Alarm, Roberts, Bruiser, Prince David*, Isle class, *Adamant, Prince Robert*

For each category there is an informative and accurate text and, in most cases, the inboard profile and all deck plans are reproduced. In a few cases there are sections and sketches of rig. Sheer draughts are not shown. The original drawings were at a scale of 1/8in = 1ft for larger ships, 0.25in = 1ft for destroyers and below. Here lies the problem; *Nelson* was 710ft long and hence the original drawing was 88.75in long. Reproduced it is 16.5in long, a reduction of 0.20, and hence virtually all lettering is illegible and fine detail is unclear. The author was clearly aware of the problem and has tried to minimise its effect, firstly by choosing original drawings for their clarity (*Nelson* is a poor example) and by providing very detailed captions drawing attention to salient points - the captions for each of the *Nelson* drawings run to about half a page. The problem is less serious for the smaller ships drawn at 0.25in + 1ft.

Despite this problem, the book will be of great value to enthusiasts for the last great era of the RN though I would certainly advise prospective purchasers to examine a copy first. The idea of making the great plans collection of the Museum more generally available is superb and I hope a clearer solution can be found. It would also be interesting to have a luxury, colour book, reproducing the beautiful tinted drawings of the last paddle Cunard liner *Persia* have often been reproduced successfully in colour.

Eur Ing David K Brown, RCNC

John Roberts' book looks at a selected series of official 'as fitted' drawings from the Admiralty archives housed in the National Maritime Museum at Greenwich. As someone who lived among the Admiralty Collection of ships' plans, this volume gives me great personal pleasure. The main problem of the book is its dependence on the quality of drawings, which sometimes lags behind the technical interest; the *Nelson's* 'as fitteds' are a particularly bad example, but Roberts guides us through the detail discernible, explaining it and putting it into its correct context. His deep background knowledge makes the process almost like reading a book.

For the layman and the modeller in particular, the big ships' drawings are bewildering, being drawn at very large scale and then reduced to fit the page, whereas the smaller warships, particularly destroyers are much easier to understand. Submarines must have been a headache, even to the Admiralty draughtsmen, driving them to adopt a unique double inboard profile projection - one looking from the centreline to port, the other to starboard. Both books are produced to the high standard we expect from Chatham Publishing, a joy to the eye and valuable additions to the technical literature of the 20th Century warship.

Antony Preston

Leonard C Reynolds, Home Waters MGBs and MGBs at War 1939-1945
Stroud: Sutton Publishing, 2000.
215 pages, 100 illustrations, £20
ISBN 0 750992 518 3

This is the third in a series covering all MTB and MGB operations in World War II (*Dog Boats at War* and *Mediterranean MTBs at War* have been reviewed and are still available). According to the author there were 266 'short' boats fighting 308 engagements in Home waters with the loss of 76 boats and 285 men. There were few suitable craft available at the outbreak of war and the author makes much of this apparent neglect. However, up to 1940 there was no enemy coastline within range of these crafts and with so many other shortages, the admiralty may be excused in this area. There were specific problems in engines and in weapons.

Pre 1940 designs had favoured the Italian Fraschini engine, which ceased to be available when Italy joined the war, or the Rolls Royce Merlin of which 107 marinised versions were built. Only when the US Packard became available did these craft again develop worthwhile speeds. Originally, Motor Torpedo

Boats and Motor Gunboats were seen as separate types but later the more powerful engines and stronger hulls enabled both guns and torpedoes to be carried. The effectiveness of their torpedoes was greatly enhanced when the Mk VIII with the CCR magnetic pistol was introduced.

This is a book of actions and of people and makes thrilling reading. The 'Aces' are still remembered; Robert Hitchens ('Hitch'), Peter Dickens and 'Harpy' Lloyd, but many others did their share or more.

The numerous photographs are well selected though, perhaps, with too many 'family groups'. On a personal note, I am delighted to see how many come from the remarkable collection of Geoff Hudson who has been studying the history of Coastal Forces since we were at school together more than half a century ago.

The author's trilogy forms a remarkable record of these flimsy but powerful craft, which, it is claimed in one Admiralty press release, fought 780 actions in European waters, firing 1,169 torpedoes and sinking more than 500 vessels for the loss of 170 of our craft. There seem to be only a few minor errors. If you enjoyed the earlier books hurry up and get this one.

Eur Ing David K Brown, RCNC

Peter Hore (ed), Seapower Ashore: 200 Years of Royal Navy Operations on Land
London: Chatham, 2001.
288 pages, many b/w illustrations, £25
ISBN 1 86176 155 4

As Sir Julian Corbett succinctly noted, although naval forces can influence conflicts by presence alone, in order to have the greatest influence naval force must have the capability to project power ashore. As this excellent collection of essays assembled by Peter Hore reminds us, this fundamental principle of maritime strategy is as relevant for the Royal Navy of today and the future, as it has been for the past 200 years.

The thirteen essays here range from Tom Pocock's assessment of Sir Sidney Smith's famous defence of

Acre in 1799 (his continual reminiscing earned him the nickname 'Long Acre') right up to the vital contribution of the TLAM armed RN submarine HMS *Splendid* in attacking Serb targets in land locked Kosovo as highlighted by Lee Willett.

In between these parameters Michael Duffy provides an overview of the RN's contribution to land operations, 1793-1815. Colin White examines Nelson's experiences ashore in the Mediterranean and seapower in the Anglo-Japanese war of 1863-64. Andrew Lambert assesses two naval bombardment operations at Syria in 1840 and at Sweaborg in 1855. The naval contribution to the relief of Lucknow in 1857-59 and the Sudan and Chinese campaigns 1896-1900 are examined by Richard Brooks, while, in similar vein, Arthur Bleby examines The Second Boer War, 1899-1901. Chris Page details the operations of the Royal Naval Division in the First World War, the editor provides a similar assessment of the Norway Campaign of 1940 and Ivor Howcroft examines the assault on Walcheren in 1944.

History provides a guide from which current and future generations can learn and then make educated decisions. As Admiral Sir Jock Slater concludes in his foreword, although the Royal Navy has a glorious and famous tradition of seeking, and usually winning, decisive sea battles the less well-known tradition that forms the basis of these essays provides the precedent for the future operational activities of the RN.

Martin Robson

Eric J Grove, The Price of Disobedience: the Battle of the River Plate Reconsidered.
Stroud: Sutton Publishing, 2000.
180 pages, 21 b/w photographs, 6 maps, drawings etc., £19.99
ISBN 0 7509 0927 7

What a refreshing change to read an analysis of this famous cruiser action which is thoroughly researched, objective *and* readable. Too many accounts (and the 1956 film) are banal recyclings of British wartime myths. Captain Langsdorff was a member of the Nazi Party, and did not commit suicide wrapped in the old Imperial ensign as a gesture of defiance against the Führer and all his works. He was chivalrous, but he followed a course of action which led inevitably to disaster.

Many naval enthusiasts will be surprised to learn that the River Plate battle was much less of a David vs Goliath affair. Professor Grove shows convincingly that the *Admiral Graf Spee* was much more seriously damaged than the Admiralty realised, and when the Government of Uruguay made it clear that it would enforce the provisions of international law, Langsdorff had only two choices: to lead his men on a death-ride or to scuttle the ship. The author probes his motivation for his disastrous decision to risk action against other warships, and concludes that he hoped to emulate his ship's famous namesake and win another Battle of Coronel by sinking a Royal Navy cruiser. If so, he forgot that Spee had brought about the destruction of his entire squadron by making an ill-judged attack on the Falklands.

To a large extent the reputation of the *panzerschiff* was inflated by the British press, which invented the spurious term 'pocket battleship' for what was really an overgunned, relatively slow and lightly armoured heavy cruiser. Perhaps the unfortunate Langsdorff believed the propaganda.

Antony Preston

Iain Ballantyne, Peter Hore et al, Submarine, 1901-2001 *St Leonards-on-Sea: HPC Publishing, 2001. 48 pages, many illustrations, £8.50* ISBN 0 9531 4212 4

This A4 format glossy volume is a special publication from *Warships International Fleet Review* to mark the centennial of the Royal Navy Submarine Service. The publication provides a brief history of the submarine service. Beginning with an examination of pre 1901 submarine developments, the narrative follows chronologically into the First World War and inter-war years, progressing through the Second World War, the Cold War, Anti-Soviet peacetime

operations and finally ends by looking at the new *Astute* class and the future of the submarine arm. Complementing the text are many excellent images primarily drawn from the Goodman Collection. Overall, a useful introduction to the history of the service.

Martin Robson

Harry Plevy, Battleships Sailors: The Fighting Career of HMS Warspite *recalled by her Men London: Chatham Publishing, 2001. 256 pages, 16 photos, £19.95* ISBN 1 86176 151 1

The author is a retired engineering lecturer who has put a lifetime's obsession with *Warspite* to good use in this, his first book. The story is told using letters from her officers and men together with extracts from published works, including those from the enemy.

After commissioning with all its 'housekeeping' problems, the story moves rapidly to Jutland where *Warspite* was amongst the most heavily hit of British ships. There are harrowing accounts of the dreadful injuries to her crew. After the war it was back to peacetime routine with a great gulf between the life style of officers and men. This gulf and a most insensitive treatment of a major pay cut led to the Invergordon 'mutiny', handled tactfully by the author. Then came her great modernisation in which protection and armament were greatly improved as a result of the weight and space saved by replacing her original machinery with more modern boilers and engines. This made her almost the equivalent of a modern battleship and made it possible for her to play a major part in the Second World War. Those who claim that battleships were obsolete before 1939 should read this book and think hard.

Present at the second battle of Narvik where her Swordfish float-plane sank a U-boat, *Warspite*'s finest hour came as Cunningham's flagship in the Mediterranean. In July 1940 she hit the Italian battleship *Giulio Cesare* at 26,000 yards, the greatest range at which a naval gun ever

scored a hit. The triumph of Matapan was followed by the tragedy of Crete where *Warspite* was again seriously damaged.

Repairs and update in the USA made a pleasant interlude before she joined the Eastern Fleet off Ceylon. She came back to the Mediterranean to accept the surrender of the Italian fleet but was very badly damaged by a 3000lb FX1400 guided bomb off Salerno. She was never fully repaired and went to support the Normandy landings with one turret and one boiler room out of action. Returning, she was mined, with damage to her shafting. She supported the landing at Walcheren with one good shaft, two damaged and the other out of action and speed down to 15.5kts.

By the end of the war she was worn out with a great deal of damage never made good. The decision to scrap her was inevitable but she broke away from the tow in 1947 and came to her last rest in Prussia Cove close to Devonport where she had been built 35 years previously.

Eur Ing David K Brown, RCNC

Iain Ballantyne, Warspite *Barnsley: Leo Cooper/Pen & Sword, 2001. 209 pages, over 200 b/w photographs, maps and drawings, £19.95* ISBN 0 85052 779 1

Judging by the sub-title *Warships of the Royal Navy* this is intended to form part of a series. HMS *Warspite* can claim to be the most famous battleship in the Royal Navy, certainly in the Second World War, when the 'Old Lady' seemed to bear a charmed life. Paradoxically, she was known as something of a 'jinx' ship from the time she joined the Grand Fleet in 1915 until the outbreak of war. The famous 'stunt' at 'Windy Corner' during the Battle of Jutland, caused by a jammed rudder, nearly got her sunk. Her numerous collisions broke the careers of several Captains, and in the late 1930s she narrowly missed a Royal Mail liner while carrying out a full-calibre shoot, and fired a burst of pom-pom shells into Valetta. But nobody got hurt on either occasion, and as soon as war broke out in 1939 her 'jinx' decided to leave her alone.

She won her first laurels in Norway, when she intervened decisively in the Second Battle of Narvik, but her greatest achievements were as Admiral Cunningham's flagship in the Mediterranean Fleet. Her hit on the Italian battleship *Giulio Cesare* with a 15in shell during the Battle of Calabria still stands as a record for firing under way at a moving target. At Matapan she and her sisters *Barham* and *Valiant* destroyed three Italian heavy cruisers, putting paid to the Italians' hope of dominating the Eastern Mediterranean.

Even in adversity she was lucky. She sustained bomb damage off Crete in 1941 and at Salerno she was hit by glider-bombs, and during the Normandy invasion she set off a magnetic mine. It was a very weary 'Old Lady' that was finally paid off in Felenerry in 1945. A previous biographer of HMS *Warspite*, Captain Stephen Roskill, said, 'She and her sisters represented remarkably good value for the money spent on them.'

This is a well-produced book, and many of the illustrations have not been seen before.

Recommended.

Antony Preston

Jim Ring, We Come Unseen: The Untold Story of Britain's Cold War Submarines. *London: John Murray, 2001. 251 pages, 24 b/w photographs, 6 maps, drawings etc., £20*
ISBN 0 7195 56909 2

Jim Ring has provided a long-overdue tribute to the unseen and unappreciated missions undertaken by Royal Navy submarines during the Cold War. They maintained discreet surveillance of the Soviet Northern Fleet, took underwater photographs of ships' hulls, and recorded noise signatures, to name only part of their work. The operational theatre stretched from the Barents Sea down to the Greenland-Iceland-UK (GIUK) Gap.

The author's approach is unusual; he takes the candidates for command who did the notorious 'Perisher' in 1963, the 'Class of '63', and looks at background, personality and performance. The 'Perisher' is widely regarded as the most rigorous selection course for potential commanding officers, and it takes its name from the fact that a failed candidate gets no second chance and cannot do any more seatime in submarines. Most of these who fall by the wayside choose to leave the Navy, and only a few tough-minded people take shore jobs.

Critics say that the Royal Navy wastes a lot of talent by such ruthless weeding-out, but the Navy says that it wants an elite; second best or adequate is not enough, so this is a story of an elite within an elite. If I have a complaint it is the author's determination to give the reader every bit of geopolitical and domestic background possible. He also assumes no technical knowledge in his readers, and some of the descriptions are over-simplified, but it is a good read, and lifts the veil on a long campaign, which made a major contribution to winning the Cold War. And the Great British Public knew absolutely nothing about it!

Antony Preston

Gerhard Koop and Klaus-Peter Schmolke, Heavy Cruisers of the *Admiral Hipper* Class. *London: Greenhill books, 2001. 208 pages, 310 photographs and line drawings, £30*
ISBN 1-85367-43-6

This book shares the style of the authors' three earlier books dealing with the *Bismarck, Scharnhorst* and the pocket battleship classes. Agreement was easily reached at Washington that cruisers should be limited to 10,000 tons and 8in guns as most countries were thinking of, or even building, ships of about this size. Later, Germany was to accept these limits.

However, there seems to have been no intention to adhere to the limits; the first two *Hippers* were over 14,000 tons and *Prinz Eugen* was 16,277 tons. They are often claimed to be the finest examples of the '10,000 ton cruiser' but at their true displacement they look unimpressive. Big cruisers of all navies were lightly armoured but the *Hippers* were very weak for such big ships of late date, with a 3in belt, 1-2in deck.

The machinery used high-pressure, high-temperature; Wagner boilers in *Blücher*, La Mont in the others. It seems that this machinery was unreliable with numerous steam leaks and the machinery spaces were so cramped that maintenance was difficult. The authors suggest that diesels would have been a better choice in the light of their primary role of commerce raiding. Preliminary trials showed bow with sheer and a clipper stem.

Blücher had the shortest life, being sunk by the 19th century guns and torpedoes of the fortifications of Oslo Fiord. *Hipper* lasted most of the war; British readers will find the encounter off Norway on 8 April 1940 when she was rammed by the *Glowworm* of interest. Damage was extensive but not serious; there is a fine photo of *Hipper* in dock. Then in 1941 *Hipper* sank seven ships from convoy SLS 64. In December 1942 she was in action with escorts of JW 51B badly damaging *Onslow* before being beaten off by *Jamaica* and *Sheffield*. She was effectively destroyed in an air raid on Kiel in April 1945. *Prinz Eugen* will be remembered for her cruise with *Bismarck*, finally abandoned due to machinery problems, and for the Channel Dash. She finally succumbed to the atom bomb tests at Bikini.

The photographs are superb. There are 'official' shots of high quality mingled with unofficial photos of lower quality but rich in atmosphere. There were two uncompleted ships: *Seydlitz* blown up in 1945 and *Lützow*, there is a good photo showing conversion to an aircraft carrier nearly complete.

There is an interesting concluding chapter based largely on post-war German technical reports. The main conclusion is that the big cruiser was an inappropriate type for the German navy of the war but, if they had to be built, they should have had diesel engines.

Eur Ing David K Brown, RCNC

Richard Knowles Morris, John P.
Holland, 1841-1914: Inventor
of the Modern Submarine.
*Columbia: University of South
Carolina Press, 1998.*
245 pages, 46 b/w, $16.95
ISBN 1 57003 236 X

John P Holland, the son of a coast-
guard officer, was born in a remote
part of SW Ireland. The family was
Gaelic-speaking and John did not
learn English until he went to school
at the age of five. The father was in
government employ so that the family were never at risk of being evict-
ed and almost certainly were not
directly affected by the great famine
but the boy must have witnessed the
events, while a brother and an uncle
died of cholera. When John was
twelve his father died, the family was
left with a small pension so, in order
to reduce the burden on the family,
John became a novice with the
Christian Brothers teaching order
providing food, clothing and educa-
tion; although a gifted teacher he
was physically frail so that in 1873
he was released from his vows; sailing to the USA in 1877 to join family members in Boston. Once there
he continued to work on the problems of submarine navigation, a
topic which had occupied his mind
for some years. In order to raise
money for building he made contact
with the *Clan na Gael* or United
Brotherhood, also known as the
Fenians, who wanted to end British
rule over Ireland by force and who
recognised the potential threat
posed by submarines to the Royal
Navy. Holland, although a patriotic
Irishman would, because of his background, never have countenanced
one of his submarines being used by
Clan na Gael as offensive weapons.

His first boat *Holland 1*, 14ft 6in
long displacing 2.25 tons, was
launched into the Passcia river at the
Paterson New Jersey in May 1878. It
foreshadowed the development of
the submarine over the next 20 years,
always having a small reserve of
buoyancy propelled by an internal
combustion engine and unlike contemporary submarines did not
descend vertically by means of horizontal propellers but was forced

down by horizontally mounted
hydroplanes, centrally placed in
Holland 1 but stern mounted thereafter and with much attention being
paid to horizontal stability; however
it and many of its successors had no
periscope. In the event the Brayton
engine refused to work with petrol so
that power was supplied by a steam
pipe leading from an accompanying
steam launch to the engine. After a
number of successful trials Holland
removed the engine and scuttled the
boat in the river from where it was
salvaged many years later and now
has a final resting place in a park in
Paterson.

Holland's next boat was the so
called 'Fenian Ram', a name coined
by a newspaper reporter with an
overheated imagination. It was larger
and propelled above and below water
by an external combustion engine
which apparently functioned at moderate depths by a combination of
high air pressure inside the hull and a
non return valve on the exhaust.
There was a dispute among the
Brotherhood and one faction stole
the 'Ram' together with a 16ft working model and the pair were towed to
New Haven, the model (No 3) being
lost *en route*. Holland made no
attempt to regain No 2 and severed
his connections with the Fenians.
His next boat was designed to test a
dynamite gun powered by compressed air invented by a Lt Zalinski,
but this sank while being launched in
September 1885.

There followed a long fallow period while Holland tried to interest
the USN and in 1895 the 85ft
Plunger was laid down to Navy specifications including steam-powered
triple-expansion engines which rendered the boat uninhabitable with lit
boilers; eventually it was bought
back by the newly formed Holland
Torpedo Boat Co when Holland produced his final design No 6, 53ft x
10ft, originally armed with one torpedo tube and two dynamite guns,
the latter later removed. Propulsion
under water was by electricity and
surface by a petrol engine launched
in 1897. No 6 was bought by the US
government after modification,
renamed USS *Holland*, the model for
the first submarines both for the
USN and the Royal Navy and the

progenitor of all succeeding submarines.

The story had no happy ending for
Holland. The company which bore is
name had been set up by a lawyer,
Elihu Root, who took care that
Holland should not have a controlling share and by the time the firm
became a subsidiary of Issac Rice's
Electric Boat Co, Holland was left
with one percent of the shares and
was then squeezed out with another
promoted over his head and he
resigned in 1904. Attempts to set up
on his own were thwarted by Rice
taking legal action and Holland only
designed two more boats for Japan,
dying in 1914.

This book originally appeared in
1966; this paperback edition incor-
porates fresh material collected since
then by the author and covering all
stages of Holland's life but unfortunately not incorporated into the text
but relegated to a supplement at the
end. This is a fascinating well-writ-
ten book never likely to be supplant-
ed. There are many photographs and
diagrams but their clarity is seriously
diminished by not being printed on
glossy paper.

Peter Brook

Bryan Perrett, Gunboat! Small
Ships at War
London: Cassell & Co, 2000
216 pages, 35 b/w photographs,
plus maps and drawings, £18.99
ISBN 0 304 35302 7

The author casts his net wide,
including the Union Navy's fleet of
river gunboats, which gives a good
balance, but some of his definitions
of gunboats' are sometimes dubious.
By no stretch of the imagination can
the frigate *Amethyst* (1949) be
described as a gunboat, and her
escape down the Yangtse be
described as a gunboat-type action.
As a pedant I cannot see the destruction of the German light cruiser
Königsberg by a pair of monitors as a
gunboat action either. It does,
nonetheless, shed much useful light
on number of minor actions which
get ignored by many historians.

Antony Preston

Geoffrey Till (ed), Seapower at
the Millennium
*Stroud: Sutton Publishing and
Royal Naval Museum
Publications, 2001. 370 pages,
£40*
ISBN 0 75092 458 6

Several hundred naval officers, aca-
demics, seafarers, engineers, museum
curators and enthusiasts gathered
together in Portsmouth over three
days in January 2000 to debate developments in seapower as we entered a
new millennium. This book is the
result of that conference. The
Conference was held under the aus-
pices of the Royal Navy, the Royal
Naval Museum, the Society for
Nautical Research and the
Greenwich Forum and was intended
to explore Man's relationship with
the sea in all its guises. Hence conference sessions (and book chapters)
on such diverse topics as 'maritime
safety across the globe', 'fisheries
management', environmental issues,
'renewable energy from the sea', 'the
globalisation of the seafaring labour
force and mixed nationality crews'.
All this as well as sections on the
more traditional subjects that we
think of as seapower, the roles of
navies and maritime trade.

Whilst a cursory glance over the
contents might not instantly make
this book a bestseller amongst
Warship's readership, despite a chapter dealing with the RN's procurement issues, this is an important work
that deserves as wide an audience as
possible. Indeed the decision to publish the conference proceedings was
taken to facilitate just such an occur-
rence. Although there is not a chapter that specifically addresses the
design of either naval or merchant
vessels, it is to deal with the subject
of this book that vessels are designed
at all.

The book attempts to take a holis-
tic approach to seapower in its widest
context. It examines the political,
economic, military and social drivers
that shape the environment in which
warships operate. At the turn of the
last century the Navy League cam-
paigned for more Dreadnoughts
under the slogan 'we want eight and
we wont wait' and gave out prizes to

pupils in state schools for essays on
the need for seapower in relation to
the British Empire. Perhaps its modern manifestations are to be found
somewhere in the chapter on 'Selling
the Sea'. Libby Purves, for example,
explores the place of maritime issues
in the media. Whilst Charles Payton,
Director of the 1996 Festival of the
Sea held in Bristol, argues events
such as the festival encourage, support, promote and demonstrate the
publics healthy enthusiasm for maritime issues.

The book devotes its first six chapters, however, to topics that might be
classified as more orthodox military
issues. The challenges faced by
navies in the Atlantic region, how
the European Union is developing a
maritime strategy, the ways in which
the US Marine Corps is responding
to greater calls on its expeditionary
capabilities. Despite this, the book
maintains its objective of seeing maritime matters as a cohesive whole.
The interactions between differing
users of the sea, environmentalists
and oilmen, fishing boats and submariners, may well be characterised
by competition but as Geoff Till
explains, civil and military spheres
are so interdependant that to consider eithers place in the grand scheme
without the other is almost meaningless.

In the realm of technology comer-
cial pressures are driving forward ino-
vations that are adapted for military
use. Develoments in infomation
technology, communications and
sensors make it harder to discuss the
characteristics of single vessels.
Rather attention is now focused upon
the intergrated nature of platforms
and systems to assess efficiency.
Together with new propulsion systems, hull designs and weapons, a
new generation of lean manned
stealth ships is being developed to
meet changing requirements.

The importance of the sea as an
economic arena is nothing new.
Maritime trade has always had a symbiotic relationship with the navy, fish
have always been a major food
resource. Increasing globalisation
means more vessels and more varied
cargoes, both legal and illegal. Navies
will be required to address threats to
legitimate shipping such as piracy

and terrorism, and intercept illegal
ones, whether that be in support of
UN sanctions or national customs.
Increasing population will put a pre-
mium on not only fish stocks but
other natural resources. Fifty years
ago the offshore oil and gas industry
hardly existed it now accounts for
billions of dollars worth of economic
activity. Added to this economic
aspect of the sea is the growing realisation of how important the worlds
oceans are to the Earth's environment. Both the monitoring of the
environment, particularly in areas of
interest to the military like the
worlds littorals, and enforcement of
safeguards to protect the environment, are likely to develop as important roles for navies.

These and other debates concerning changing requirements will clearly come to influence ship design and
construction. It is a tribute to the
conferences organizers that such a
wide and distinguished collection of
speakers were assembled to bring
their collective wisdom to bear upon
the sea as we embark on a new century. Ultimately all the contributors
make articulate arguments for the
vital importance of seapower to all
aspects of our diverse lives.

Jon Robb-Webb

Antony Preston, The Royal
Navy Submarine Service, A
Centennial History
*London: Conway Maritime
Press, 2001. 192 pages, heavily
illustrated, £19.99*
ISBN 0 85177 891 7

Produced with the assistance of the
Royal Navy Submarine Museum at
Gosport this book has been published
to mark the 100th anniversary of the
birth of the British submarine service. Considering the extent of the
subject matter, the coverage is
remarkably detailed. It paints a clear
picture of the evolution of the British
submarine from the laying down of
the first Royal Navy boats of the
Holland type in February 1901, to
that of the latest attack submarines of
the *Astute* class in January 2001,
almost exactly 100 years later.

The book begins with an introductory chapter covering the evolution of the submarine in general from Tudor times to 1900. The author describes this as a 'brief historical outline', which, while not incorrect, is perhaps a modest description of a carefully researched and readable account of the many attempts to produce a workable submarine. It is in effect the first of several essays of equal quality that begin each of the book's five chapters. Each of these chapters covers a specific period in chronological order, starting with the 1901-1914 era and, after covering the two World Wars and the period between them, ends with the last half century. The bulk of the text is an interesting combination of an underlying diary of events, covering both technical and operational history, interspersed with boxes containing more detailed information.

The boxes provide specifications, with short notes, for all RN submarine classes and a variety of expanded notes on various aspects of British technical and operational submarine history. The latter include short biographies on three of the RN's most famous submarine officers (Bacon, Horton and Wanklyn) and expansions of various historical events from the use of old 'C' class submarines in U-boat decoy operations 1915-16 to *Conqueror*'s sinking of the *Belgrano* in 1982. There are also some comments on the technical aspects of the subject, such as escape methods, midget submarines and peroxide fuel and even an amusing tale of the gift of a young reindeer to HMS *Trident* by the Russians in 1941.

The Royal Navy Submarine Service is profusely illustrated, primarily with photographs, although a number of line drawings are also included. Some of these are a little on the small side but, given the subject, this is more forgivable than it would be with the more complex exteriors of surface ships. Some of the photographs will be familiar but many others have not, to the best of my knowledge, been published before. They have obviously been chosen with care and provide a variety, which is not normally to be found in a subject of this nature. In general Antony Preston has provided a book which serves its commemorative purpose well. Those wishing to expand their knowledge of British submarines, be they expert or beginner, will find here an ideal starting point which combines both the value of a reference book with a really good read.

John Roberts

THE ROYAL NAVY SUBMARINE SERVICE
A CENTENNIAL HISTORY
ANTONY PRESTON

IN ASSOCIATION WITH THE ROYAL NAVAL SUBMARINE MUSEUM, GOSPORT
FOREWORD BY REAR ADMIRAL R P STEVENS CB, FLAG OFFICER SUBMARINES

The year 2001 witnesses the 100th anniversary of the foundation of the Royal Navy Submarine Service. *The Royal Navy Submarine Service: A Centennial History* presents a day-by-day account of the Royal Navy's submarines throughout their first 100 years in operation, celebrating the heroic feats and everyday life above and under the sea. It examines the development of the submarine arm from the keel laying of the solitary *Holland One* in February 1901 right up to the keel laying of the Royal Navy's new HMS *Astute* exactly 100 hundred years later in February 2001.

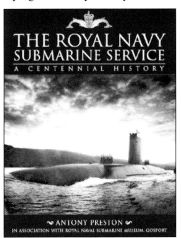

Important technical developments and specification tables, analysis of single submarines or a whole class of craft, notable actions, important individuals and more unusual events are all examined in authoritative detail. Also included are details of all fourteen submariners who have won the Victoria Cross and information on all preserved Royal Navy submarines currently open to the public. Complementing the text are many images and drawings of the men and vessels that have shaped the first hundred years of the Royal Navy Submarine Service.

The Royal Navy Submarine Service: A Centennial History, supported by the Royal Navy Submarine Museum, Gosport and Rear Admiral R P Stevens, Flag Officer Submarines, provides an authoritative and stimulating complement to the centennial celebrations programme.

Hardback, 246 x 189, 192 pages
220 b/w illustrations and line drawings
£19.99
ISBN 0 85177 891 7

WARSHIP GALLERY

In this section, we publish photographs of warships which are unusual, remarkable as images, or otherwise of special interest to readers. The section is not intended for standard ship portraits, but for out-of-the-ordinary pictures, which illuminate aspects of warships not evident in the usual views. This year's annual includes a special feature on British operations in North Russia in 1919-20, the so-called Intervention War. The were taken by Victor de Sarigny, an army officer serving at Archangel, and came into the possession of the Editor through the generosity of his granddaughter Lavinia de Sarigny, now living in Fremantle, Western Australia. Some of the identifications are tentative, and if any reader can throw any more light, please contact the Editor.

The Editor will be happy to hear from readers with any other unusual photographs for publication in future issues.

Shipping in the Dvina River, which runs into the White Sea at Archangel. (Antony Preston)

What appears to be a kite balloon barge (left) and one of the small monitors M.24-27. (Antony Preston)

A puzzling view of a 'Racecourse' class paddle minesweeper with what appears to be a hangar aft. HMS Eridge and HMS Melton carried out trials in 1916 but there is no evidence linking them to the White Sea. (Antony Preston)

Probably the old Russian predreadnought Chesme on the left and possibly an old RN light cruiser on the right. (Antony Preston)

Two views of salvage work on the mined ex-War Office tug Sword Dance, *serving as a minesweeper.* (Antony Preston)

Two views of the tunnel minesweeper Sword Dance, *mined on 24 June 1919.* (Antony Preston)

HMS Sword Dance *refloated*. (Antony Preston)

The minesweeper HMS Morris Dance towing a lighter carrying two floatplanes. (Antony Preston)

The old battleship HMS Glory (left) was sent to Archangel as a depot ship in 1917. The liner (right) is the Braemar Castle, *probably serving as a troopship.* (Antony Preston)

The 'Insect' class gunboat HMS Cockchafer slipped for maintenance. (Antony Preston)

Starboard quarter of HMS Cockchafer, *her sisters* Cicala, Cricket *and* Glowworm *also served in North Russia.* (Antony Preston)

'Insect' class gunboat with a small monitor beyond. (Antony Preston)

An 'Insect' and a floatplane on a lighter beyond. (Antony Preston)

The forward 6in gun of an 'Insect', with assorted ships beyond. (Antony Preston)

INDEX

Page references in *italics* refer to illustrations and those in **bold** refer to diagrams.